The German Jew

The German Jew

A Synthesis of Judaism and Western Civilization,
1730–1930

by H. I. Bach

Published for
THE LITTMAN LIBRARY
by
OXFORD UNIVERSITY PRESS
1984

Oxford University Press, Walton Street, Oxford OX2 6DP
London New York Toronto
Delhi Bombay Calcutta Madras Karachi
Kuala Lumpur Singapore Hong Kong Tokyo
Nairobi Dar es Salaam Cape Town
Melbourne Auckland
and associated companies in
Beirut Berlin Ibadan Mexico City Nicosia

Oxford is a trade mark of Oxford University Press

Published in the United States
by Oxford University Press, New York

© Littman Library 1984

British Library Cataloguing in Publication Data
Bach, H.I.
The German Jew.—(The Littman library
of Jewish civilization)
1. Jews—Germany—History—1096–1800
2. Jews—Germany—History—1800–1933
I. Title   II. Series
943'.004924   DS135.G33
ISBN 0–19–710033–3

Printed in Great Britain
at the Alden Press, Oxford

CONTENTS

FOREWORD
by *Albert H. Friedlander*

The history of German Jewry cannot be encompassed in one volume; nor can it be understood by one individual. There are too many trends and countertrends, Hegelian currents of the World Spirit and economic developments, which any historian must compress within a specific theory and vision where clarity is achieved at the expense of depth. All historical writing can be exposed to that criticism—and each historian has a specific reply to this attack. In the end the historian cannot be silenced. The encounter with an identifiable entity must be recorded and transmitted, whether or not a memorial is established for a world that has vanished, or an introduction given to an existing reality that still shapes the self-awareness of the totality.

Hans Bach has presented us with his encounter with German Jewish life from Mendelssohn to Rosenzweig—two centuries of flourishing, creative life, which were then swallowed up by the darkness of the greatest destruction ever visited upon Jewry. Much was taken; and much abides. Hans Bach himself was a participant in the work of the Leo Baeck Institute, with its distinguished Yearbooks and more than a hundred scholarly publications dealing with that living entity which is the German Jew. Yet in the end he wanted to establish his own vision of the German Jew as his own monument. This must be understood and appreciated. Jewish scholarship delights in writing commentaries and supercommentaries upon the texts of its teachers. Yet, in this instance, Hans Bach was his own commentator. We understand the composition of the mosaic once we understand his vision, his thinking, and his passion for the entity he was portraying. The very concept of an anthology of original texts states the need for the participating actors in the drama of history to speak to us without intermediaries. The same privilege must be accorded to Hans Bach.

At the same time, a few biographical words must be said, if only to emphasize that he was what he described: the quintessential German Jew. He was a scholar equally at home in philosophy, Germanistics,

7

art and music, the humanities, and the world of Jewish thought. One
need not argue that every German Jew was a Hans Bach; but Hans
Bach was certainly a German Jew, totally at home with all the thinkers
who found their way into this text, able to argue with them, to
correct them, to love or to hate them, to record them for posterity. He
was born in Stuttgart in 1902 and completed his formal studies in 1928,
in Berlin. An academic career began there which, in terms of German
culture, can be typified by his share in the historical critical edition of
Jean Paul's writings. His work within Jewish thought is most clearly
seen in his editorial work for the journal *Der Morgen*, still used as a
treasure trove for contemporary Jewish writers.

Hans Bach escaped to London in 1939. One of the strongest imprints
upon contemporary Jewish self-awareness is the image of the German-
Jewish refugee, the emigré-scholar. These were not the wandering
scholars of other times and places, who found students waiting for
them in every land they entered. The teachers and the students of these
refugee scholars had died or were about to die; there was no public for
them. Often their language was not spoken and their words were not
heard. Hans Bach started as a factory worker. In time his mind and his
knowledge came to be appreciated—at the Foreign Office, at the Board
of Trade. And the Jewish community came to appreciate that the editor
of the *Synagogue Review of Great Britain,* a journal of the Progressive
Jewish community, had edited *Der Morgen* and was one of the great
scholars resident in the land. Comparisons might be drawn between
Hans Bach and Jacob Bernays, once his definitive biography of Bernays appeared in 1974. The comparison would be in terms of scholarship and learning, of creativity and relationship to the culture of his
time. Yet, in terms of commitment to the world of Jewish thought,
Bach must be credited with greater achievements. His work in the
scholarly Jewish journals in Germany up to the moment of his departure, and his studies published during his last years in England—all
give us the assurance that we could not have a better guide into the
world of German-Jewish thought. Listening to him, we begin to understand that the world of the German Jew did not end with the coming of
the dark days. And we begin to understand why we must listen to the
testimony of the two hundred years of creativity limned within the
pages of the text. There are other dimensions to the life of Hans
Bach that can help us understand his work: his marriage to Susan
added a partnership in which a wise scholar guided him in the exploration of the human mind and heart. This is not an ancillary but an
essential thought as we move into these texts: the dreams of children
recapitulate the experiences of the centuries behind us. The dimen-

sions of the past would shrink into nothingness if we did not relate them to the future.

Mendelssohn wrote *Jerusalem*. Rosenzweig wrote *The Star of Redemption*. Hans Bach takes us on a journey between these poles that ultimately leads to a future where the creativity of the German Jew endures as a constellation of hope against a universe that must still lie open to us.

London, England

PREFACE

In contemplating the life and thought of the German-speaking Jewries during the two centuries prior to the Hitler years, one cannot help being struck by an almost unprecedented record of creative achievement of so small a group, never more than five percent of the population: Karl Marx, Sigmund Freud, and Albert Einstein are some of the best-known examples.

The tragic destruction of these Jewries by the Nazis has terminated an epoch that extended from Roman times to the present century. This fact may enable the historian to visualize and evaluate this epoch as a whole, against the background of both European and Jewish history.

The period from 1730 to 1930, with which this book is concerned in particular, is characterized by the gradual emergence of Jews from the ghettos of the late Middle Ages and by their entry into, and direct confrontation with, Western civilization.

The catastrophe of the expulsion of Jews from Spain in 1492, after centuries of brilliant achievement, had shaken all other Jewish communities as well. This shattering of the security of their leading group, however, astonishingly did not break their spirit but threw them back to the very core of their religious roots. In the course of time a deep response to the disaster emerged: the fervent hope of bringing about the coming of the Messiah by mystical contemplation and purification—the hope of *redemption from within*. This mystical doctrine, known as Cabbalah, became the chief inspiration of Jews all over the world for more than a century. It reached its peak when, in the mid-seventeenth century, an oriental Jew, Sabbatai Zevi, proclaimed himself the Messiah and was widely hailed as such. These hopes were exploded when, under duress, he forsook his religion. The consequences of this disappointment bordered on nihilism.

Two generations later, however, the hidden, indestructible spark of messianic hope for God's kingdom on earth, prepared by man's devoted endeavor, lit up again. This time, participation of Jews in European culture came to offer a new, constructive aim. Its problems and achievements are represented in the life of an outstanding man, Moses Mendelssohn.

A few years after his death the French Revolution held out the prospect of the emancipation of Jews into a universal brotherhood of man—of their *liberation from without*. Emancipation became their new messianic aim. Yet the price for thus being emancipated as "individuals" was to give up their distinctiveness as a group, to sever their Jewish roots—a demand almost akin to spiritual suicide. The high tension inherent in this situation called for a reassessment and reformation of Judaism in modern terms, and the delay of full emancipation, shelved during the period of political reaction after the Napoleonic wars, gave the time to bring it about. German Jews, subjected to the strongest stress, were the leading representatives of this development, and they illustrate both the problems and the response evoked by them with particular clarity. Once again, while taking root in their environment, they expressed their religion by their way of living, like the "pious men of Germany" of the Middle Ages.

The second half of the nineteenth century saw the fight for emancipation won. The age of realism and materialism, however, appeared to erode religion altogether, while the anti-Semitic wave of the 1870s and 1880s, fanned by nationalisms competing as Favored Nations, threatened the standing of Jews within their environment anew. Yet, in their widespread participation in Western culture, Jewish religious ideas and attitudes proved capable of being secularized in new fields. For example, Ferdinand J. Cohn, identifying God and Nature on the lines of Spinoza's philosophy, searched for the unity of nature in its smallest parts with the same single-minded devotion that Jews of old had devoted to beholding the unity of God, and became the founder of systematic bacteriology. Moritz Lazarus and Heymann Steinthal created, within the cult of the individual, the academic discipline of a psychology of national groups. Ferdinand Lassalle, who as a teenager had dreamed of liberating the Jews, came to organize the oppressed workers in a trade union. Emil Rathenau, transferring the aim of enlightenment to a technical application, fought tirelessly for the introduction of electricity. Above all, Theodor Herzl, deeply shocked by the Dreyfus affair rekindled the powerful messianic hopes by his plan of a secular Jewish state and became the founder of Zionism, whose national aims could enable non-religious Jews to retain an inner identity with their past.

With the decline of Liberalism in the twentieth century, Western culture no longer held the fascination it had exerted a hundred years before. Now Judaism reappeared on the horizon of fully assimilated

Jews almost as a new discovery. A synthesis of Judaism and Western civilization was achieved which, represented above all by four men, Hermann Cohen, Leo Baeck, Martin Buber, and Franz Rosenzweig, still holds prospects for the future far beyond its origin.

The German Jew

German Jews in the Middle Ages

From Roman Times to the Medieval World

By the closing stages of Jewish nationhood in the Hellenistic period, colonies of Jews had sprung up all along the Mediterranean, in Italy, in France, and in Greece. Even in the pre-Christian era there were settlements of Jews in Rome, in Marseilles, and in other places. This colonizing movement increased when the Temple of Jerusalem was destroyed in the year 70 of the Common Era and Jewish national sovereignty came to an end.

Wherever Jews went they carried with them their belief in the One God, their own particular customs, their specific way of life. Trust in an invisible, seeing God, the creator of the universe and the ruler of life, gave them an inner security beyond the visible world. This made them independent yet flexible and adaptable to changing circumstances and surroundings, and prevented them from being absorbed by whatever external contacts they met.

The history of Jews on German soil covers a continuous period of two thousand years. They came in the wake of Roman armies, as craftsmen or merchants, some perhaps as soldiers—so excavations appear to suggest—others maybe as captive slaves who were later freed. A decree of the emperor Constantine, of December 321, refers to a well-organized Jewish congregation at Cologne, the members of which owned houses and land and were eligible for municipal offices. A seven-armed candlestick, the old symbol of Judaism, and terracotta heads with markedly semitic features, excavated at Treves, are relics of a life of which otherwise we know little.

From the time of Charlemagne onward (ninth century) this history becomes continuous. In his empire Jews were held in high esteem, secured by imperial privileges, living among their neighbors in an atmosphere of friendliness. This Holy Roman Empire of the German Nation felt itself to be the successor in the spirit of Christianity to the peace-promoting Roman rule of the world. Within this supernational,

17

universal conception Jews could render valuable services by mediating between East and West. This became their main contribution to the tender growth of Western civilization, by trading, by personal service, and above all by transmitting in translations from Greek and Arabic the heritage of antiquity in medicine, science, and philosophy.

An embassy that Charlemagne sent from Aix-la-Chapelle to the caliph al Rashid at Baghdad consisted of two Franconian Counts and a Jew, Isaac. Since both Germans died during the long voyage, he was the only one to return after four years, in July 802, and to bring back the precious gifts of the oriental ruler, among them an elephant called "Abulabaz" and the magnificent tapestry-elephant cloth in which Charlemagne chose to be buried.

Judaism too enjoyed high prestige. Charlemagne was said to have attracted Machir, a most learned and distinguished Jew, from the home of the Babylonian Talmud, to teach the Jews he had allowed to settle throughout his realm. It caused a great stir when leading Christian priests such as Bodo (in 837) and Wezelin, the confessor of the emperor Henry II (in 1010), became converted to Judaism.

From about the middle of the tenth century we find schools of Jewish learning at Mayence and Worms, which became Western centers of scholarship for over a hundred years. Gershom, son of Juda of Metz, called *Rabbenu* our teacher and the "light of the Dispersion" (ca. 950–1028), established biblical and Talmudic studies at Mayence. Such was his authority that his "ordinances" were permanently accepted by Jews all over Europe. These ordinances mark the beginning of the Western Jewries. For oriental custom allowed polygamy and gave a wife no rights in divorce proceedings and, although no longer practiced in the West, it was still permitted by Jewish law. Rabbenu Gershom's ordinances, codifying the prohibition of polygamy and introducing the agreement of the wife as a necessary condition for divorce, raised the status of women in the West in significant difference from that of the East.

The schools of Mayence and Worms attracted disciples from afar, the most famous of whom was Solomon, son of Isaac (1040–1105) from Troyes, commonly known as Rashi (*Ra*bbi *Sh*elomo *I*zhaki). He studied at Worms for ten years and received there the knowledge and inspiration for his straightforward, lucid, and wise commentaries on the Bible and the Talmud. These are still printed with the Hebrew texts and have made his work the indispensable basis for textual understanding. Legend has even made Rashi teach at Worms, where a twelfth-century synagogue bore his name, reflecting the close cultural ties between German and French Jews at a time when language and nationality had not yet become barriers.

Piety and international trading as well as learning flourished in these Jewish communities on the Rhine. Both sides were represented in the Kalonymos family that came from Lucca in Italy at the end of the tenth century and had settled at Mayence. Members of the Italian branch of this family were among the distinguished translators of Greek classics. The ancestor of the German branch, having saved the life of the emperor Otto II, was invited to ask a favor and chose residence on the Rhine. For several centuries his descendants not only maintained wide trading connections but also became political and spiritual leaders. Many of the hymns they wrote still grace the Jewish prayer book today. Most of them, alas, are laments.

For in the middle of a widespread movement of preparation for the coming of the Messiah, for redemption and return to the Holy Land, disaster struck among the Jews. The knight adventurers of the First Crusade (1096), on their way to liberate this self-same Holy Land from the infidels, descended on the Jewish communities, "more numerous than a host of locusts", and wrought havoc among them. Eager to seek revenge for the charge of having crucified the Savior, and hoping that their own sins would be forgiven if they killed the Jews, they were as ready to sack their possessions as the property of the Moslems. No local protection sufficed, no imperial warning prevailed. In their last strongholds the Jews preferred to kill their wives and children and commit suicide rather than fall prey to these rapacious hordes, with death or compulsory baptism as their fate.

In the course of time the deserted houses were reoccupied by new settlers, the schools of learning reopened, and in the Second Crusade (1146) Bernard of Clairvaux himself averted an impending similar disaster. Yet a sense of danger remained ever present.

The answer of German Jews to this outer insecurity was a mystical movement—not, however, as well one might expect, merely a withdrawal from outward reality but, on the contrary, one that led back to a heightened sense of social responsibility, to piety as expressed in daily conduct. This movement was brought about by three members of the Kalonymos family, Samuel "the Hasid" (devout), son of Kalonymos of Speier (active around the middle of the twelth century), his son, Jehudah the Hasid of Worms (died at Regensburg in 1217), and the latter's relative and disciple, Eleazar, son of Jehudah.

In particular it was Jehudah the Hasid, comparable to his Christian contemporary St. Francis of Assisi and becoming a legendary figure during his own lifetime, who molded this movement. Jehudah was acquainted through his Italian family traditions with the older Jewish mysticism; he was widely traveled and, although freely adopting the influences of Spanish-Jewish Neoplatonists and other sources, was yet of a rare independence of mind. Whereas among Jews Talmudic studies were universally regarded as the noblest activity of the mind independent of legal application, he was impatient of scholars who "ponder too much upon the Talmud without ever coming to an end." Thus he set out to reinterpret the meaning of Jewish life in terms of great simplicity and of immediate appeal, centring round the two biblical commandments "Thou shalt love the Lord, thy God, with all thy heart, with all thy soul, with all thy might" and, for the sake of the Lord, "Thou shalt love thy neighbor as thyself."

The love of God, raised to a consuming passion, is described in a passage by Eleazar, Jehudah's pupil and friend.

"The soul is full of love of God and bound with cords of love, in joy and lightness of heart. The pious is not like one who serves his Master unwillingly, but so that even if force tries to stop his hand, the love of service burns in his heart and he is glad to fulfill the will of his Creator. . . .Not, however, does he serve Him for the sake of his own advantage nor for the sake of his own honour, but he speaks thus: Who am I, "despised and rejected of men" (Isa. 53:3), today here and tomorrow in my grave, "behold I was shapen in iniquity" (Ps. 51:5) and am full of filth,—how then have I been chosen and created to be a servant to the King of Glory? For when the soul in its depth is thinking in fear of God, then the flame of heartfelt love flares up in it, the exultation of innermost joy delights the heart, inner jubilation abounds, and wisdom illuminates the face. Hence those who love His name delight in Him. . . .And the loving one cares for . . . nothing except that he may do the will of his Creator, do good unto others, hallow the Lord's name and sacrifice himself in His love."

In its inward expression this love of God meant a ritual of prayer, exegetical speculations and, above all, contemplation of the mystery of God's unity in beholding the secrets of the *Shekhinah,* or divine glory, in all its radiance. With an intense feeling of God's omnipresence, it was experienced as a spirit inherent in all creation, formless but endowed with a voice, and as "the soul of the soul" in man himself.

The social application of his teaching that raised piety above scholarship was given by Jehudah the Hasid in a long series of practical examples in his (and his followers') *Sefer Hasidim* (Book of the Devout). Piety was shown to lead to a meaningful life in which even the most ordinary activity, such as eating a piece of bread or taking a sip of water, could be raised to a holy act. Yet his guidance, while including the usual edifying precepts of piety such as serenity that renders the devout impervious to suffering or derision; humility; friendliness regardless of social distinction; truthfulness, honesty, compassion even to animals, did not stop there. On the contrary, it was particularly outspoken and strict on those points of private and business life where everyday temptations are greatest:

> If one has to turn down a loan to a Jew or a Christian, because one mistrusts his solvency, it is not permissible to justify such an action by saying that the money be not available—white lies are only allowed in describing happenings of the past for the sake of peace, but not in regard to the present and future.
> If you have a guest and you open a bottle of wine, as you would have done anyway, do not let him believe that it was done for him.
> Do not praise a rich man in the presence of another rich man or a skillful scribe in front of another so that he may not feel slighted, but you may well praise a pious man in front of another.
> If your wife hurts you and you hate her, ask God not to give you another but to turn her heart to you in love.

Such detailed instructions extend throughout the range of human relations, combining social realism, a loving care for the community, and level-headed regard for human frailty with an uncompromising devotion to the values of human life in an admirable blend of reverence and common sense.

Jehudah's teaching immediately became popular and remained so for centuries. Molding the character of German Jews, it created a new type. Whereas the distinction of the Spanish Jews rested on their philosophers and poets, the German Jews became known as the *Haside Ashkenaz,* the devout of Germany. Their unobtrusive piety, scorning ostentatious asceticism, rendered them independent within themselves but at the same time socially responsible. Without this ultimate certainty of faith and the ability to adapt they would not have been able to weather the storms to come.

The Standing of Jews in the Middle Ages: the Emperors

The standing of Jews in the Middle Ages was primarily dependent on two powers, the Empire and the Church. As long as the supranational, universal outlook of the Holy Roman Empire of the German Nation prevailed under the strong emperors of the Carolingian and Staufen dynasties, Jews were welcomed because they fitted well into this all-embracing conception. Their adherence to the strict requirements of Talmudic law and the absence of any other political allegiance made them reliable; freedom from alcoholic excesses and from prostitution made them socially acceptable. Among a largely illiterate population they maintained a scholarly tradition. Their usual residence at centers of trade and communication, their own widespread connections, their knowledge of foreign languages and customs, their financial proficiency (the arithmetic of division was still a closely guarded trade secret) made them valuable in a clumsy and slow economic system. A privilege of the emperor Frederick I Barbarossa of September 1182 put them under imperial protection by placing them, within the feudal system of the age, in the emperor's retinue:

> It is Our Imperial Majesty's duty, being at the same time demanded by reason and equality before the law, that to each of Our subjects, not only the adherents of the Christian religion but also of those who are not of Our faith and live in accordance with the traditions of their fathers, We safeguard their property after just examination and that We provide for the continuance of their customs; furthermore, that We procure them peace for their person as well as their property. Wherefore We make known that We shall zealously care for all Jews residing in Our empire and who, by a special privilege of Our dignity, have been recognized as belonging to the Imperial Chamber.

Under subsequent emperors, however, who for lack of an independent dynastic power, both military and financial, found it hard to maintain their position, the revenue from taxes on Jews had to be pawned to princes, bishops, or towns. In 1356 Charles IV's Golden Bull handed the Jews over to the German princes. Arbitrary cancellation of debts to Jews, special Jewish taxes to raise funds for the interminable wars marked them out as milch-cows without the benefit of lawful protection. A cruel proverbial saying expressed the situation: "If you beat my Jew I hit your Jew."

The fate of R. Meir, son of Baruch (born at Worms around 1215), the outstanding Jewish scholar of his time, may illustrate both the spiritual strength of the man and the insecurity of the Jewish position. Founding a flourishing school of Talmudic studies at Rothenburg on the Tauber near Nuremberg, he became the leading authority among the *Tosafists*, or Talmudic casuists, of his time, using his authority to consolidate religious practice that, until his time, had been subject to many local variations. Over a thousand of his decisions on points of religious law or custom have been preserved. Asked whether it be permitted to light candles in the synagogues even during the day when they would not be required for the light itself, he replied:

Lights in the synagogue, even in daylight, are not useless as they serve to increase joy and solemnity. The joyful mood is advanced and increased by the lighting as, on the other hand, it is banished from places where darkness reigns. . . .In the Temple they used to kindle the lights long before the beginning of the night. They served for the glorification of the Sanctuary, although they were not necessary for lighting during the whole night, and the Lord does not need our light.

On the question of how to punish a man who has maltreated his wife:

I have a tradition according to which a husband who beats his wife is to be punished more severely than one who hits his neighbor, for his wife he is to hold in higher regard than any other human being. Maltreatment of wives is not seldom met with among non-Jews. A Jew, however, should refrain from it, God forbid. If there be one so devoid of feeling as to persist in this, he should be chastised and excluded from the community—his hand should be cut off if he does not desist from such despicable conduct.

On how to withstand torture:

If a man is firmly resolved to remain steadfast in his loyalty to God according to his faith and, if need be, face martyrdom for its sake, he will not feel any pain on being tortured. Whether he be stoned or burnt, buried alive or hanged, he will remain insensitive, not even a moan escaping his lips.

Toward the end of his life R. Meir drew the line at senseless sacrifice and, despite his age, decided to emigrate to the Holy Land with his family. On his way southward, he was recognized by a baptized Jew, detained and, on the charge of prejudicing the interest of the royal exchequer, imprisoned in the fortress of Ensisheim in Alsace. He refused to be ransomed lest a dangerous precedent be established, and he died at Ensisheim in 1293. Fourteen years after his death a wealthy Jew, Alexander Wimpfen of Frankfurt, had to pay a high ransom for the body in order that he himself might be buried next to the famous scholar.

The Church

In the present century Christians and Jews alike share the firm foundations of their belief in Holy Scriptures. It needed the common threat of a savage neopaganism, as exemplified by Hitler, to bring about an appreciation of the far greater importance of this common basis as compared with the remaining differences of belief.

In the Middle Ages the situation was far different. Because the Empire needed the spiritual sanction of the Church and the latter prevailed in the long struggle between emperors and popes, the attitude of the Church toward the Jews was even more important than that of the emperors. In analyzing the motives of the Church we may find some of the reasons for the otherwise bewildering persecution of Jews through the greater part of the following five centuries.

The medieval attitude of the Church is expressed on the face of Strassburg cathedral (ca. thirteenth century) by two stone figures contrasting the victorious Church with the defeated Synagogue, the latter blindfolded and carrying a broken wand. These statues exemplified an aim rather than a fact. By the end of the thirteenth century, the Church had indeed come to dominate the European world. Politically, the Pope prevailed over the Emperor after a long struggle. Spiritually, the Church, by successfully incorporating Aristotelian philosophy in the works of Thomas Aquinas and by the merciless extermination of heretics, had succeeded in encompassing and holding the whole of European civilization.

Yet toward Judaism and the Jews the Church was in a far more difficult, indeed an irritating and ambiguous position. Had they been long extinct, all would have been well; they might just have been made the precursors of Christianity. Every living Jew, however, was considered to be a challenge to the Church's doctrine that she herself held the absolute and exclusive truth—the notion of *nulla salus extra Ecclesiam* (no salvation outside the Church). On the other hand, the experience of Marcion's Gnostic attempt in the third century to divest Christianity of its Jewish inheritance had shown this path to be highly dangerous, for it would leave the Christian religion suspended and cut off from its basis, the Old Testament.

In the thirteenth century, as many times later in the case of nations and even races, it seemed inconceivable that the community of Christians, as represented by the Church, could rightfully feel themselves to be the Chosen People without the Jews abandoning this conviction. It took centuries to reach the insight that from the candle of a great experience many other candles can be lit without dimming its own light.

This dilemma might have been less acute had Christianity been greatly and evidently superior to Judaism. Yet the latter, organically developed from roots in ageless antiquity, evolved by the prophets, a galaxy of religious geniuses almost without parallel in human history, smoothed and polished by intimate contact with most of the great religions and philosophies of history, was in its majestic simplicity amazingly true to life and difficult to surpass. Its faith in the indivisible unity of God challenged the notion of divine unity as represented by the Trinity. The Jewish doctrine that guilt can be redeemed by genuine repentance and by trusting the divine power of forgiveness stood out against the Christian precept of original sin and the need of a savior.

Above all, the originator of the Christian religion himself was the stumbling block to any possible agreement. Aroused by the stubborn refusal of the Jews to recognize Jesus as the Messiah, the Messiah as expected and forecast by the prophets, Christians could only take it as a complete denial of their highest belief. Neither side ever stopped to reflect on the possibility that there might indeed have been a mission by a human being incorporating the essence of Judaism, invaluable and indispensable to the heathen throughout the globe—a mission creative and valid for all but Jews, who had the best of reasons for continuing this selfsame, their own, tradition.

For to Jews, Jesus neither set out to nor did he ever bring the factual political liberation from the foreign yoke expected of the Messiah by the prophets, nor yet did he fulfill the corollary of their forecast, to promote peace among all the nations on earth. The belief in redemption by his sacrificial death has indeed meant peace and comfort to millions of individual hearts, while to nations and peoples he brought, as he said he would—the sword. Hence to Christians and to Jews this part of the Messianic expectation still remains to be fulfilled.

The Christian Church of the Middle Ages could therefore hardly be expected to show sympathy or understanding, let alone love, for Jews. Even had the Church wished, it could probably not have afforded to do so because it would then have been left with the alternative either of dominating or of being swamped, but with no chance of admitting any proposition such as multiple aspects of religious truth. These reasons lay in the position of the Church toward the pagan religions that Christianity had replaced. Though Christian churches might be built upon the foundations of pagan temples, the doctrinal edifice of Christianity was not. No attempt was made to interpret pagan religious notions as true, though limited, experience, and pagan religions themselves had been driven underground as superstitions. Had the Church seen fit to admit any truth outside her own, they might have raised their heads again.

In the second century Justin had formulated the Christian doctrine toward the Jews. They were recognized as having been the people to whom God had allied Himself and from whom salvation had come. Destined to survive till the end of days to fulfill God's oath to them of eternal life, they would revert to the glory of their divine task at the millennium, yet for their disbelief in Christ they were meant merely to subsist, without value or claim, throughout the course of history.

The policy of the Church toward the Jews in the Middle Ages thus had a twofold aspect. On the one hand, their survival was justified, not to say explained away, as witnesses of the truth of the Christian faith, and in a number of critical situations threatening the mass extermination of Jews, papal bulls intervened to prevent the worst. On the other hand, the Lateran Council of 1215 ordered Jews to wear a yellow badge of discrimination and for centuries the Church saw to it that the Strassburg statue of the Synagogue with the broken wand was never far from representing the true state of the Jews. They were made into models of unbelief, into stubborn materialists who, so near the truth, refused to open their eyes to it, and hence into arch-enemies of Christianity. A ceaseless barrage of sermons trying to prove from scriptural quotations the superiority or, indeed, the inevitability of the Christian way of interpretation of the Bible was directed against the Jews, in particular by the popular preachers of lay orders such as the Predicants. The conversion of Jews was eagerly pursued, and often enough Jews were compelled to listen to such sermons, sometimes with the alternative of death. Occasionally their children were taken away from them, and successes of conversion even among the poorest in body, spirit, and morals were turned into triumphs.

Quite apart from this double aspect of the policy of the Church toward the Jews, their mere presence among Christians provided a safety valve, a target upon whom to deflect unresolved agresssion, feelings of guilt and despair caused by unrealizable demands on their own saintliness, and plain greed. It was all too easy and tempting for bad Christians to recover their self-esteem by Jew-baiting, by punishing their own sins, as it were by proxy, on those held to be altogether godless, and to feel meritorious into the bargain. However, Jews, with their messianic hope and trust, could not have survived had they not also been protected by a spiritual armor of awe and respect felt for the people of God, people secretly credited with hidden wisdom of immense value, with powers of blessing and curse. At the height of persecution, Christians of both high and low social standing never hesitated to entrust their lives into the hands of Jewish doctors.

Life of Jews in the Middle Ages

Even so, these ambivalent feelings were sufficiently charged to explode at the slightest friction. And there was a constant source of friction, based on theological grounds, in practically the sole occupation open to Jews: money-lending. Christians were not allowed to take interest on financial loans. This did not prevent the emergence of great Gentile bankers who were compensated by trading facilities, mining monopolies, and the like. On the whole, however, money-lending based on or supported by trading became the chief economic function of Jews, on both a large and a small scale. By law they were excluded from agriculture and from all the crafts covered by the system of guilds, from public and municipal service, from all professions except medicine—without, however, being admitted to its study in German universities. However respected Jews might be as traders, from the small village peddler who combined his sales with the buying of hides or cattle, bringing news of the day, carrying messages, and making suggestions for a husband or bride, to trading houses of international repute, as money-lenders they were as indispensable as they were hated and despised. Neither honesty nor piety on their part could prevent debts from often being burdensome, and the more insecure the times, the more severe became the conditions under which loans could be granted. The harder these conditions, the greater the friction. Thus there was a vicious circle that every now and again led to riots against the Jews, to bloodshed and murder.

These conditions were, however, only the everyday background of the life of Jews in the Middle Ages. Yet any uncanny or frightening event was still more dangerous. For instance, when sacramental wafers were found to be covered with red spots—due in fact to a bacterial culture—Jews were tortured and executed on the charge of desecration. Any crime such as a murder that could not be elucidated tended to be charged to the Jews, often leading to the punishment of whole communities.

Far worse, however, were those irrational charges of ritual murder which would spring up time and again despite the most thorough examination and the most authoritative refutation. The first recorded case of this kind occurred in 1235. A mill was burnt down at Fulda and, in the absence of the miller and his wife, their two small children perished in the flames. Crusaders happened to be in the town and spread the tale that Jews, requiring the blood for ritual purposes (later on the Passover festival was singled out for special mention), had killed the children. Thirty-two Jews, both men and women, were killed outright and all the Jews of Germany were charged with murder. In great excitement the bodies were brought to Hagenau where the Emperor Frederick II happened to be residing. Well acquainted with leading Jewish scholars and convinced of the absurdity of the charge, the emperor ordered a most careful investigation.

A large assembly of princes and grandees and of dignitaries of the

Church, advised him to send to all the kings of Europe and bring together a commission of all the learned Jews in their realm who had been converted to Christianity. After long search and consideration, this commission reported that neither the Old Testament nor the Gospels contained any suggestion that the Jews needed or used human blood. On the contrary, the Noachic laws forbade the comsumption even of animal blood, while the laws of Moses and the Talmud emphasized the contaminating effect of any blood. Thus, in view of the horrid and perverse character of the charge, it was inconceivable that any Jew would risk his life and possessions on such an undertaking. The emperor accordingly acquitted the Jews of the charge and solemnly forbade it to be repeated by whomsoever or on any occasion whatsoever. Yet neither his edict nor a bull of Pope Martin V (1422) to the same effect could stop the charge from being repeated time and again, invariably with disastrous consequences.

Indeed, it is only modern psychology that can elucidate the character of this charge, which lacked any foundation in fact. It was what in modern terms is called a projection, the phenomenon of seeing outside what in reality is unconsciously in the beholder's own mind—originally discovered in the parable of the mote and the beam of the Gospel. Not that Jews needed the blood of Christian children, but on the level of inner reality, Christians, one could say, needed the blood of a "Jewish child," Jesus of Nazareth, for the expiation of their sins, and the unconscious pagan part of their souls was mindful thereof.

How did Jews live under such conditions? Danger was never far away, yet this did not prevent life from being serene and even gay. General suspicion and mistrust never prevented friendly personal relationships with their Christian neighbors next door. And inside, among the Jewish communities themselves, there was a bustling social life. Butchers and bakers catered for daily needs, girls and women were busy with weaving, with embroidery, and with millinery. Scribes and illuminators, masters of their craft, were constantly in demand, for copying the scrolls of the Torah and other manuscripts was high on the list of charitable activities. Silversmiths and goldsmiths made the beautiful and elaborate ornaments used in the religious services, as well as candlesticks and goblets for home consumption. Jews in country districts cultivated orchards and vineyards, those in towns their own gardens. Scholars were engaged in never-ending studies and discussions of points of religious law and doctrine, on teaching children, and on adding their share to the voluminous store of treatises and books. Yet while there were degrees of learning, the whole community participated. No pressure of business was allowed to interfere with the

time dedicated each day to the sacred books, their study being regarded as the real purpose of Jewish life; a party was given to mark the
completion of study of each of the parts of the Talmud. Hence no
distinctive barrier arose between scholar and layman, the wealthiest
feeling honored to marry off his daughter to a poor scholar of great
promise. At weddings and parties musicians performed, and care had
to be taken lest fashionable tunes should intrude into the sacred liturgy,
or innocent-sounding lullabies contain undesirable references to pagan
myth or Christian custom.

Gay and daring Jewish students wandered from one seat of learning
to the next, picking up songs and tales on their way, as well as scholarship. There was a colorful profane literature, incorporating much of old
oriental fairy tales as well as European folklore. In this age of the free
exchange of cultural goods we also know of the Jewish minnesinger,
Süsskind of Trimberg in Franconia. In the late thirteenth century, he
made his way as a poet-composer around the feudal courts, composing
a hymn to honor the glory of the Lord, singing in praise of married
women as against the lady loves of fashion, of thought free as the
eagle's flight, of charity, contrasting nobility of conduct with nobility of
birth—and finally, in hardened times, when the great lords spurned his
song, realizing that it had been a fool's hope and vowing to turn back to
the old Jewish ways, growing a long beard, donning the long coat under
a pointed hat, and walking in humility.

Organization of Jewish Communities

The Jewish communities were interlinked by a flexible but effective
system of organization, their representatives meeting to confer and
decide on problems of common concern, not only of liturgy and administration but also of economic matters such as fixing a ceiling to rates of
interest. In the absence of anything like postal services, Jews had a
system of communication of astonishing simplicity, reliability, and
speed. It simply consisted of anyone traveling taking letters on his
way, no matter how far beyond his destination they were addressed.
On arrival he would hand on the letter to someone else going in the
same direction and thus, through a chain of bearers, the letter would
reach the addressee in a matter of days inside Germany, within a few
weeks if it were, say, from Kiev in southern Russia to Cordova in
Spain or from Italy to the North Sea coast.

Travels were mostly but not invariably trading trips. From 1175 to
1190, for instance, R. Petahia, son of Jacob, traveled from Regensburg

through Poland, Russia, Armenia, Persia, Babylonia, and Palestine. Returning via Greece, he wrote a record, edited by R. Jehudah the Hasid, that is still attractive for its mixture of shrewd observation and earnest credulity. It was only natural that travelers would settle permanently when, somewhere on their way, they encountered especially favorable conditions of work or life. Thus we find colonies of German Jews in Italy in the eleventh century and, later on, in Spain and Portugal as well, although the regular trade connections with the European East and Russia did not for the time being lead to established settlements.

The life of Jews in the Middle Ages was summed up in a memorable passage by Leopold Zunz, the founder of the Science of Judaism:

> The position of the Jew, as it had to take shape in the States of central Europe, of the Jew with the old faith, with his unappreciated culture, with his longing for Jerusalem, living in the midst of Celtic barbarians and Romance enemies, superior to them in spirit, subject in life, individually obliging, inexorable as a community, sought after and avoided at the same time, confidently suffering for a tremendous future and uncertain of the morrow:—this tragic position produced the contrast of unchangeable perseverance and of ceaseless change. People who, when their houses are ablaze, are not saved but thrown into the flames; above whom, their human right being contested, the sword is constantly poised, for whom no suffering is unattainable and who at every moment have to weep for their fathers, their children and themselves—these people needed a gift of courage, of a courage that gave significance to their life. Raised above the accidental and individual, this had to be more powerful than the mainsprings of our civilization, of the fabric of what is agreeable to the individual, useful to the community. To be a pious Jew, so as to be purified by suffering for the time of the Messiah and a blessed life, this was the task of their human existence. This determined the content of life, this alone mattered. Everything else was deemed a passing accessory, and what time and life affected, since it happened unconsciously, accidental. What maintained and activated the Jewish religion, this alone was the fully intentional, the free deed of one's own. . . . The splendour of the faith of the "devout of Germany" illuminates the synagogues of half the globe still to our days.

The Catastrophe of the Black Death

In the mid-fourteenth century anarchic conditions developed in central Europe. Peasants revolted against the towns, the guilds of the towns plotted the downfall of their ruling families and municipal councils. Both peasants and guilds also turned against the Jews, and the roads were strewn with victims. It was an apocalyptic time. Hordes of flagellants, fanaticized by a guilty conscience, swarmed through Germany from Styria and killed who ever they found on their way, turning against the Church as well as against the Jews. Then, in 1348, the country was hit by a severe epidemic of the plague, the "Black Death." The mode of infection and sanitary precautions being unknown, any explanation was plausible enough for a populace nearly insane with fright. The Jews were charged—as had been lepers in France earlier— with poisoning the wells and thus producing the epidemic, regardless of the fact that they drank the same water and suffered as much from the disease. Pope Clement V immediately refuted the charge by a bull—to no avail. And greed was allied to fear. The emperor Charles IV entered into agreements with towns, as, for instance, Frankfurt, transferring to them his financial rights in their Jews and granting them in advance immunity for whatever outrages might be inflicted on the Jews, "it be wherefrom it be, and may come about however it may come about," but claiming his share of the spoils. Regensburg and Vienna steadfastly protected their Jews. But tens of thousands in over 350 congregations were massacred, from Lake Constance to Prussia, from Flanders to Silesia. Their houses were burned down, their goods and chattels confiscated, their gravestones overturned. Not even the names of the martyrs could be recorded for lasting memory, only sad lists of congregations no longer in existence. "Can you, O Lord, how can you bear it?" asks one of the hymns of the time commemorating the terrible catastrophe.

The Ghetto

This seemed to be the end of Jewish life on German soil, and in the sense of the specific culture of medieval Jews, it was. Yet, surprisingly enough, there were survivors, some returning from foreign travels, others hidden away by Gentile friends. Many of them emigrated to Poland, where a liberal government was glad to offer them favorable conditions; there they tenaciously maintained their middle-high German language, the Yiddish of today. The flames had hardly died down and a maze of interminable legal suits regarding not only debts and claims owed to Jews but also pledges they had taken as well as their own debts, had only just begun, when towns and innumerable small principalities claimed rights on "their" Jews and clamored to have them back. Their absence had become far more conspicuous that their presence had previously been. Still, there was a difference. Feelings being mixed on both sides, the approach was one of strict utility. In the towns Jews were now segregated in closed quarters, commonly referred to as ghettos.

The word *ghetto* designates, not inappropriately, the gun-powder magazine and arsenal of Venice after which the nearby Jewish quarter had been named. The burghers wished to protect themselves as much as the Jews against a recurrence and consequences of their own excesses.

This measure had, in the long run, the effect of making the ghettos almost intolerably crammed; their high, narrow houses, with upper stories jutting out to use every inch of space, let hardly a ray of sunshine penetrate down to the street. Inwardly, Jews lived as they always had, their gaze fixed on the sole reality, the lasting word of God, turning away from the surrounding world, yet ever attentive to its fortunes and dangers. Still, the seclusion had its effects. The spiritual wall was raised every inch as high from within as from without. Participation in external affairs became more remote, because a distinctive garb and the development of a Jewish dialect impaired spontaneous relationship with the environment. Although in many small village settlements Christian and Jewish children still grew up together, Jews on the whole were not only felt to be alien, but looked it. Otherwise there was little change. The political stability of the empire did not improve; impoverished Jewish communities were faced with ever-increasing financial demands; preachers incited the masses; the old, long-refuted charges reappeared periodically; and while in the country districts life sometimes went on without disturbance for generations, the inhabitants of whole ghettos, now here, now there, were burned alive or else expelled, survivors readmitted only later. By a subtle and gradual change, Jews came to be even more despised than hated, straining their hardy vitality to bear their burdens without becoming too embittered.

The Age of the Reformation

In September 1509 Johann Pfefferkorn, a convert of Jewish descent, entered the synagogue of Frankfurt, the largest Jewish community, and threatened to ransack the houses of the ghetto as well, with an imperial warrant to confiscate all Jewish books except the Bible, on the charge that their contents were directed against the Christian faith. The dangers inherent in this charge and its possible consequences exceeded anything that had happened before. This time, however, help came from an unexpected quarter: European Science intervened to protect the Jewish faith.

The new humanism of the Age of Renaissance in Italy had evoked interest in a knowledge not only of ancient Greek but also of Hebrew; Elia Levita, born at Neustadt near Nuremburg, had emigrated to Italy and, as editor to the Bomberg printing house at Venice, became the father of modern Hebrew philology. A special messenger from Frankfurt to the Emperor procured the setting up of a commission of enquiry, and Johann Reuchlin became one of its members. Reuchlin, too, had learned his Hebrew in Italy, from the Emperor's Jewish personal physician, Yehiel Loans. He was the first Christian in Germany to become a Hebrew scholar but, above all, he was a man of upright character who did not mind arousing the hatred of Christian writers by his defense of Jewish books. In his memorandum to the Commission he mentioned that he had never been able to buy a copy of the Talmud but that it could only serve to bear witness to the Christian faith.

> The prayer-books and hymnals of the Jews are inviolable according to the decisions of the Emperors and Popes that the Jews should be left to carry on peacefully in their synagogues, customs, usages and devotions. None of these books shows, as has been alleged, any hostile intent towards the Christians. For the Jews have created their scriptures for their own edification and the protection of their faith, in case anyone, be he heathen, Christian, or Mohammedan, should attack them, but not to anyone's hurt, detriment or disgrace. . . . It is forbidden to baptise Jewish children by force. From this we can deduce that one must not take away their books against their will, for some love books more than children. The Jew is a creature of God, like ourselves; if he stands, he stands before his Lord; if he falls, he falls before his Lord. Each one must account for his own person. How shall we judge another man's soul? That is in God's power alone.

Despite all the attacks against Reuchlin, his views prevailed. Through the intervention of the Duke of Brunswick, who had pawned his jewels to the Jews of Frankfurt, the confiscated books were returned.

The Reformation, the fruit of the humanistic movement, heralded a new—the modern—age. Heaven-aspiring cathedrals had previously expressed the prevailing longing for a world beyond. Now the emphasis shifted to regarding life in this world, divinely created and ruled, as meaningful, and the world itself worthy of being made a better place, worthy of becoming the kingdom of God. This feeling, permeating the

Christian nations in the course of time, created a common basis of sympathy and understanding between Christians and Jews that had not existed in the Middle Ages, greatly diminishing the importance of such differences of outlook as still remained.

Subsequent development, above all the progress of science, had a share in this outcome. yet religion paved the way. Both Luther and Calvin took the Bible to the people, with a new emphasis on the Old Testament. Luther's translation of the Bible, influenced through an intermediate source by Rashi's commentary, made it a household book and the basis of a common German language, cutting across all dialects. Putting the lay believer on an equal footing with the priest and giving secular rulers power over the Protestant Church, it transferred numinous significance from the Church to a national community of Christians, however strong the tension remained between a nation of Christians and a Christian nation. Yet by making faith the sole justification for redemption, irrespective of conduct, that is, of active social responsibility, Luther deprived his nation of the backbone of social conscience. In recent times even the "faith" of National Socialism was able to have recourse to his justification.

In his early days Luther had a sincere feeling for the Jews, not without hope of succeeding in their conversion where the Church had met with so little genuine success. In his pamphlet "That Jesus Christ was born a Jew" (1523) he wrote:

> Our fools, the popes, bishops, sophists and monks, have hitherto dealt with the Jews in such a manner that he who was a good Christian would rather have wished to become a Jew. And had I been a Jew and seen such dolts and knaves govern and teach the Christian faith, I would sooner have become a sow than a Christian, for they have dealt with the Jews as though they were dogs and not human beings, have not been able to do anything with them but chide them. . . . Had the apostles who were Jews too dealt with us heathens as we heathens have dealt with the Jews, none among the heathens would ever have become Christians. Since they have treated us heathens in so brotherly a manner, we in our turn should treat the Jews in a brotherly manner, hoping we might convert some among them. For in the faith we ourselves are not all yet up the crest, let alone across.

The Jews too had high hopes that this sudden interest might lead to some better understanding; during Luther's stay at Worms, where he defended his doctrine before the Diet, two Jews contacted him for a religious discussion. Yet nothing came of it. Even in these early days some of the Reformers, such as Butzer in Strassburg, competed with the Dominicans in anti-Jewish writings, whereas the latter charged the Jews with having inspired the Protestant movement. Twenty years later Luther himself, irascible and disappointed in his hopes to win over the Jews, wrote two anti-Jewish pamphlets, full of insults and threats, worse than anything the old Church had done before. The Protestant Church in Germany—as distinct, for example, from Calvinism—adopted his later rather than his former line, becoming more severe as time went on.

That the fabric of Jewish life, now threatened by both religious parties, could be maintained at this period was largely due to the untiring efforts and statesmanship of one man, Joselman (ca. 1480–1554) of Rosheim, a small town in Alsace. Without special distinction of either learning or wealth, his official standing was merely that of a representative of the Jews of his local district. Yet as a boy he had experienced the effects of torture and expulsion within his own family. A burning zeal to stem all this injustice was matched by the politician's grasp of essentials, by deep conviction of the truth of his own faith, and by a candor capable of appreciating merit where he met it. He went to listen to his Christian friend Capito's famous sermons in the cathedral of Strassburg for the brilliance of learning they showed, but left when points of doctrine were expounded. Thus, in a position of moral equality and personal authority, he could plead the Jewish cause with towns and princes and, time and again, with the Diet and the Imperial Court.

Wherever there was danger and distress he appeared to meet it, riding without regard for his personal safety to Pressburg on the lower Danube, to Silesia, to Flanders, where for generations no Jew had been allowed to live, to see the Emperor. Justified complaints against the Jews he met by internal reforms. On the other hand, he calmly used the Protestant theologian Butzer's anti-Jewish pamphlets to refute the charge that the Jews had a hand in the Protestant movement. Against Butzer himself he quoted the example of the leading Protestant theologian, Melanchthon, who in 1539 had proved to the Elector of Brandenburg that the charge on which, in 1510, thirty-eight Jews were burned under his father's reign, had been faked. This proof enabled Joselman to achieve the readmission of Jews to Brandenburg. Quite capable of meeting theological points when it came to it, Joselman refuted at the imperial court an apostate, Antonius Margarita, so effectively as to procure his banishment. Yet he preferred quiet good sense. When Butzer demanded that all the goods of the Jews should be taken and given to the poor, he merely asked him to search his own conscience whether he acted out of love of God or out of wrath. If the latter: "then it is not the spirit of God, for where there is wrath, there God does not reside." In the same vein he reminded the town of Strassburg that "we are human too, created by God Almighty to dwell on earth, to dwell and be active among you and with you." Joselman attended every imperial Diet, "standing on the watch-tower of Israel," as he felt he had the confidence of Emperor Charles V, having been able to convince him of the loyalty of the Jews in the face of the Turkish armies advancing in the Balkans. It was also to his credit that in 1544 the Emperor reaffirmed and even extended the old medieval privileges, granting Jews the protection of the Empire once again, while at the same time once more refuting the blood libel.

The imperial protection thus regained was indeed effective in preventing a recurrence of the worst excesses. After Joselman's death, however, Butzer's advice prevailed, namely that the Jews, though being protected against iniquity, derision, and spite, "should indeed be put on the lowest rung with their living and their political position." Thus even local riots were by no means at an end, and the life of Jews in Protestant states remained at least as hard as formerly under the Church.

In Bohemia and Poland, among Unitarians and Calvinists, a much more liberal regime attracted a stream of emigration from Germany in the sixteenth century. The epoch-making discoveries of natural science, above all those of Galileo, found an echo in the Jewish community. David Gans, born in 1541 in Westphalia and active at Prague, became a mathematician, an astronomer of the circle of Kepler and Tycho Brahe, and a historiographer. The Chief Rabbi of Prague, the "tall" R. Jehudah Loew, son of Bezalel (ca. 1525–1609), was a representative of this age. An initiate of the secret knowledge of the Cabbalah, astrologer to the court, he was also interested in the study of mechanics and tried to reintroduce philosophy, forbidden to Jews since their expulsion from Spain. A legendary tradition of old standing credited him with having the services of a *golem* or mechanical robot, a servant that only he could master by affixing on, or removing from, its forehead a slip of parchment inscribed with the Holy Name.

Absolute Rulers and Court Jews

The secularization of political and economic life, so characteristic of modern times, began in the seventeenth century as an outcome of the split of Christianity by the Reformation, which could no longer be resolved by force. The Thirty Years' War (1618–48), which started with the intention of crushing the territorial strongholds of Protestantism, ended in undisguised power politics. It was a cardinal of the

Church, Richelieu, who as Prime Minister of France announced the principle of a new, secular state as the *Raison d'état* or, put more plainly, as national self-interest unmitigated by religious considerations. The impossibility of restoring religious unity among Christians led to the idea of tolerance. At first limited to the Christian denominations, it could not in the long run fail to become applicable to Jews as well.

The Thirty Years' War left large parts of Germany ravaged and depopulated for almost a century. From within the decaying empire sovereign national states emerged, of which Prussia came to be a European power. Each of these many sovereigns, both great and small, regarded himself as "absolute" after the model of Louis XIV of France, and wished to equal the splendor of his court. The feudal system of fealty, which gave each order of society specific rights as well as duties, clashed with the conception of absolute monarchy. Modern types of army and civil service were evolved in the image of mechanisms, each link within its order being interchangeable except for the head, who could handle the institution like an instrument. The new economic system of mercantilism aimed to make each country self-sufficient, producing everything it needed within its own national boundaries. As a means of procuring wealth for depopulated and impoverished countries by a maximum of export and a minimum of import, trade gained an increased importance.

The example of Amsterdam with its flourishing trade, boosted by the participation of Jewish refugees from Spain and Portugal, was duly noted in Europe. Hamburg, too, admitted a colony of these "Sephardic" Jews. When Jews were expelled from Vienna and Lower Austria in 1670, they were received not only by the adjoining districts of Moravia, Bohemia, and Bavaria, but also by the Elector of Brandenburg, who invited fifty families to settle in his realm. Not the least reason for the success of the annual trade fair held at Leipzig was the large and regular contingent of Jewish visitors.

The old-established guilds, opposing the new regime as best they could, were unwilling to respond to the new opportunities. The rulers themselves and their professional civil servants came to appreciate the Jews, who were only too glad to be allowed to manufacture textiles and leather goods, to found printing presses, to cultivate hops, or to plant tobacco. Yet beyond filling such gaps in the national economy by introducing new industries, by using their personal and trading connections for building up valuable exports, Jews came to be esteemed individually for the initiative and versatility they brought to bear on new tasks. The pomp and splendor of the courts, the costly buildings

being erected, and the maintenance of armies all required ready
money, and more of it than the countries themselves could yield. Jews
were in demand as bankers and financial advisers on a wide and varied
scale. They were always ready to provide an army with food,
transport, horses, and fodder, and the mint with metal, also to satisfy
the demand for choice furniture and fine jewels, or to cater to personal
predilections.

Court Jews became an established institution, enjoying the
confidence of princes and grandees, respected as advisers, not seldom
entrusted with delicate missions, and freed from the special restrictions
and taxes imposed upon their less fortunate coreligionists. The emergence of these Court Jews created a plutocratic top layer of the Jewish
body politic. Yet their position was usually too precarious to be stable.
The greater the confidence they enjoyed and deserved, the greater was
the number of enemies they made, so that each succession to a throne
endangered their safety, and their fortune dwindled as quickly as it had
grown.

The career of Joseph Süss Oppenheimer, perhaps the most gifted
among these Court Jews, illustrates this danger. He became Minister of
Finance to the Duke of Würtemberg, consolidated the finances of the
country, which were in a bad state owing to the luxury of the Court,
and reorganised its administration, some of his ideas being far ahead of
his time. Yet in achieving all this he antagonised the old-time forces.
When the Duke's death left him without protection, his fall was as
meteoric as had been his rise. Convicted of having accepted bribes,
and without receiving credit for his solid achievements, he went to the
gallows in 1738.

On the other hand, Court Jews could easily be ruined by advancing
in the course of their service all their capital without being able to
recover it. This happened, for instance, to Samuel Oppenheimer of
Heidelberg, readmitted to the Imperial Court at Vienna as early as
1673, who after providing food, artillery, ammunition, horses, and ox-
wagons to the Austrian armies fighting the Turks and French, went
bankrupt with a claim of six million florins against the Imperial exchequer.

His successor, Samson Wertheimer of Worms, represented a new
type. In his dealings with the Imperial court he had learned the lesson
of limiting his activities solely to financial matters. As respected for his
character and learning as for his financial and diplomatic skill, he used
his influence to become the spokesman for the Jewish community to
the authorities, averting danger wherever it threatened. This was in
striking contrast to Court Jews before his time who, for the sake of

furthering their own interests, had tried to dominate their coreligionists.

Like Samson Wertheimer, the best among the court Jews were *shtadlanim* or representatives of their communities, continuing the work of Joselman of Rosheim under new conditions. However, whereas the latter had been but an isolated figure, Samson Wertheimer's son inherited his father's position. Other families too were able to maintain their connections with the same Court for generations, stabilizing and expanding their financial interests in the process. The most successful and famous, yet by no means isolated, instance from the mid-eighteenth century onwards, of Court Jews branching out into international finance was the House of Rothschild, originating within the ghetto of Frankfurt.

The Inner Life of the Ghetto

However important this development might become in the course of time, it caused barely a ripple inside the ghetto, where the great mass of Jews were hardly affected, their lives becoming more rather than less difficult in the seventeenth and eighteenth centuries.

The inner life of the common Jew indeed retreated farther inward than ever before. His chief concern was an almost desperate hope and expectation of Messianic redemption, to be brought about by mystical self-purification, meditation, and speculation.

The catastrophe of the expulsion of Jews from Spain (1492) had engendered an apocalyptic feeling that even the persecution of the Crusades had failed to evoke. This feeling found its expression in a mystical fervor rarely equalled. The founder of this new school, Isaac Luria (1534–72), born in Jerusalem of a family of German extraction, lived and taught at Safed in Upper Galilee.

His teaching included a mystical interpretation of Exile and Redemption as symbols of an evolution affecting the Divine Being itself, yet assigning man a function in this process of reintegration. The "vessels of creation" having been broken—so the doctrine may briefly be summed up—the divine sparks they contained were scattered throughout the world. Their recovery from the most unlikely, unobtrusive, and even unseemly places where they had fallen, was within the means of prayer, meditation, and daily conduct of the individual, if only directed toward the unity of God, so helping to return to its origin the *Shekhinah*, the divine glory and also the soul of Israel, and thereby achieving the primordial order and beauty of creation. The Exile, formerly regarded as a temporal punishment for Israel's sins and as a test of faith, now took on the character of a Messianic mission: "And this is the secret why Israel is fated to be enslaved by all the Gentiles of the world: in order that it may uplift those sparks which have also fallen among them . . . And therefore it was necessary that Israel should be scattered to the four winds in order to lift everything up."

It was this task of introspective self-redemption, meant to bring about external liberation of Jews and even the salvation of the world, that held the attention and fired the imagination of Jews all over the world. Against this Messianic background the Amsterdam rabbi Menasseh ben Israel successfully pleaded for the readmission of the Jews to England in 1656.

A further line of development tended to raise this movement of mystical self-redemption to a high pitch of intensity and Messianic expectation. It had its origin in just one work. A follower of Isaac Luria, Joseph Caro, had a vision in which he was enjoined to collect all the biblical and traditional ordinances regulating Jewish religious practice, which he did in a methodically arranged textbook entitled *The Prepared Table* (*Shulhan Arukh,* 1564). It was immediately accepted as the authoritative code of Jewish religious observance throughout the Jewries of the world. In practice, even though not in theory, this had a strange effect. Once codified, religious observance lost the flexibility and power of adaptation which, for all its central unity, it had shown throughout the ages. Every custom included in the *Shulhan Arukh,* whether old or new, now appeared as final and sacrosanct.

Talmudic learning, hitherto needed for decisions on finer points of everyday religious practice, lost much of its direct bearing on actual life once it sufficed to look up the reference in this single work. Even where, as in Poland, this learning did not decay, it took on an air of sophisticated, rational brilliance yet of emotional shallowness. Its method, called *Pilpul* ("peppery"), consisted in finding real or apparent inconsistencies in a given biblical or Talmudic quotation and in resolving them, with dramatic effect, by another quotation. In older Jewish literature this method of cross-reference had developed much fine and profound insight. As a method of disputation it raised to perfection dialectic skill, the art of finding flaws in any argument. Yet, since it had no regard for the significance of a quotation in its original context, it tended to blunt the sense of meaning up to the point of degenerating into a game of wit. The emotional energy that it did not satisfy reinforced the mystical intensity of the Lurianic movement.

German Jews were deeply affected by this development because, in the late seventeenth and the early eighteenth centuries, Polish Jews came to dominate their spiritual life. From 1648 to 1658 the flourishing

Polish Jewry had suffered a series of disasters unprecedented since the time of the "Black Death" in Germany. Beginning with the violent incursion of the Don Cossacks under Hetman Khmelnietsky into their densely populated settlements, they continued with Russian aggression. Now the direction of migration was reversed. The old German seats of learning gladly offered shelter and fields of activity to the famous lights of Jewish learning from the east, and for a century Polish rabbis were thought superior and were usually appointed by German congregations as their spiritual leaders. Naturally they found it incumbent upon them to maintain in Germany that spirit of seclusion which had become advisable in Poland after the Jesuits recovered the country. Knowing the German language and reading a German book were punishable offenses. Hence the Court Jews, a small minority everywhere despite their considerable total numbers, could not have altered this state of affairs even had they wished to do so. The gaze of Jews remained firmly focused on the hope of Messianic redemption.

Sabbatai Zevi

This hope, and the expectation of its imminent fulfillment, made the appearance of the widely accepted "Messiah," Sabbatai Zevi (1625–76), the decisive event of the seventeenth and eighteenth centuries in the Jewish sphere. As a young Cabbalist of the Lurianic school, with alternating elevated and depressive moods, he believed himself to be the redeemer. More important still, he found in his disciple Nathan of Gaze a "prophet" of rare propagandistic skill. His fame spread like wildfire through all the Jewish communities in Europe and the Near East. Sober merchants of the Court Jew type sold their houses and belongings and prepared barrels of clothing and foodstuffs so as to be immediately ready for his call. All the more profoundly disappointing was the outcome of his mission. In an interview with the Sultan, confronted with the alternative of publicly proclaiming his faith in Islam or death, he chose the former, and left as a royal pensioner with his name changed to Mehemet Effendi.

The explosion of such high-flung hopes by the spectacle of a redeemer turned apostate was crushing—so much so indeed that many of his adherents preferred to give him their continued allegiance. For they had experienced a full year of spiritual ecstasy, and this inner experience could not be false—only its external corollary of actual liberation had failed to materialize. For a time this could be got over by pointing out that, in order to fulfill his work of separating good and evil forever, the Messiah himself had had to penetrate into the depth of seeming iniquity, had to be imprisoned by the forces of the dark—but would in time emerge again. When, however, Sabbatai Zevi died ten years later, the movement took on heretical, anarchic, and even nihilistic forms. Certain licentious transgressions of religious observances indulged in by Sabbatai Zevi in his manic state, incomprehensible to himself at other times, were introduced among his followers as a ritual. A whole theory of "holy sin" was evolved as indicating the path to salvation. A radical wing of Sabbatians held that, in order to sprout and bear fruit, the Torah as the seed-corn of Salvation must rot in the earth—hence a kind of subversive morality was required to make the Torah appear in its true Messianic glory. Outward reality and inner meaning had to differ in order to put things right. Sabbatians in Turkey and the Balkans, maintaining their belief in Sabbatai as the Messiah, followed him into Islam in the thousands, forming a distinctive sect called Doenmeh, descendants of which survive to this day.

In the second half of the eighteenth century, the sinister Jacob Frank of Podolia, posing as a Messiah, as a "reincarnation" of Sabbatai Zevi, evolved a whole theology of inverted morality. He had a large following in Poland and Moravia. Excommunicated by a Rabbinical synod at Brody, he formally went over to the Roman Catholic faith with his adherents, provoking a disputation in consequence of which thousands of copies of the Talmud were burnt.

Here one of the highest and most lasting beliefs of Judaism had indeed decayed. The Rabbinical authorities were fully justified in regarding Sabbatianism as a danger of the first magnitude, the adherents of which could expect no sympathy. Yet there was also a moderate wing of Sabbatianism that believed that it was incumbent only on the Messiah himself, not on his followers, to bear all the suffering and be subject to all the paradoxes that the work of salvation implied. They could, and did, remain within the fold of observant Jewry, although their continuing belief in the coming of redemption had to remain dormant for almost a century.

The moral twilight under the severely repressed condition of German Jews in the eighteenth century that Sabbatianism brought about was epitomized in Jonathan Eybeschütz (1690–1764), of Moravian origin. He was an outstanding Talmudic scholar, a successful teacher, an inspiring preacher and, at the same time, owing to his divided personality, a dangerous character. As a young man he had sworn to shed his Sabbatian belief. Yet despite great success as a rabbi at Prague, he felt uneasy and accepted a call to Metz, incurring such suspicion of political treason—Austria being at war with France—that not only was he himself expelled but the whole Jewish community of Prague was threatened with imminent expulsion (1744). It took the concerted efforts of German Jews, directed by Wolf Wertheimer of Vienna, and of British and Dutch diplomatic representations inspired by the Jews of London and Amsterdam to avert the danger. From Metz, Eybeschütz went as rabbi to the combined community of Hamburg-Altona-Wandsbek. There R. Jacob Emden charged him with crypto-Sabbatianism, alleging that Eybeschütz had sold amulets of barely veiled Sabbatian content. This was strenuously denied. The fight, extending over a period of years, split the congregations of Germany and Poland into two camps. The parties excommunicated and expelled each other; the civil authorities had to intervene. When in the end Eybeschütz was confirmed in office by the king of Denmark (Altona being under his jurisdiction), it appeared that this was largely due to a memorandum by a baptized follower of Eybeschütz who held his teacher to be a secret adherent of Christianity. The whole fight could not but bring the moral authority of the rabbis into disrepute.

The effects of Sabbatianism, however, went much deeper. Before the rise of Sabbatai Zevi, belief in the Messiah had been simple and clear. It not only meant that the Jews would be liberated and led back to Zion from all the corners of the earth, but also that all the nations of the world would rejoice with them, would help them on their way, and would themselves be redeemed as well. With this belief violated by a false Messiah, perverted into nihilism by his followers, the central core of Jewish feeling was numbed by bewilderment. This disillusionment, combined with the difficult external situation, produced an atmosphere of frustrated entanglement. Only an extraordinary personality, strong enough to rise above this atmosphere, could lead the way to a new age, to the hope of salvation from without—to emancipation. This was Moses Mendelssohn.

Moses Mendelssohn (1729–86)

A slightly built man of delicate health, a stammering hunchback with a noble, wise, and kindly face, he did much of lasting value and initiated more. Yet far beyond what he *did,* it was by what he *was* that he created a novel type of Jew that, throughout the range of Western civilization, transformed the Gentile idea of what Jews are really like. In the generations before him it had become unthinkable that a Jew could be noble-minded, disinterested, or even honest, or that he might have a significant contribution to make to the life of Gentiles through his illuminating insight, wisdom, or style. Moses Mendelssohn was, and did, just this. His humanity gained him the love and affection of some of the noblest men of his time, his writing the respect of his most critical contemporaries. That such a man could be, and could remain, a Jew; that the transition from the secluded life of medieval Jewry to participation in Western civilization could be achieved without loss of faith or damage to mental stability; that this faith could be expounded in terms both intelligible and acceptable to the surrounding world—all this had to be seen to be believed. What one Jew had been and done, others could also be and do. Without such an example the emancipation of the Jews, the freedom to take their place as valued citizens of the Western world, could never have been contemplated. The same trust, since justified by results, still forms the basis of the continued existence of Jews, in the Jewish State of Israel as well as in the Dispersion.

"Moses Dessau," as he called himself in his youth after his home town, grew up in a little Jewish community not far from Leipzig. The Jews of Dessau provided cooks, musicians, and a burial ground for Jewish patrons of the great trade fair. His father, Menahem Mendel, was a scribe who copied scrolls of the Torah and drew up marriage contracts, besides teaching infants to read and write the Hebrew script. The social standing of his profession, despite its spiritual dignity and strict discipline, was of the lowest; great piety, near-starvation, or both together, would normally lead to this occupation. Moses' mother,

44

Sarah Bela Rahel, came from one of the most distinguished families of the little town. Her father was a direct descendant and namesake of that half-legendary Saul Wahl who, for one night, had ruled as king of Poland; her mother claimed descent from the famous R. Moses Isserles of Cracow. It was after the latter that young Moses was named.

The boy received his first tuition from his father. As soon as he could write, however, he was handed on to the *Beth Hamidrash,* the proper school where the Talmud and its commentaries were studied. He recalled that while he was still of tender age, his father would get up at three or four o'clock in the morning, even in winter, and would carry him to school on his back, wrapped in his own overcoat. It is a story of symbolic significance: through his life he was borne forward to tasks overtaxing the strength of his frail body but, wrapped in the cloak of warm fatherly love and secure in his undivided belief, he could face these tasks and master them.

His teacher was R. David Fraenkel, a stern disciplinarian but ever ready to help his pupils, putting his books at their disposal day and night. He had been a businessman in Berlin and Hamburg before taking up this post, and he was of uncommon independence of mind, the first man in modern times to write a commentary on the Jerusalem Talmud, on which he was then working.

As was usual at the time, the curriculum of the school was confined to the Talmud and its commentaries. Moses was left to discover the Bible for himself, and he soon knew long passages by heart. The method of teaching, the Polish way of *Pilpul* or "peppery" discussion, while giving a first-rate training in lightning repartee and great subtlety in defining the exact meaning of terms, may have appeared one-sided even to the boy, overstraining the intellect but starving the heart. When ten years old, and never having been allowed to play, he began to write Hebrew poems.

He cannot yet have been thirteen when he had an experience that determined his whole life. A copy of Maimonides' *More Nebuhim,* the *Guide of the Perplexed,* fell into his hands. With great courage, R. Fraenkel had authorised the reprint, the first for nearly two centuries. The town of Dessau had the distinction of owning a Hebrew printing press at nearby Jessnitz, and the work was published there in 1742. Yet the more spectacular the opportunity, the more tantalizing it must have been to the boy that it was also so elusive. A solemn four-hundred-year-old ban forbade every Jew to touch this work before the age of twenty-five, for its Aristotelian framework and its free-thinking method rendered it suspect. Yet Moses could not resist its fascination. He broke the ban. How difficult it was to obtain a copy we do not know, but most likely he had to read the work in deepest secrecy, after a hard day's work. He studied it thoroughly. It opened up to him a new realm of serene contemplation, glowing with the passion of the heart to understand God's creation as an ordered universe of related laws. "Reason granted to us by God," he read there, "is the link between Him and us. . . . This link will be strengthened if you use it to love Him and if you strive after this with all your might; it will be weakened if you turn your mind to other objects." Small wonder that the daily dose of Talmudic legal texts, hardly ever relevant to living reality, could not compete with this experience, transforming the outlook of the budding personality and setting him a new standard.

Yet the adolescent had taken on a spiritual burden he could not yet bear and it bent him. The strain and overwork, aggravated by a guilty conscience for having broken the ban, coincided with a severe illness, probably a tubercular infection of the spine, that left it crooked all his life. We do not know whether his stammer also dated from this time. It may well be so, for he had to hide his dangerous knowledge. At any rate he himself was fully aware of the connection between his discovery of Maimonides and his illness. "To Maimuni it was due," he later used to tell his friends, "that I got so deformed a body. In spite of it I love him dearly, for he has iluminated many gloomy hours of my life. Even though, unintentionally, he harmed and weakened me physically, he has rewarded the injury sevenfold by invigorating my soul with his high wisdom."

Moses had hardly recovered when R. Fraenkel left Dessau, having been appointed Chief Rabbi of Berlin. Being now thirteen years of age and expected to earn his own living, Moses had to escape from the fate, customary in view of his family's poverty, of taking up the trade of a peddler. It took him four months to win his parents' and the community's consent to let him follow his master.

The penniless fourteen-year-old youth who in October 1743 demanded admission at the Rosenthal tollgate of Berlin—the only gate through which foreign Jews might enter the city—could merely state as his purpose his desire to learn, yet he passed the scrutiny because he could refer to R. Fraenkel. He did indeed continue his Talmudic studies at his teacher's school, and through his influence obtained a small attic room free of rent in the house of a wealthy and cultured Jew. He was also included in the rota of free, though frugal, meals served on specific days of the week that customary charity in Jewish families offered to indigent students. Better still, R. Fraenkel was able to use the fine hand his pupil wrote for copying parts of his own work. All this, however, could only just maintain the youngster above starvation level. He had to ration his bread by marking the loaf with incisions; a small silver coin found in the street that meant a new shirt was bliss to be remembered to his last years. He was too shy to beg support from wealthy Jews, holding that his desire to learn was no concern of theirs.

Perhaps he was right in feeling that his and their ideas of what he ought to learn were by no means the same. To have confessed that he was irresistibly attracted to that serenity of outlook, to that lucidity and coherence of thought which had made his acquaintance with Maimonides' work so glowing an experience—in other words, that he wished to become a philosopher—would only have meant his immediate expulsion. For since the catastrophe of the Jews of Spain, any interest in philosophy, being held to have been the cause of their expulsion, was discouraged.

Yet though the road to philosophy was nowhere in sight, the road to wisdom could be taken forthwith: "He who strives after the highest grade of human perfection, he who aspires to the bliss of uniting the lower powers of his soul with the higher ones in perfect harmony, has to go about the laws of nature just as the artist does about the rules of his craft. He has to continue training himself until his principles have been transformed into predilections and his virtue appears to be more a natural impulse than the product of reason." This was the course that he adopted, identical almost to the word with a direction in the medieval *Book of the Devout*. He became the first object of his willpower, as hard and flexible as a blade of steel. He had to try and control his stammer, to hide his shyness; he disciplined his quick and biting wit; he trained his passionate temperament into quiet, calm, deliberate, slow reaction. Yet throughout his life he was healthy enough not to try to control his feelings the way he controlled their expression.

After a day of Talmudic studies the young man in his garret indulged in voracious reading. He deepened his knowledge of Hebrew letters and developed a liking for the mystic writers, sensing a hidden "philosophical" meaning behind their metaphorical language. One day he found, as a pledge left with the host of one of the houses he visited for his meals, a German book, a stout volume of Protestant theology. With only the little German that he might have picked up from R. Fraenkel, who could read and write the language, he plodded steadfastly through the unpromising subject, yet mastered it stubbornly and was rewarded by finding a philosophical proof of the existence of God—his very first glimpse of comparatively modern European thought.

For all his youth, Moses was secure in himself because of his quest.

Yet the mere reading of German books, let alone a book on Christian theology, was felt to be too dangerous to be permissible within a Jewish setting, and the danger was unmistakably brought home to him. At the Talmud-Torah school he had taken under his wing a boy three years his junior, tutoring him and often sharing with him such meager food as he had. One day, while fetching a German book for Moses, this boy was caught in the street by a Jewish overseer of the poor and expelled from Berlin on the spot. With "foreign" Jews the community had considerable powers of self-government and for the time being all that Moses could do was to get his young friend a place at some other school elsewhere.

Hence it was prudent to see what help he could get within the Jewish environment. A schoolmaster who had had to leave his Polish home town because of his mildly independent views, taught him elementary mathematics, essential for anyone intent on conquering philosophy. There were also some Jewish students of medicine, the only ones allowed to acquire worldly sciences without incurring suspicion. One of them, from Prague, gave him tuition in Latin—a quarter of an hour a day. Moses went without food until he could afford an old secondhand grammar and a dictionary. After six months the student had to leave, yet Moses had learned just enough to decipher, word by word, sentence by sentence, a Latin translation of Locke's *Essay Concerning Human Understanding,* the first modern philosopher he met, and whose work remained of lasting influence upon him.

Acquaintance with another student of medicine proved to be the door into a wider world. Aron Salomon Gumpertz, six years his senior, had had a Jewish education similar to Mendelssohn's own. However, being the scion of a wealthy Berlin family, he had also had the opportunity of learning English and French, of studying philosophy, and of meeting educated Germans and Frenchmen. He sensed the burning zeal as well as the superior intelligence of his young fellow-student and helped him along with such friendly care that Mendelssohn felt forever indebted to him for the European side of his education. Gumpertz taught him languages and lent him the works of Leibniz and Wolff, the leading philosophers of the time. Gently and unobtrusively, he introduced him to a group of masters and pupils at a Gentile public school who at regular intervals held philosphical discussions, thus giving him an opportunity to learn to speak German, to express himself clearly, to test his own knowledge and judgment, and to widen his horizon.

The young man's solid Jewish training and his knowledge of languages were valuable assets, combined as they were with shy modesty and a friendly heart. In 1750—he was just over twenty years of age—a wealthy Jewish silk manufacturer, Isaac Bernhard, offered him the post of tutor to his children. The job meant relief from the utter distress of the past years, a social standing of sorts but, above all, security. As the employee of a *Schutzjude,* or holder of the privilege of residence, he could no longer be expelled from Berlin. And the care of the children left him time to continue his own studies.

The problems confronting the young scholar were, to start with, to obtain, read, and digest a large number of works written in the four languages he had only just begun to master. To assimilate these works, however, he had to grasp the essence of European philosophy. His Talmudic training had given him the mental tools he needed, yet even the meaning of basic terms in Hebrew and in the European languages was by no means always identical. He himself recalled a striking instance of this difficulty, in the term *accident*. Having started out from Hebrew, he referred every new term he read or heard to its equivalent in that language. Yet all the old Hebrew words for *accident* meant something like "*divine* ordinance," almost the opposite of the European concept of *accidental* that is, lacking any particular cause or reason, having come about by a chance arrangement of circumstances. Such were the challenges of learning to move on to new ground without losing his own basis.

The Age of Reason

The philosophers and scientists who attracted Mendelssohn's interest were all associated with the "Age of Reason," with the movement of the Enlightenment. To describe it briefly, their achievement was a creative response to the problems raised by the expansion of the European horizon that followed Christopher Columbus's discovery of a new, unknown continent, America, in 1492. In the world of science Copernicus's revolutionary concept of the earth moving round the sun—that is, that man's earth was not, as hitherto believed, the center of the universe—and the demonstration of the laws of motion by Galileo and of gravity by Newton—to mention only the most important of the discoveries of several centuries—led to an unprecedented increase of knowledge and skill in the recognition and handling of natural forces that opened the gateway to modern civilisation and established the material supremacy of the Western nations. The medieval vista of spiritual powers, that is, qualitative values, gave way to the conception of a quantitative universe of calculable forces and measurable bodies, determined by causality—a soulless mechanical world.

The new approach, supremely successful in the scientific and technical field, also raised very grave problems. A boundless universe with no beginning in time seemed to leave no room for the biblical view of a divinely created world. With laws of nature conceived as deterministic and allowing of no exceptions, a sense of human freedom based on an awareness of exemption, however partial, from the rules of nature could not be felt to exist. Nor could the correlate notion of human responsibility, the very basis of social order, be easily reconciled with the view of a system of mechanical laws equally applicable to the terrestrial and the celestial spheres. Above all, the old conception of the earth as the center of the universe, with the sun and moon as her attendants by day and night and man as the center of life, the kingpin of creation, had fulfilled an essential function. It had balanced man in himself, given him spiritual security and an instinctive feeling of human dignity, whatever his station in life. Now, with the notion that the earth was a comparatively insignificant satellite of the sun, itself but a tiny spot in an infinite universe, man was rudely shaken out of his former sense of security, feeling displaced from his supporting center, lost and disorientated.

The Christian Church, as custodian of traditional values, though weakened by the rift of Reformation, was not nearly flexible enough to try to adapt, let alone incorporate any of the rapidly changing scientific views. It was outside the Church that the humanist Hugo de Groot based his Law of Nations on the Noachic Puritans thus reuniting nation and religion, "as a heritage of the Jews," in the idea of a Favored Nation—the Chosen People.

The human need for an interpretation of the universe, and of man's place in it, in the form of a consistent, comprehensive, and reasonable set of ideas could not for long remain unfulfilled, and it found an answer through philosophers. In a world full of doubts and illusions, Descartes established the thinking individual as the one safe and certain reality with his formula *cogito, ergo sum,* "I think, therefore I am," providing man with a provisional, secondary center within himself, a sense of existence confined to thinking but allowing orientation in, and exploration of, the strange new universe widened by the magnifications of the telescope and the microscope.

While Descartes managed to keep his new scientific thinking neatly apart from his traditional religious feeling, Hobbes declared the religious view to be untenable in the light of advancing science and even derived moral conscience from man's egoism. Spinoza followed him to the extent of regarding moral feelings as the recognition of an order of life useful to human society.

On the basic question of combining science and religion, however,

Spinoza found his own bold solution. In his view new insight into the laws of nature altered the human understanding of God. His *Deus sive Natura* is the God whose power is shown in the mathematical laws of nature—indistinguishable to the limited human power of penetration from nature itself. This view retained the biblical understanding of the creator and ruler of the universe at the price of discarding its correlate, the King and Lawgiver manifesting Himself in the human language of revelation, of the Ten Commandments—the God near to the human heart. Spinoza's God could not be reached by prayer, although possibly by "intellectual love" humbly adoring the impersonal laws of nature; he might be grasped by looking at the world *sub specie aeternitatis*, from the viewpoint of eternity. Nevertheless, Spinoza's conception of the laws of nature as being modes of God enabled man to find the divine rule behind the regular, familiar life of nature, whereas in times of old it had been seen rather in the grandiose and extraordinary, in the starry sky, in monsters like the leviathan, in earthquakes, eclipses, and miracles. The guidance of human society, which previous generations had considered entirely dependent upon divinely revealed laws, Spinoza left to human rule.

For all their difference of approach, thinkers such as Locke, Leibniz, and Shaftesbury all agreed in regarding the law-determined organization, the order and beauty of this world, as proof of its being the work of a Creator not only powerful but also benign and wise. In this way their philosophical systems, while based on science, left room for religious views.

In achieving a synthesis between the new scientific views and the essential part of religious tradition, these philosophers had indeed found an answer to the acute danger that threatened Western man when he saw his world disintegrating into incompatible parts. The Age of Reason was therefore one of the happiest and proudest periods in European history. Its aim, Enlightenment, meant a belief in universal laws of nature accessible to human reason, which was considered as the counterpart of God in man. From this belief there sprang a confidence in human nature's ability to act in accordance with reason, to fashion the world anew in the light of rational knowledge. In the human field, the movement of Enlightenment believed in the rational unity and the intrinsic goodness of human nature, overriding distinctions of nationality, race, and creed, and hence uniting man in mutual tolerance for a common purpose.

These beliefs inspired a movement that determined the outlook of rulers and statesmen throughout the Western world. To have been educated was almost synonymous with having been trained in the phi-

losophy of reason, this discipline acquiring the social significance that
theology had held in the sixteenth century. The brilliant and ambitious
king of Prussia, Frederick II, prided himself on being a philosopher,
without however letting this interfere with the training of his armies.
He surrounded himself with a circle of French scholars and writers,
preeminently including Voltaire, each of them an exponent of the Age
of Reason in his own field.

To "Moses Dessau" the study of philosophy meant therefore first of
all acquiring the common educational background of the leading groups
of society of his time. The intensity with which he embraced these
studies, enabling him to overcome all the difficulties of languages and
ideas, was understandable enough as his own part in a universal movement for the betterment of mankind. This movement, idealistically,
welcomed the Jew in him in a spirit of toleration, however few of its
rays of enlightenment ever penetrated as low as the daily realities of
Jewish life. He could hardly have realized how fortunate he was in
meeting European thought at the time he did. For either before or
afterward he would have had to cope with a veneer of Christian ideology that would have been incompatible with his Jewish upbringing.
During the Age of Reason such ideology was in temporary eclipse,
more or less relegated to the background and away from public attention. The beliefs he met coincided to an extraordinary degree with
those with which he had grown up, so that he did not even have to
consider surrendering any of his own. Jewish doctrine had taught him
to regard man as a rational being, the Law as compatible with reason,
human action as efficacious. The notion of tolerance was potentially
implied in the traditional Jewish respect for the outstanding men of
other peoples. The novel element in his studies of European philosophy was the widening and strengthening of its scientific and mathematical side, the fruit of the developments of the past two centuries,
and an ordered assembly of ideas, linking God and the world—the
exciting element in Maimonides' work—in contemporary shape. Combining ideas of Locke, Spinoza—still abhorred by Christians and Jews
alike—and French philosophers with the leading systems of Leibniz
and Wolff, he felt no need to evolve a system for himself, finding plenty
of scope for work of his own.

To return to Moses' personal situation as seen against the contemporary background: he had hardly attained the relative security and independence of his tutorial post when, together with a friend, he started,
anonymously, a periodical, *Kohelet Mussar (Preacher of Morals)*,
written in lucid and elegant Hebrew. Far from promoting "dangerous"
philosophical or nonorthodox views, it revived in a modern form (in-

spired perhaps by the famous English moral weeklies) the edifying books most popular among Polish and German Jews of the late Middle Ages. Its chief purpose was to kindle in young Jews the love of classical Hebrew, to revive the old tongue as a contemporary means of expression. Mendelssohn demonstrated its ability to express poetry by his brilliant translation into Hebrew of the first nine stanzas of Young's *Night Thoughts,* but he found to his regret that the language did not equally lend itself to rendering philosophy. Thus he gave up the attempt after the second issue of the little periodical, even though it had met with some approval. This did not impair his standing within the community nor his identification with it, yet it deprived him of a means of self-expression, of an opportunity for sharing his new findings, of a platform for discussion. For a long time this experience deterred him from further efforts at widening the horizon of his fellow Jews, and indeed it may have drawn him closer to the outer world than he might otherwise have dared to go. It put Moses Dessau on the path to becoming Moses Mendelssohn.

In 1754—he was twenty-five—his tutorial post came to an end, the children having outgrown the schoolroom. Yet what might have been a crisis or at least a major problem, if only because of the security of residence that his employment had provided, worked out as a smooth transition. The Bernhard family had come to regard Moses as being one of them. He took on the post of bookkeeper and correspondent in the silk factory and warehouse, so that his activities were merely switched from the home to the business. He became its manager on his principal's retirement and the widow's partner after his death. Devoting himself as conscientiously to this new task as he had previously to the children's tuition, the scholar became a businessman as well. It molded his character, giving him the solid, matter-of-fact outlook of a manufacturer who would stand no nonsense, whether it be in his own workshop or in the field of studies. His salary now made him independent and even allowed him to indulge to some extent in the giving of charity after having received it himself for so long. Yet his leisure time was restricted. Although he kept a few books on his office bureau and tried to read in spare moments, these were few. His thinking and writing too were conditioned by this factual approach. Even abstract speculations were kept related to common sense, and he was ever watchful to ensure that conflicting standpoints would not, on closer investigation, resolve themselves into disputes over mere words.

Mendelssohn's social contacts widened. His former tutor and friend, Gumpertz, had taken his medical degree and traveled widely. On returning to Berlin he married a banker's daughter and, rather than set up as a medical practitioner, he decided to continue his literary studies. He became secretary to the Marquis d'Argens, a member of King Frederick's intimate circle and of the recently founded Prussian Academy. The friends took up their joint readings and discussions once again, and Dr. Gumpertz continued to take his shy friend under his wing by introducing him to such interesting people as he knew.

One of these was Gotthold Ephraim Lessing, in his mid-twenties like Mendelssohn but already well on the way to making his name as a critic and playwright, though at the time he only held a minor post as literary sub-editor of the *Vossische Zeitung*. Even if, according to the recollection of a common acquaintance, Mendelssohn was only introduced to him as a good chess player, this was probably just a convenient pretext; indeed, contrary to his usual shyness, it may well have been himself who wished to meet Lessing. For among Lessing's plays to which Gumpertz had drawn his attention was a little comedy *The Jews,* of no particular literary merit in itself but unique in German letters of the time for putting forward a strong plea for toleration toward the Jews. Mendelssohn would have been eager to know a writer with such unusual freedom from prejudice. He found even more than this. The young man in a small room on the second floor of a house in a side street, where a highly varied stream of friends and visitors seemed to go in and out continuously, preferred to conduct the flow of talk from his bed. His was the most original mind Mendelssohn had ever met or was ever to meet, a brilliant conversationalist, a penetrating critic and, young as he was, an accomplished scholar with a formidable range and depth of knowledge handled lightly and flippantly. Impulsive, full of jokes, ever ready to defend outrageous paradoxes with imperturbable stubborness, juggling with ideas, yet behind all those fireworks a lonely soul, touchingly humble, unobtrusively helpful and tireless where he sensed an earnest endeavor—such was Lessing.

Moses and Lessing had known each other for but a few months when a review of Lessing's comedy *The Jews,* just then published among others of his early plays, objected to the main character on the grounds that such noble-mindedness could not possibly be found in a Jew. Mendelssohn flamed with fierce indignation. Lessing, a clever journalist along with his other gifts, got him to express his indignation in a letter to Dr. Gumpertz—who, paradoxically enough, had probably served as model for that character—and obtained the right to use the letter in his reply to the review. Hence, apart from the ill-fated periodical, the letter was the first of Mendelssohn's writings to be printed, though anonymously:

Sir,

I herewith send you [the review] of Lessing's plays which we so often read with pleasure. What do you imagine the reviewer had to find fault with in the comedy "The Jews"? The chief character which, as he puts it, is much too noble and magnanimous. The pleasure, he says, which we feel in the beauty of such a character, is suspended by its improbability, and in the end nothing remains in our soul but the desire for its existence. These ideas made me blush for shame. I am unable to express all the feelings they roused in me. What a humiliation for our hard-pressed nation! What an excess of contempt! The common folk of Christians have always regarded us as the refuse of nature, as a sore upon the body politic. Learned men, however, I should have expected to judge with greater fairness; I looked to them for the unqualified propriety of judgment, the lack of which is generally blamed on us. How much was I mistaken in crediting every Christian writer with the measure of sincerity he demands from others!

In truth!—with what brazen-facedness can a man who has any feeling of honesty left in him deny to a whole nation the probability of producing one single honest man? To a nation out of which, as the author of "The Jews" says, rose all the prophets and the greatest of kings? Is this cruel judgment sound? What a shame to humanity! It is unsound! What a shame to the judge!

Lessing, in his reply to the review, merely quoted the letter as having been written by "one of the [Jewish] nation" whom he "knew too well to deny him the character of a witty, learned and honest man." In a letter to the reviewer whom he knew, he was more outspoken: "[The writer] really is a Jew, a man in his twenties who, without any tuition, has become proficient in languages, mathematics, philosophy and poetry. I regard him in advance as an honour to his nation, if only his co-religionists whom an unhappy spirit of persecution has always prompted to go against men of his kind, will allow him to mature. His honesty and his philosophical spirit make me regard him as a prospective second Spinoza who, to equal the original, will lack nothing but his errors."

Lessing, though never out to offend, was impatient of conventions. A rebel by heart as well as in mind, he conversed with actors, Jews, and officers, all of them not commonly regarded as polite company. Yet the fighting spirit that directed a hard-hitting pen against all kinds of pretense and pomposity had as its counterpart a delicate gentleness, a tender compassion that, in his writings, made him the protagonist of lost causes and altogether a lovable human being.

Mendelssohn, "fortunate enough to be loved in return by all those I love," soon became Lessing's friend—a friendship that became one of the decisive events in his life. It was a relationship based, first and foremost, on high mutual respect. Moral earnestness and a dedicated search for truth as well as a deep-rooted love of mankind were their common bond. Mendelssohn, sensing in Lessing the man who was to become the protagonist of Enlightenment in Germany, gained self-confidence from his regard. Lessing found in his friend a match for his wit, which was new to him, and more than a match for him in dialectical skill, yet allied to this there was a steadfastness of thought as against his own preference for "logical feuding tricks and flights of fancy." Solid results emerged from conversations where previously his blaze of brilliant improvisations had left a glowing memory but no tangible conclusions. It was also a novel experience to him to find the innumerable ideas that he so carelessly threw out seriously considered by his friend and either objected to or else returned in a form that suddenly made them look sensible and practicable. Mendelssohn's voracious but amateurishly diffuse reading and study received tactful guidance from Lessing's scholarly mind, and his writing took on some of the vivid, concise, and personal touch of this master of style. Above all, however, Lessing's stimulating company gave him an unheard-of elevation and broadening of all his interests: he felt "mind and heart bettered and amused" by every conversation.

One day Lessing brought him a newly published essay by Shaftesbury and asked him what he thought of it. Mendelssohn, after reading it, said: "Not bad, but something like this I could do myself." "Well then, why not do something like it?", asked Lessing. After some weeks, Mendelssohn gave him a manuscript to read. When some months later he enquired of his friend whether he had yet had time to glance at it, Lessing smilingly handed him a slim book. He had had Mendelssohn's manuscript printed as a surprise.

This book, entitled *Philosophische Gespräche (Philosophical Conversations)*, reflected real talks between the two friends, discussing philosophical points of topical interest. A reviewer, ironically enough the same one who had been the object of Mendelssohn's wrath on behalf of Lessing, ascribed the anonymous book to the latter—no mean praise for a first book in a foreign language, however much it had profited by Lessing's editing.

A second book, again published anonymously, followed within the same year, 1755, entitled *Briefe über die Empfindungen (Letters on the Sentiments)*. It was a contribution to aesthetics, then only recently established as an independent discipline of philosophical theory, and it contained germs of future work that was to win its author a permanent place in this field. He distinguished clearly, and for the first time, between ethics and aesthetics in respect to morality:"The stage has a morality of its own," demonstrating that, suicide say, though morally reprehensible, could be acceptable in a play. "I am partial to any writer," Mendelssohn wrote, "who cannot but consider with a certain regard for the heart even the most abstract concept of philosophy, and I have to violate my feelings if attempting to investigate with cold blood truths affecting man's moral dignity." Critics of his book did indeed point to a "language of the heart" as its distinctive quality. The book was quite a success, and the author of the *Letters on the Sentiments* became a literary figure.

While thus embarking on a literary career, though still under the double protection of anonymity and of Lessing's guidance, Mendelssohn became painfully aware that his ear was "not yet German enough to judge correctly the weight of words and the regular usage in putting them together." He therefore welcomed Lessing's suggestion that he should translate Rousseau's just-published prize essay, "Discours sur l'inégalité parmi les hommes," for its own sake as well as for literary exercise in rendering the brilliance of this "divine eloquence." No one foresaw at the time what dynamite this essay was yet to become under different cultural conditions. While condemning Rousseau's verdict on all civilization in favor of a return to nature, idyllically felt to be "innocent," Mendelssohn was "in secret respect" attracted by his uncompromising assertion of the equality of men. He consoled himself, however, with the thought that it could not possibly have been the writer's intention "to trample on the true dignity of humanity and to raise the unreasonable beast above himself."

Lessing had left Berlin for Leipzig, and his letters, warm and brilliant like himself if and when they came, were as unpredictable as his movements. Hence Mendelssohn attached himself more than he might otherwise have done to a friend of Lessing's, F. Nicolai. He was a little younger than either of them, self-taught like Mendelssohn. A bookseller and publisher by trade and a man of independent means, he had a personal and professional interest in literature and poetry. Mendelssohn soon came to share these interests, "growing quite a disposition to bel-esprit," as he wrote to Lessing. It was by no means easy to combine these interests with a bookkeeper's post but, encouraged by Lessing to secure sufficient time for his own studies, Mendelssohn came to an arrangement with the business that fixed his working hours from 8 A.M. to 2 P.M., leaving his afternoons free.

Together with Nicolai he took Greek lessons for several years. Men-

delssohn came to know Plato's dialogues in the original—a delight to
him and a lifelong model of style. "I am in the middle of a transformation," he wrote during these studies, and added jokingly "and
when it is completed, who knows whether I might not even have
wings?" Indeed, Plato's style, with its "inimitable lightness of touch,"
weaned the young writer from Lessing's help and gave him a style of
his own, a combination of scientific precision, elegance, and warmth
that, admired by his contemporaries, has kept his mature writings fresh
and alive for two hundred years. Yet, even though less and less de-
pending on Lessing's guidance, he could still do with his encourage-
ment, and he got it in no uncertain terms: "Do write, my dear Moses,
write as much as your healthy hand ever can, and be certain and
convinced that you cannot write anything mediocre—for I have said
it!"

Nicolai was one of the most enterprising publishers of his time as
well as the most successful. When he started in an atmosphere still
weakened by the aftermath of the Thirty Years' War, French influence
in literature, tragedy, philosophy, aesthetics, and architecture was
dominant in Germany, the example of the Prussian Court merely
reflecting and reinforcing the general opinion. Nicolai's publications of
periodicals and books established the "Berlin school" as the leading
force of German letters, helped above all by Lessing's genius as a
literary critic of constructive suggestiveness. Yet Lessing's contributions, essential as they were, could never be counted on. For years
Mendelssohn became Nicolai's chief adviser and collaborator.

Toward the Emergence of a Middle Class

Beyond their immediate aims, these periodicals came to represent
and foster the common social outlook of a middle class just about to
come into existence. This outlook might be described as a specific set
of values, differing from those both above and below their station, such
as steadiness, thrift, honesty, patriotism, as a sense of community, and
a practical idealism leading to the assumption of responsibilities outside the range of personal interests.

By intuitively sensing, representing, and formulating this middle-
class approach, by helping to bring the belief in Enlightenment,
hitherto confined to courts and universities, within the reach of a
vaguely defined group of "educated" people and to make it one of its
distinctive features (just as a belief in progress was to be in the
nineteenth century), Mendelssohn's writings fulfilled a social function.

Ahead of Lessing Mendelssohn discovered Shakespeare's plays, scorned by the French critics as "monstrous gothic barbarities," and welcomed them as an antidote to the straight-laced rules of Racine's tragedies. He did not mind criticizing the French verse of King Frederick himself and justified his daring by saying: "Whoever writes verse, plays at skittles, and whoever plays at skittles, be he king or peasant, must suffer the 'setter-up' to tell him how he bowls."

Mendelssohn's conviction of the superiority of the German philosophy of his time to that of the French and his criticism of the frivolity of the French circle around the King, in particular Voltaire's, did not prevent him from establishing social contacts with his group. Introduced by Dr. Gumpertz to Maupertuis, the president of the Prussian Academy and a distinguished mathematician, Mendelssohn, though disliking the pomp and circumstance surrounding His Excellency, impressed him sufficiently for Maupertuis to remark that he lacked nothing but a little foreskin to be a great man. In fact, his major writings were translated into French within a few years of their publication.

Mendelssohn came to be known in academic circles as well as being familiar with Lessing's and Nicolai's friends in Berlin. Most to his liking were the Monday Club and the newly founded Learned Coffee House, a society whose members met informally at a coffee house where local and foreign newspapers and periodicals were available and where the latest publications would be discussed. Once a month a learned paper was read by one of the members, restricted in number to forty. The Society included not only mathematicians, physicists, philosophers, and theologians but also doctors (among them Gumpertz), army officers, artists, and a few businessmen such as Nicolai and Bamberger who, in Mendelssohn's beginnings in Berlin, had been the first to offer him shelter.

In the Berlin of the seventeen-fifties and sixties small groups such as these were of an importance quite disproportionate to their actual size and even to their combined learning. For, unlike London or Paris, Berlin was still a small town within a country that, only a hundred years before, had had more than half its inhabitants either killed or abducted in the Thirty Years' War. Prussia itself, never touched by the civilizing rule of the Romans, had only been colonized and Christianized in the late Middle Ages. Its culture owed much to foreign immigrants who had found refuge from religious persecution—in the seventeenth century French Calvinists and Bohemian Brethren, and since the eighteenth century, Jews. The acceptance of Mendelssohn and his fellow Jews as members of learned societies, while breaking an unwritten taboo that for long centuries had kept Jews as such, except for doctors and sometimes Court Jews, outside polite company, was quite unobtrusive because the very composition of these societies lacked any precedent. Hitherto members of a profession, trade, or craft would have kept to themselves as did members of medieval guilds. Even one generation before, scholars would not have been willing to mingle with businessmen, and army officers would neither have wished to be, nor would have been, admitted. In finding his bearings in this new type of society, Mendelssohn was not merely welcomed as a most respected member; he also did not meet any strong competition in the fields in which he entered. He had to oust no one in order to find his own place, nor did he have to compete with standards above his own reach. On the contrary, while growing himself, he could at the same time slowly and steadily raise the cultural level around him.

Yet for all his success Mendelssohn was lonely. Lessing had taken a post as secretary to the Prussian garrison commander of occupied Breslau—it was in the middle of Frederick's Seven Years' War against Austria—and was writing few and unhappy letters. Nicolai was more and more absorbed in his growing business. Dr. Gumpertz had lost his first wife and, having set up in practice in Hamburg, was once again engaged to be married. His fiancée and one of the daughters of the Bernhard family, formerly Mendelssohn's pupil and now married in Hamburg, were both friends of Fromet Gugenheim, one of the six children of a related family with whom Gumpertz himself was staying. Mendelssohn went on a visit to Hamburg, fell in love with the blue-eyed girl, and married her in the spring of 1762.

An anecdote makes quite a dramatic story of the engagement. Mendelssohn came to press his suit, but the girl, frightened of marrying a hunchback, would not have him. At their final meeting he asked her whether, according to old Jewish belief, she thought that whenever a child was born, his or her future marriage partner was announced in heaven. On her nodding agreement he told her that it had actually been decided that *she* should be a hunchback on earth, but that on his insistence that such a misfortune would only embitter a girl, he had been allowed to carry the burden instead—whereupon she embraced him.

This is one of those stories which, though but highlighting a character, can make him truer than reality. Yet in this case reality also had its points. Fromet, charming and witty but "neither beautiful nor learned," as Mendelssohn wrote to Lessing, had grown up in luxury, her father being a great-grandson of the imperial Court banker, Samuel Oppenheim. Her family's fortunes had turned for the worse, however, and they were in great financial difficulties, her father having tried in vain for months to refloat his business in Vienna and other cities. To marry off one of his four daughters to a man of Mendelssohn's solid though modest worth and good business connections could only be a welcome relief. The girl herself had certainly been forewarned that he was no prince charming in outward appearance but had ample compensations of heart and mind, just as he knew in advance that he could not expect a dowry. He went to see her, trusting the judgment of his friend and the young lady's family. He saw her every day for four weeks, but could open his heart to her only on the very last day of his stay—he had been too shy before. And he explained that her worst handicap, the family's sudden distress, was rather a virtue in his eyes: "I believe, my dearest Fromet, you would by far not be as lovable had God left you in your brilliant station."

This confession resulted from a discussion about whether it would be politic to make use of the advances that the Court Jew, Veitel Ephraim, had made to Mendelssohn in order to further both his own interests and those of his fiancée's family. Ephraim had amassed great wealth by issuing debased currency in the newly won province of Silesia so as to comply with the king's demand that he should finance some of the cost of the war. Yet Mendelssohn had warned Lessing, who was officially concerned with the project, to steer clear of it. And he replied to Fromet's—or rather her mother's—urging: "I take it for granted that our rich men are not disposed to friendship. One has to live with them on no other footing than that of good acquaintanceship. Friendship, however, requires a middle station." He firmly included Jewish society in his middle-class approach.

The marriage was a very happy one. Mendelssohn bought a house in which Lessing, Nicolai, the poet Ramler, and other members of his intimate circle had lived. He referred to it as "our house" and lived there until his death. The Bernhard family insisted on having it decorated; they had also taken over the wedding arrangements. The privilege of residence in Berlin, which was needed to enable him to marry, had been obtained with some difficulty and only for himself and his wife, not so far for any children.

In the very first weeks of his married life he sat down to compete for the prize essay of the Academy, "On Evidence in Metaphysics."

Maupertuis had stated that only the mathematical sciences, because of their quantitative proofs, were capable of producing strict evidence. Mendelssohn held that metaphysics could not fulfill the function of acting as a guide to life, since reliance had to be placed on a "practical conviction" that was independent of metaphysics and accessible without recourse to it. To metaphysics, however, he ascribed the function of *defending* truth, which "to the unspoiled, not misdirected human reason is as clearly obvious, as undeniably certain as any geometrical proposition." Metaphysical evidence is thus "like fortresses that protect a country against enemy incursion while, to peaceful inhabitants, they are neither the most convenient nor the most pleasant dwelling places." His essay was awarded the Academy's prize in preference to Kant's, which contained the germs of his revolutionary philosophical ideas, probably because, brilliantly written, it answered more the needs of his day.

In the summer of 1763 Lessing returned to Potsdam for a short visit, with all the fascination of personal intercourse. Mendelssohn contributed important notes to the former's draft of the "Laocoon" essay, which analyzed the rules governing the art of the sculptor, painter, and poet, During this decade, however, his own main work was "Phaidon or On Immortality, in three dialogues," published in 1767. Its central problem was fitting to a time when people were no longer able to believe, yet craved rational certainty, people for whom above all the problem of death meant a great question mark. Combining a partial translation of Plato's dialogue with a survey of philosophical opinion on the problem and his own ideas into a "solid yet beautiful, profound yet human" explanation of popular appeal, Mendelssohn for the first time carried philosophy into the realm of literature. His work had a European success.

For years he had been one of the most famous scholars in Berlin. Visitors from abroad would not miss the chance of seeing him in his office, standing at his desk, directing weavers and foremen, drawing patterns, advising fashionable ladies, yet ever ready to talk philosophy or literature. Beyond this, his house, populated by a growing number of children (of whom six survived), became a meeting place novel to Berlin and unique in its time, where people from all walks of life would get together and converse in a peaceful atmosphere of animated interests, being satisfied with very modest entertainment—the housewife would carefully count beforehand the almonds and hazelnuts to be offered each time. Mendelssohn had the gifts of welcoming every contribution to the conversation, of talking to people at their own level while giving their remarks a roundness and brilliance that made them suddenly sparkle with wit or wisdom. His withdrawing to say his prayers was treated with deep respect. His guests loved the evenings in his house because each of them felt raised, in his own eyes, as much by what he had contributed as by what he had received. After the appearance of his "Phaidon," Mendelssohn commonly came to be called the

German Socrates, the ideal of his time of a wise man, friendly and honest, uniting Jewish and classical traits. He became a kind of confessor for people of all stations and religions, from Ministers of State to unknown students.

Lavater's Challenge

A bombshell upset this quiet state of affairs. As far back as 1763, one of Mendelssohn's many foreign visitors had been J. C. Lavater, a young deacon from Zurich. Greatly impressed by his host, Lavater had directed the conversation toward religious matters, and Mendelssohn had had no hesitation in pronouncing his appreciation of the moral character of Jesus as a human being, although obtaining the promise that his qualified remark would be kept within the bounds of private conversation. Lavater was a fervent Christian revivalist, believing in his own mission and in the power of prayer to work miracles. In 1769 he heard from Berlin that "philosophical" Jews there were inclined toward the unitarian view of Christianity, emphasizing the human nature of Christ while denying the divine. He dedicated his translation of Bonnet's *Palingénésie philosophique,* an exposition of Christian doctrine, to Mendelssohn as an expression of his respect and gratitude, asking him publicly either to refute its proof of the truth of Christianity or else "to do what wisdom, love of truth, and honesty enjoin you to do—what Socrates would have done had he read this book and found it irrefutable."

This placed Mendelssohn in a most difficult position. It was not the first time that well-meaning Christians had wondered how such a man could be, and remain, a Jew and had desired him to become a Christian, yet never before had this been in the form of a public challenge that could neither be ignored nor be accepted. For, however alien Lavater's proselytizing zeal was to Mendelssohn's mild tolerance, to disregard this demand would have been tantamount to a confession of inconsistency or of inability to represent his own convictions. A full-fledged religious disputation, on the other hand, even if Mendelssohn had wanted it, was out of the question in Frederick's Prussia where, for all the philosophical talk of toleration, Jews were only just tolerated.

The Protestant Consistory, asked whether the reply would have to be submitted to ecclesiastical censorship, replied that Mendelssohn could have his writings printed as and where he wished, since they were convinced that his wisdom and modesty would prevent him from writing anything to cause offense.

The reply was quiet and dignified. On the main points Mendelssohn stated that he had "not merely since yesterday" begun to examine his own religion and he could not see why, if not convinced of its truth in his own heart, he should have held on to it. "His whole soul would have to take on another nature, should he give up his principles." He could not see a need to establish the truth of Judaism which, as he held, did not claim validity except for Jews and which he would demonstrate by conduct rather than by argument. Nor could he agree that he would have to refute Christianity in order to remain a Jew. In matters of faith Mendelssohn distinguished between harmful prejudices or errors, which would indeed have to be combated, and speculative or theological points that, however erroneous they might appear to an individual, any friend of virtue would have to hold "almost sacred" as long as what he held to be right had not yet become generally accepted. He protested against publicizing private remarks on Jesus without first mentioning the qualification under which they had been made. Wrongly assuming that Bonnet himself had backed the dedication, Mendelssohn stated that his work was neither the best apology for Christianity that he had read nor did he admit of his proof of its truth through miracles, since the truth of every religion could so be proved.

The very moderation of this reply, highlighting the insinuating nature of Lavater's demand, won Mendelssohn general sympathy, all the greater because of the general excitement that had accompanied the discussion. Lavater himself was sharply rebuked by Bonnet, who had written his book to strengthen Christian faith in Christians, and Lavater's theological friends in Berlin also felt most uneasy lest his implied attack on the spirit of Enlightenment might provoke Mendelssohn's circle, above all Lessing, into joining forces with him. Hence Lavater apologized for the form of his request while maintaining his good intentions, Bonnet dissociated himself from Lavater while defending his own position, and Mendelssohn answered once again. The discussion went on for a whole year; however, both parties now tried to avoid giving offense, and several critical stages were overcome by contact behind the scenes.

It was a full moral victory for Mendelssohn, notwithstanding the fact that anti-Jewish pamphlets also entered the whirl of publications occasioned by the fight. The Prussian Academy elected him as an ordinary member, though King Frederick refused to sign the decree.

But his victory was bought at a high price. The responsibility for defending his community as well as his own reputation that the public discussions implied, had strained the nervous energy of the scholar who was "an athlete neither in the physical nor moral sense." As soon as the clamor had subsided he collapsed. Any attempt to read or write meant dizziness and blackouts. Attacks of physical paralysis at night and on awaking from sleep did not impair his consciousness but were accompanied by thumping heartbeats, by anxiety, by the feeling of a scorching liquid streaming from his brain down and over his back and meeting with resistance, and by the sensation of having his back scorched with red-hot rods. Only external shaking restored the flow of his blood and the mobility of his limbs. Just as in his adolescence he had clearly appreciated the connection between the illness that twisted his spine and his reading of Maimonides, so he was now well aware that these attacks were related to Lavater's importunity—and the accompanying sensations were indeed those of torture, not so long past in Jewish experience. Inability to do any serious thinking or any reading or writing at all felt to Mendelssohn like "having his soul put in fetters." When his doctor inquired how he spent his day, he answered sadly: "Counting the tiles of the house opposite." This unhappy state of affairs continued for two months. One day, reentering his study on the first floor, Mendelssohn found his writing desk desolate, the curtains drawn, and jam jars on his bookshelves; he fled in terror, feeling like his own ghost.

However, a strict diet and his own iron will put him on his feet again. The business, so often complained about as burdensome, was now the only activity open to him; even letter-writing remained a great effort: "Like that king [Nebuchadnezzar, Dan. 4:33], I am to be deprived of my human part to recover my reason among wild animals," he wrote to Lessing.

For seven years Mendelssohn felt unable to do any philosophical thinking, reading, or writing. This period of semi-withdrawal from the outside world became an opportunity for inner reassessment. The Lavater affair had shaken his inner naiveté and security, had called into doubt his assumption that the transition from the Jewish sphere into the world of European letters was as smooth and natural to his contemporaries as it had appeared to him. He could now see that his motives and whole position still remained to be explained. More important still, had he perhaps strayed too far afield? Had not Maimonides too gone outside the "fence round the Torah" in order to study Aristotle, but returned to write his *Guide of the Perplexed?*

Reorientation

Not that Mendelssohn had lived in an ivory tower within the Jewish community during these long years. In strict observance of ritual practice he did not differ from his coreligionists, in Talmudic discussions he could stand his own ground, and sermons in German from his pen had enhanced special Jewish services to celebrate victories during and after the Seven Years' War. Hebrew writings, such as a commentary on Maimonides' *Logic* and even an extract from his "Phaidon," indicated that he had resumed his educational work. Holding a position of high respect within the Jewish sphere, he had been freed from all internal taxes and been made a representative of the Berlin congregation. Henceforth, however, there was a shift of emphasis on his own part to matters of Jewish concern. The writer of European fame, having been challenged as a Jew, became fighter for human rights and religious freedom, against prejudice and intolerance. His deep convictions and their personal expression, unlike the objective tone of his former works, moved his contemporaries and kept his voice alive across the centuries.

Some of the most important works of this decisive last period had their origins in his own personal condition and needs. During his prolonged illness Mendelssohn, like the generations before him, had found consolation in the Psalms, which he would "pray and sing." In thirteen years' work he translated them into German, viewing them as masterpieces of religious poetry, and studying in the process the long-neglected rules of Hebrew prosody.

Translation of the Bible

Of even more lasting influence was his translation of the Old Testament into German, with a Hebrew commentary. This was originally undertaken for the tuition of Mendelssohn's own children. Printed in Hebrew letters, this translation taught German to a whole generation of Jews—as later on, to generations of Eastern Jews—while at the same time leading them back to the center of Jewish religion, which was somewhat obscured by the prevalence of Talmudic studies during the early stages of education. The many first-rate Jewish writers in German during the next generation would have been impossible without this translation. Even more than this, it bridged the transition of Jews to a new spiritual home within European civilization. Without such a bridge their participation could never have become completely wholehearted. A focal center was, however, still maintained in the Hebrew commentary, written by Mendelssohn himself and four collaborators on strictly traditional lines despite its modern and philosophical treatment. Nonetheless, this work evoked a storm of indignation from the old rabbinical quarters, which Mendelssohn bore with equanimity and weathered with diplomatic skill.

Externally he was now in a position to use his personal authority and widespread connections on behalf of communities threatened with persecution or expulsion. He successfully invoked Lavater's intercession in favor of the Jews of two communities near Zurich, and that of the Prime Minister of Saxony for those of Dresden, apart from many other instances. A similar request from the Alsatian Jews, politically subject to France, he preferred not to deal with himself, but handed on to a young and enthusiastic Christian friend, Counsellor C. W. von Dohm. His treatise "über die bürgerliche Verbesserung der Juden" (On the Improvement of the Civil Condition of the Jews, 1781) became a classic because of its calm and lucid discussion of the advantages to the national interest in removing the senseless restrictions on Jews. When the old anti-Jewish arguments were raised against this treatise, Mendelssohn got his friend and medical attendant, Markus Herz, to translate Menasseh ben Israel's *Vindiciae Judaeorum,* which had achieved the admission of Jews to Cromwell's England, and accompanied it with a passionate introduction. But the project for a Jewish State, proposed by an anonymous correspondent of high standing, Mendelssohn, with realistic levelheadedness, thought to be impracticable because of the pitiful condition to which Jews had been reduced after centuries of persecution. He added prophetically that without a European war such a project would never stand a chance of success.

These external activities were combined with measures of internal reform designed to raise the educational level of Jews, and with it, their confidence, so that, secure in themselves, they could participate more readily in the surrounding civilization. To this end Mendelssohn took part in the foundation of the Jewish Free School in Berlin. Some of his pupils published a periodical, *Meassef (The Gatherer)* which, written in correct and lucid Hebrew, carried the message of Enlightenment far and wide into Eastern Europe. The feeling for purity, correctness, and beauty of language, which Mendelssohn shared with his friend Hartwig Wessely, proved even more important than the actual content of the periodical. Conscious culture of Hebrew became the distinctive characteristic of the *Haskalah* movement of enlightenment in Russia and Poland throughout the nineteenth century, and formed the bridge over which Hebrew, grammatically neglected for centuries, could become the national tongue of the State of Israel.

Mendelssohn insisted with equal determination on the use of pure German, as against the Jewish jargon then prevailing. For the use of German legal authorities as well as to protect such independent jurisdiction as remained to the Jewish community, he collected the *Ritual Laws of the Jews* (1778). The Prussian minister of education frequently consulted him on candidates for academic posts, and the Government also sought his expert opinion on the silk trade.

During his years of forced withdrawal from active participation in German letters and philosophy, Mendelssohn had traveled more than hitherto, both for reasons of health and for business. Several times he met Lessing, now librarian at Brunswick-Wolfenbüttel; he attended Kant's lectures at Königsberg and found an enthusiastic welcome wherever he went, making new friends among both the famous and the unknown. Yet it was no longer his world. Sterne's *Sentimental Journey,* young Goethe's *Werther,* foreshadowing the romantic movement, put feeling above reason. Kant's crushing *Critique of Pure Reason* seemed to render all the preceding philosophies dogmatic and obsolete. Mendelssohn's younger Jewish friends willingly adopted this philosophy, while their wives and daughters were enthusiastic over Goethe's poetry. Mendelssohn became sadly aware that the Age of Reason that he had helped to create was no longer in the dawn of permanency but in its evening glow. He no longer felt at ease in his time.

Lessing's death, after one short year of happy married life, came as a heavy blow. "Once I was a healthy slender tree, now I am such a rotten gnarled trunk! Oh, dear friend, this play is over. If only I could speak to you once more!" was the end of his last letter. In his last play, *Nathan the Wise,* Lessing, deeply convinced that to strive after truth is better than to possess it, had put forward his strongest plea for religious toleration. The central character of the play, portraying Mendelssohn as a strong and wise personality, was his lasting memorial to his friend.

Jerusalem

Yet, curiously enough, this blow seemed rather to revive than reduce Mendelssohn's energy, since it reminded him that, although only in his fifties, he still had to garner his crop. In 1783 there appeared his chief work, *Jerusalem, or On Religious Power and Judaism,* containing that justification for his remaining a Jew which he had only hinted at when replying to Lavater. Distinguishing between the State, which has to control and if need be to enforce action, and Religion, the teachings of which, being a matter of human conscience, neither should nor can really be enforced, Mendelssohn pleaded for the separation of State from Religion, assigning to the former the right to proceed only against convictions of a socially harmful nature, such as atheism, fanaticism, or Epicureanism. "True divine religion," however, "assumes no power over opinions and judgements . . . it needs neither arms nor fingers, being all spirit and heart." On this basis Mendelssohn characterized Judaism as a religion not of revealed religious beliefs but of divinely revealed religious *laws*. In respect to beliefs, he held that Judaism had none that were contrary to reason, none that were inaccessible to the natural, untutored mind, and that no beliefs at all, only actions, were enjoined by Scripture. "The spirit of Judaism," he wrote, "is conformity in action and freedom of theological opinion, except for a few fundamental doctrines on which all our teachers agree and without which the Jewish religion itself could not exist." These fundamental doctrines, however, he held to be of universal validity, while "ceremonial laws" were enjoined and binding, by divine command, upon Jews alone as a means of preserving the original true beliefs of mankind against pagan polytheism, anthropomorphism, and religious usurpation, and thereby a national link in the dispersion. While necessarily continuing to keep Jews apart as a community, these laws, "a tie linking together action and meditation, doctrine and life forever," in no way prevented Jews from taking on the duties and rights of citizens. Ordained by God, these laws could not be abrogated by any human authority, yet non-Jews, if they observed the Noachic laws and the demands of virtue, could just as safely expect salvation.

To demand religious tolerance without in any way blunting the sharp outline of Judaism was characteristic of Mendelssohn's inner freedom. This freedom was based on his striking conviction that the religious truth of Judaism not only did not clash with reason, did not subjugate reason to belief, but was even within reach of ordinary common sense without any necessity for divine revelation. It might easily be assumed that, while maintaining the observances, he had won this freedom by surrendering the spiritual independence of Judaism, by adopting the chief tenets of the Enlightenment. Yet, in fact, this cardinal feature of Mendelssohn's synthesis of the Jewish faith with the beliefs of the Enlightenment did not require any intellectual sacrifice on his part; they just happened to coincide. Jewish teachers of the Middle Ages had held the truth of the Bible to be evident to reason. Revelation had been explained by Maimonides as an intuitive anticipation of insight that, although more slowly, could also have been attained by rational deduction. Hence it was not surprising that no immediate contemporary Jewish protest was raised against his position.

The problem, however, did not rest there. Mendelssohn's emphasis on revelation as divine legislation enabled him to represent Judaism as the religion of reason, as being free from dogmatic beliefs and open to scrutiny on rational grounds, and thus to defend the independence of his religion in the light of his time. Yet this approach had itself been conditioned by a development that, while rationalizing revelation, accorded reason a somewhat metaphysical dignity. In this sense Spinoza, in his *Theological-Political Treatise* (1670), held the Bible to be a national Jewish work of legislation rather than of religion, of which only the moral precepts were of universal validity, human reason being sufficient to conduct individual and communal life. By retaining the latter and inverting the former argument, Mendelssohn succeeded in making it the basis of his apology. But in claiming the binding force of Jewish observance to be on Jews alone, he omitted the fact that almost cosmic importance, namely, a potentially universal validity, had been ascribed by former generations to the divinely revealed Torah as a combination of doctrine and law. Indeed, this view was so generally accepted that even Abraham could only be visualized as having had a secret revelation of the Torah-to-come. Mendelssohn still shared this timeless, nonhistorical view of the basic and immutable laws of human conduct, the outlook of medieval Judaism. In fact, his virtual identification of Judaism and reason simply expressed this conviction in a new way. To later generations, however, with the tremendous authority that his works attained, Mendelssohn's assertion could only mean that the spiritual characteristics of Judaism could or should even merge and become dissolved into those of mankind. His personal synthesis, a beacon for his own times, could in times to come become a will-o'-the-wisp.

Contemporary reactions to *Jerusalem* could hardly have been more varied than they were. Kant admired the work, "an irrefutable book" for its acuity, subtlety, and wisdom: "I see in it," he wrote, "the proclamation of a great reform that, though slowly, will come and continue and will apply not only to your nation but to others as well. You were able to combine your religion with a degree of freedom of conscience with which one would not have credited it and which no other religion can boast of. At the same time you have demonstrated the necessity of unlimited freedom of conscience for every religion with such thoroughness and lucidity that, on our side, the Church too will have to consider how to sort out whatever can burden and press the conscience, which in the end must tend to unite man in respect of the essential points of religion; for all the religious doctrines that weigh heavily on conscience come to us from history, belief in their truth being made the condition of salvation." But antagonism to this book was as strong as approbation. Charges leveled at Mendelssohn ranged from being an atheist to being a rationalist in his demand for religious tolerance, an "inveterate Jew" in his exposition of his religion.

If Mendelssohn could let such charges pass with comparative equanimity, there was another charge that he felt called upon to refute to his dying breath for the sake of Lessing's memory and reputation. A common friend, knowing that Mendelssohn intended to write a memorial appreciation, informed him that in the course of a conversation with F. B. Jacobi, Lessing had confessed to being an adherent of Spinoza's pantheism, adding that he had mentioned this once to Mendelssohn but, not finding any response, had dropped the matter. Jacobi only knew Lessing from this one conversation; he had brought him a poem by his friend, Goethe, entitled "Prometheus," which Lessing, despite Jacobi's doubts, had received enthusiastically. Mendelssohn, generally known as Lessing's oldest and closest friend, at first tended to disbelieve the tale altogether. He had known of Lessing's sympathies for some aspects of Spinoza's work since the early days of their friendship, and he himself in his very first book had vindicated the solitary sage of Amsterdam, still abhorred by Jews and Christians alike, as "a victim of human reason, but one that deserves to be decked with flowers." But Lessing an outright Spinozist, an unqualified pantheist, a declared atheist! This was the view of Jacobi, a "pantheist in head and mystic in heart" who, like many romantics after him, held the Church to be the sole refuge against this irrefutable philosophy. To Mendelssohn as to his contemporaries, this was a charge designed to blacken Lessing's character as well as his sincerity. To his own bitter chagrin, he found himself involved as well as his friend. Had he really to accept that Lessing had concealed a compromising secret from him while openly admitting it to an unknown visitor during an afternoon's conversation? The probability of the allegation could be gauged from Goethe's poem. Yet it could only make bad matters worse. There was the spirit of a new age, personified in Prometheus's daring Zeus with the titanic hubris of genius, believing in nothing but his own work. Could Lessing possibly have been in sympathy with what his friend could not understand? Mendelssohn had had a feeling for Shakespeare; he was far above being a mere rationalist. Yet the idea of fighting God, even a pagan god, was inconceivable to him. For him to have discarded the cloak of fatherly love would have meant instantaneous death.

An exchange of letters with Jacobi only tended to confuse matters. Mendelssohn had to fight on his own ground. For years he had given lectures on philosophy and theology to a circle of young men, including his own son and other members of his family, as well as Christians seeking his guidance, such as the brothers Wilhelm and Alexander von Humboldt. He could still use only the morning hours for creative thinking, and under the title *Morning Hours, or Lectures on the Existence of God* he published these results of his maturity, including a measured appreciation of Spinoza and referring to Lessing's attitude.

Jacobi, claiming as a prerogative of man that the law should exist for his sake and not vice versa, published the correspondence in full without authorization and without awaiting the publication of Mendelssohn's book. Embittered, Mendelssohn gathered all his strength for an immediate reply "To Lessing's Friends." "In this sanctuary of friendship," he said of himself and Lessing, as if he were still alive, "mind opens up to mind and heart to heart, allowing insight into its secret corners and recesses. The friend uncovers to the friend all his most secret doubts, weaknesses, shortcomings and infirmities, to be touched by a friendly hand and maybe even healed. He who has never tasted the delight of such an hour of opening up of the heart, has never enjoyed the bliss of life." He ended by addressing Jacobi on his despair of reason, which made him seek refuge in faith: "May he return to the faith of his fathers, reduce hard-mouthed reason to obedience by the triumphant might of belief, crush rising doubts by authorities and peremptory decrees, bless and seal his childlike turning back by words from Lavater's pious lips, pure like an angel's. I myself stand to my Jewish unbelief, trust no mortal to have lips of angelic purity, should not like to depend on the authority of even an archangel if eternal truth be at stake on which man's salvation is based, and cannot but stand or fall on my own feet in this matter. . . . Strengthened by this unwavering faith, I look for instruction and advice wherever I can find it. And, praise be to the redeeming benevolence of my Creator, I believe to have found it and I hold that everyone can find it who searches for it with open eyes and will not himself obstruct the light."

Taking the manuscript to the printer on the last day of December 1785, Mendelssohn caught a chill and died four days later of an apoplexy of the brain, sealing with his life his loyalty to Lessing's memory and to his own truth.

The Significance of the French Revolution for the Emancipation of Jews

Moses Mendelssohn had traveled a long road from the secluded anonymity of the ghetto to full participation in German letters and philosophy, to European fame. By what he was and by what he did he had shown the Jews that the ability to read and write German was perfectly compatible with maintaining and representing Jewish faith and tradition. To Gentiles he had given a living example that Jews were human beings much like themselves and were capable of valuable contributions to their cultural life.

Among Jews, Mendelssohn had opened a window into the world from the spiritual wall of the ghetto, demonstrating that Western education, in addition to their own traditions, could pave the way to social reception on a footing of equality. By the time of his death a comparatively large sector of the leading Jews in Germany and Austria, inspired by his example, had come to take an active part in the cultural life of their time. In Berlin Markus Herz, Mendelssohn's friend and physician, gave lectures on Kant's philosophy. The salons of Jewesses of Mendelssohn's circle, such as Henriette Herz, Markus's wife, had become centers of the intellectual as well as the social life of the town. Combining beauty, charm, and understanding—or, as in the case of Rahel Varnhagen, by the magnetic fascination of an outstanding personality—they continued the social function of Mendelssohn's hospitality, creating an atmosphere in which people from all walks of life could meet and converse—a unique feature of the time.

Politically, too, Mendelssohn's passionate pleas for the religious toleration of the Jews and for the improvement of their social position had begun to bear fruit during the last years of his life. The liberal-minded emperor of Austria, Joseph II, influenced by Dohm's treatise on the improvement of the civil condition of Jews, issued in 1782 his "Toleranzpatent," envisaging the gradual removal of Jewish disabilities.

73

But fearing that this decree might tend to convert Jews while setting them free, Mendelssohn inserted the following warning to the emperor in his *Jerusalem:* "For the sake of your own and of our happiness, religious union is not tolerance, it is its very opposite!"

In this respect, Mendelssohn's life and work took full effect only posthumously. Shortly after his death the young French Count Honoré de Mirabeau came to Berlin. Deeply impressed by the grief with which Mendelssohn was mourned by Jews and Gentiles alike, by the imprint of his personality on whoever he met in the salons, he read Mendelssohn's chief works. The philosopher's demand for the separation of State and Church inspired and clarified Mirabeau's own thoughts on the matter. He wrote a book *Sur Moses Mendelssohn et sur la réforme politique des Juifs.*

Only a few years later the French Revolution of 1789 proclaimed the Rights of Man, following the example set by the constitution of the United States of America in 1783. Mirabeau's book and the predominant influence and political weight that he exercised during the early phases of the French Revolution were decisive in applying these rights to Jews. The motion to this effect in the French National Assembly expressly justified the grant of full civic equality, of emancipation, to Jews by their "force intérieure" as exemplified in Moses Mendelssohn. The Jews of France were in fact granted full emancipation in 1791.

The victorious armies of the French Revolution, under Napoleon's leadership, came to occupy the western part of Germany as well as Italy and the Netherlands. Wherever they went, Jews were as a matter of course recognized as citizens with equal rights.

The clarion call of "Liberty, Equality, Fraternity" rang out to Jewish ears as the prophetic aims of Messianic redemption: liberation of the suppressed, social and spiritual equality of men, and a universal brotherhood of mankind. Even though these aims were proclaimed in the name of Reason in lieu of God, they were irresistible.

To understand the fascination that this Messianic air of emancipation had for the Jews of the time, we must cast a glance backward and recall that the Messianic hope of medieval Jews, of *redemption from within* by means of mystical purification, had been bitterly shattered by that false Messiah and apostate, Sabbatai Zevi. In the Sabbatian movement Messianic expectation had been perverted to nihilistic contradiction of belief and action, and even in its mildest form had been reduced to a prolonged state of purely passive waiting, of inward suffering with the Messiah.

Now the French Revolution held out hope of *liberation from without*. It promised its believers an active, constructive share in the betterment of mankind. What an immense relief that activity could now conform to belief instead of contradicting it! Redemption that could be worked for, the status of citizens as against that of social outcasts, settled existence after aeons of wandering, a country, a home—what hopes! For the first time in centuries divine benevolence was tangible: "We too, not only our forefathers, are being redeemed from slavery!"

Messianic expectation shifted from the future to the present: "The Messianic Age is the present era, it began to germinate with Spinoza and entered into actual world history with the great French Revolution" (Moses Hess). The corollary to political liberation in the Messianic sense was spiritual liberation—and had not Moses Mendelssohn achieved this already? His example clearly showed the way of enlightenment and tolerance, and education as the means of reaching this goal. Far beyond any immediate aims of social betterment, however urgently needed, emancipation held this twofold meaning of political equality and of personal education. In this sense it attained the emotional status of a Messianic summons, with unquestioning readiness to respond to the call whatever the sacrifice.

What sacrifice then did emancipation demand? Paradoxically enough, it almost appeared to require Jews to give up being Jews. For the French formula of emancipation that became dominant all over the Continent said: "The Jew as an individual is to be given every right, but Jews as a nation"—the word is to be taken in the limited eighteenth-century meaning of "corporation" or "community"—"are to be denied any right."

This formula, beyond its immediate interpretation of not recognizing Jews as a community, distinguished, in a social sense, between those "desirable" Jews who, by wealth and/or education, had already proved or would prove to be "individuals," and the unassimilated Jews of the ghettos. In a more subtle sense, however, the distinction extended to Jews as "individuals" and as members of the Jewish community—in fact, to Jews and their collective roots in their community. Yet, however strange such a distinction may appear to modern eyes, at the time this formula merely represented what the best men of the age were everywhere striving for—to form a unified brotherhood of man by "*overcoming the barriers* of nationhood, creed and race."

History came to compensate this rational individualism in the nineteenth century by an equally one-sided age of nationalism, and this demonstrated that the individual can outgrow national and other limitations by being more deeply rooted in his own community but not by trying to sever his roots. And if the collective traits of nationhood in an Englishman, Frenchman, or German be inextricably interwoven with his personal, individual character, how could such a separation be expected to operate in Jews whose community had been the first to attain timeless spiritual significance as the Chosen People of God?

The seemingly insoluble contradiction of an emancipation that held the quality of Messianic hope yet at the same time demanded the surrender of the very fundamentals of Judaism, caused deep conflicts and utter confusion. In the course of centuries hundreds of thousands of Jews had been ready to face torture and martyrdom for their faith. Now a whole generation of cultured and educated Jews, equally determined to respond to the call of their time, asked themselves wherein their duty lay. Looking around, they found a striking difference between the world outside and that within their Jewish environment. They were welcomed among the Gentiles, entertained them in their own homes, and found the same understanding and toleration they gave. Yet within the close confines of the Jewish quarter, centuries of segregation and persecution had left their mark on health, minds, and morals. Nothing ever seemed to change. The rabbis of the old school were of blameless character, yet, since the undignified crypto-Sabbatianic feuds, no longer above criticism as religious leaders. Frightened by the inroads of secular pursuits, they anxiously insisted on the rigid enforcement of ritual observances, despairing of their ability to impart the spiritual meaning of their faith. A representative of the Berlin congregation, when asked by a minister about the functions of rabbis, could only say "They are the guardians of *kashrut*"—of ritual cleanliness. It was hard indeed to find the living faith in such externals. And if the religion of reason was common to mankind, as Mendelssohn had held, could it be God's will that Jews should maintain an increasingly artificial seclusion, observing ritual practices that, even though divinely revealed, no longer seemed applicable?

In the light of this crude division between Jews as "individuals" and as members of the Jewish community, it was precisely Mendelssohn's position that was thrown into doubt. He would not buy social improvement at the price of inner independence and had firmly maintained the peculiar form of Jewish life in combination with the common bond of a universal ideology. But old Jewish tradition had envisaged that the coming of the Messiah would put an end to this very separation of the Jews, when all nations would unite in worshiping the One God. Since a kind of spiritual unity of mankind, though vastly different from that tradition, was already discernible in the spreading of enlightenment and tolerance, was it still justifiable to retain the seclusion built up by the elaborate system of Jewish ritual observance? Had not its basis in divine revelation been superseded by the Messianic Age?

In 1792, only a few years after Mendelssohn's death, Saul Ascher's

Leviathan, foreshadowing the movement of religious reform, advocated a "reform of the Law," arguing from Kant's "autonomy of the human will" that it could not possibly be the intention of the Lord to reveal to the Jews laws that eternally interfered with their independence. He merely wished to retain the main characteristics of Judaism—circumcision, the Sabbath, and the festivals. Yet he emphasized that biblical revelation contained the true doctrine of mankind and showed the path to human happiness—a conception of Judaism as a faith and philosophy of life as opposed to a way of living.

The general tendency of German life, however, moved against religion. The only place left by Kant's philosophy to the basic ideas of religion was as postulates of Practical Reason, and to the spirit of the time it appeared that secular notions might well be able altogether to replace religion. With Lessing, Kant, Herder, Goethe, and Schiller, with Haydn, Mozart, and Beethoven, the Age of Reason had merged with the classical period of German letters, philosophy, and music. How could the onslaught of the threatening rationalistic trends thrown up by the French Revolution be stemmed? Instead of religious ideas whose value had been undermined, the new humanism established a belief in goodness, truth, and beauty as secular ideals of human conduct.

In this humanism reason still claimed to fashion life according to its own standards. Yet its guiding concepts, its ideals, were above the level of attainable reality and immune to materialistic criticism. The component parts of this humanism were distilled from the most diverse sources. Jewish monotheism, the social ideas of Mosaic Law, the beauty of Hebrew poetry were among its ingredients, as well as Rousseau's view of nature, Christian charity, and, towering above all, the ideas of Greek antiquity. As a synthesis of such divergent contents, however, this humanism was consistent. Represented by men of genius and by works of timeless merit far superior to anything that contemporary Jewish life had to offer, it kept its fascination right into the twentieth century. It was quite understandable that Jews wanted to participate and find their place in this brilliant and humane world.

The feeling of many Jews of the time was expressed in a family letter to Mendelssohn's second son, Abraham, who had become a leading banker in Berlin: "One can remain loyal to a suppressed and persecuted religion, one can impose it on one's children as an expectancy of lifelong martyrdom, so long as one believes it to be the only saving faith. Yet once one ceases to believe this, it is barbarous." A century before, Jews had sold their property and belongings to be ready to follow the call of one whom they believed to be the Messiah. This time, hoping to be redeemed from without, many gave up their spiritual home—Judaism. A considerable part of a whole generation of the leading group of Jews, including Mendelssohn's own children with the exception of his eldest son, dropped their allegiance to their religion, either silently adopting the dominant "religion of culture" or, as Heine was to put it, accepting baptism as the "admission ticket to European civilisation." The large majority, however, became assimilated to the surrounding culture at a much slower pace and without such sacrifice.

That "particularities" of ritual law and custom, of dialect, dress, and name that Jews felt compelled to abandon in order to be admitted to the universal brotherhood of mankind included not only the traditional forms of Jewish life throughout the ages but also the feeling of a separate Jewish identity. To discard these apparent externals overnight while joining at the same time with Mendelssohn and to disclaim any distinctive spiritual features of Judaism, were bound to leave a disastrous spiritual void.

It was astonishing how blind even highly responsible Jews were to this danger. David Friedländer, a pupil of Mendelssohn and founder of the Jewish Free School at Berlin, was tireless in his activities for bettering the condition of his fellow Jews. High idealism combined with serious political misjudgment of the whole situation prompted him in 1799 to address—though anonymously—an Open Letter to one of the leading Protestant ministers. He declared the abolition of Jewish religious observance "in the now prevailing circumstances" to be, "according to our conviction, highly conformable with the spirit of the Mosaic System" and offered the conversion to the Christian faith of the "Jewish family heads" in whose name the letter was written, if such an act could be accepted as a political formality without implying any belief in Christian dogmas. He justified this step by saying that, after centuries of separation, Christians and Jews had drawn much nearer to each other. Provost Teller, the addressee, had to decline the conditional offer that had been made. Amid strong Jewish protests, Friedländer remained loyal to his faith and to his confidence in "what the best Jews and the best Christians have in common." Undaunted, he continued his efforts toward improving the social and political condition of the Jews, whose chief spokesman in Prussia he remained for over thirty years.

Progress and Setbacks of Emancipation

The difficulties of faith and conscience encountered in connection with the Messianic hope of Jewish emancipation were matched in the political fight for the achievement of civil equality by equally grave, if not even more difficult problems. As long as the aims of the French Revolution had been confined to the country of their origin they had raised universal enthusiasm. But when once carried throughout Europe by the victorious French armies, they looked and felt quite different. Napoleon, the leader of these armies, came to be as nationally hated as he was personally admired throughout the Continent.

In the Rhineland, Westphalia, and the Free cities of Hamburg, Bremen, and Lübeck, which were occupied by the French, the emancipation of the Jews had been introduced as a matter of course. The states of Southern Germany had reluctantly followed suit in improving their position, but on the whole their status remained much as before the French Revolution, with the sole exception of Prussia, the leading power in Germany.

In the course of conquering most of Europe, Napoleon had in 1806 inflicted a crushing defeat on the Prussian army, held to be invincible since the days of Frederick II. The effect was, however, an all-out effort of national enthusiasm combined with a wider, truly European spirit bringing about a spiritual as well as military resurgence. A series of far-reaching internal reforms included the emancipation of the Jews. A decree of 11 March 1812 granted Jews equality of civil rights, abolished the restrictions on residence, established their admission to academic and municipal posts, and subjected them to the newly introduced general conscription. Proudly Jews joined the Prussian forces in the War of Liberation against Napoleon.

After Napoleon's defeat, the Congress of Vienna set out in 1815 to consolidate the political framework of Europe. In the gay social life of the Congress, Jewish hostesses played a prominent part. The political problem of especial interest to Jews was the stabilization of the new status that had been accorded them voluntarily by Prussia, and under French compulsion in other states. For the first time since the Middle Ages Jewish communities sent delegates as observers to the Congress. Prussia, represented by Wilhelm von Humboldt as Minister of Education—he had been a pupil of Mendelssohn—sponsored a uniform liberal policy toward the Jews within the new Germanic Federation, including the confirmation of the rights accorded to them under the French occupation. This proposal met with reactionary opposition. The clause stating that Jews should continue to enjoy all the privileges granted to them *in* the various states was altered to read "*by* the various states." This innocuous-looking substitution retarded emancipation for fifty years, for it enabled all the newly reconstituted cities and principalities to plead that the emancipation granted under French rule had not been effected "by" them. Bremen and Lübeck actually expelled the Jews who had settled there, Frankfurt repudiated an agreement of 1810, secured by Amshel Mayer Rothschild, which granted the Jews of the town civic equality against payment of an amount twenty times the annual Protection Tax.

These setbacks were indications of the political reaction that set in after the Napoleonic Wars. The "Holy Alliance" of Russia, Prussia, and Austria, deeply mistrusting the spirit of national enthusiasm and the sense of freedom from oppression to which the victory had been due, purported a romantic restoration of Christian life as in the Middle Ages. In actual reality this meant the return to patriarchal tutelage by a despotic absolutism. In Prussia the decree of emancipation of 1812 was not abrogated but administratively limited wherever possible. It was not extended to the newly won provinces and resulted in about thirty different gradations that restricted the movement of Jews almost as much as in olden days. Outside Prussia the prevailing reaction reduced the status of Jews to utter confusion, their rights varying from almost complete emancipation in one state to semi-medieval segregation elsewhere. In general, however, it was undeniable that conditions were more liberal, which made the retention or reintroduction of the old disabilities even more resented.

The abolition of the age-old privilege of internal Jewish jurisdiction by the legislation of emancipation did not raise a murmur even in the most orthodox Jewish circles. A profound transformation had taken place even among the Jewish masses. The age of emancipation was hailed as the "New Jerusalem," as the fulfillment of Messianic hope: "The Jew should not be blamed for finding his Messiah since good princes have put him on an equal footing with his fellow citizens, have granted him the hope to attain, while completely fulfilling all civic duties, all civic rights as well" (Lazarus Bendavid).

The process of secularizing Jewish religious convictions, which had started with the French Revolution and was to extend throughout the century, had progressed one step further: education and culture became concerns of pious devotion. The diligent study of Holy Scripture that Jews had for centuries given as an end in itself now turned to the classics of German philosophy and music. The famous salons of Berlin and Vienna were but the highlights of a spiritual interest in culture that was equally deep and passionate in unknown garrets. Jews filled lecture rooms, theaters, and concert halls with a regularity of attendance and to an extent that turned such activity into a social phenomenon; they read the books of the day with such interest that the book market itself was placed on a secure footing. Education became the new meaning of individuality to Jews, the basis of their self-respect. In biblical times children had been dedicated to the service of the Temple, in the

Middle Ages to Talmudic studies. Now the sons of Jewish families were, often at great parental sacrifice, sent to the universities to advance learning in the service of goodness, truth, and beauty. The holder of an academic degree came to command the respect formerly held by a *Talmid Haham,* or Talmudic scholar, as a qualification for spiritual leadership.

Thus Jews faithfully kept their own part of the new social contract, that they would become free citizens if only they discarded the "particularities" of custom, dress, and language. Yet before their very eyes the rewards of emancipation eluded them. On the contrary, the romantic blend of Teutonic bravery and Christian saintliness appeared to leave no room for them at all, and they were told so in no uncertain terms, both officially and in propaganda publications. In 1819 anti-Jewish street rioting occurred in various parts of Germany, accompanied by cries of "Hep! Hep!", the anti-Jewish watchword of the Crusades, formed from the initial letters of the words *Hierosolyma est perdita*—Jerusalem is lost. Even those who had become converts in the first flush of enthusiasm were despised as "baptized Jews" for the deeply ingrained anti-Jewish feeling of the Middle Ages was quite as capable of secularization as were the tenets of medieval civilization. To be a Jew had been felt throughout the centuries of persecution to be the highest of distinctions: "The sin of sins is to forget that ye are children of the King of kings." For the first time in history it came to be thought of as a calamity, almost a curse. Rahel Varnhagen, whom the historian Ranke credited with "the instinct of a Pythia," a seer, whom outstanding poets and statesmen of her time judged to be "the greatest woman on earth," wrote to her brother that, despite all the gifts with which she had been blessed at birth, the fact that she was born a Jewess seemed to her like a prolonged bleeding to death.

The Jewish Reform Movement

In the pattern of Jews as individuals versus Jews as a community, which the legislation of the emancipation tended to impose, Christianity returned to the Jews its most precious Jewish heritage, the conviction of following one's individual conscience regardless of the consequences. Jesus had died in early manhood, without reaching that maturity which prompts men to come to terms with their community, to add their own insight to previous tradition without impairing either side—and this kind of maturity did not and could not form part of the Christian tradition. By combining this individualistic tendency with the rationalistic design of the Enlightenment, the emancipation of the Jews at first threatened Jewish communal life with complete disintegration, with an effect as disruptive as that of Christianity on pagan society.

Judaism had penetrated, however, more than skin deep; it was stronger than the old pagan cults and had not survived in vain amid the varied civilizations. It proved capable of resurrection and rebirth in a new form.

The German Jews of the time had become aware that the millennium of the emancipation, as a form of Messianic liberation, had dawned but had not yet arrived. They realized that abandoning the narrow walls as well as the security of the ghetto could not seriously mean abandoning Judaism itself. Yet to many of them the ghetto they had left behind seemed a terrifying memory. The newly won individuality of acquiring education, of being worthy to become a citizen of the Western world, was far too valuable a possession to be endangered. But this individuality required a new relationship to the eternal message of Judaism, its universal religious appeal. Henceforth a new trend evolved that was to remain current throughout the whole of this first phase of emancipation: the fight for the well-merited rights of emancipation as individuals, coupled with a demand that the maintenance of the Jewish community structure should be tolerated—a compromise imposed by the very structure of emancipation itself that obscured, however, the simple truth that Jews were, could be, and would be valuable citizens of Western nations *because,* not in spite of the fact that they were Jews. The unceasing antagonism, ideological even more than political, that they had to face left its mark on the new shape of Judaism in Germany and produced a much greater intensity of Jewish consciousness than was evinced by Jewries elsewhere in Europe. It forced German Jews to develop a working synthesis between Western life and Jewish values that gave them a leading position among the Jewries of the world for a full hundred years.

The necessity of distinguishing between the universal concepts of Judaism that ought to be retained, and the national side of the Jewish religion, which was felt to be an obstacle to emancipation, led to the formation of what came to be known as the Reform Movement. Its beginnings were inconspicuous—liturgical modifications of the synagogal services. Isaac Jacobsohn was a financial agent of some influence at the Court of the Napoleonic puppet state of Westphalia. He was credited with having convinced the Emperor of the difference between the lasting religious content of Judaism and its transient national tenets, which led to Napoleon's famous Great Sanhedrin of 1806. After the annexation of Westphalia by Prussia, Jacobsohn moved to

Berlin and there instituted a private synagogue which, because of its tremendous success, had soon to be moved to more commodious quarters in the house of the parents of the composer Meyerbeer. The service in this synagogue was characterized by its considerably shortened liturgy, largely in the vernacular and omitting national and Messianic allusions, by a sermon in the German language, and by the dignified manner in which it was conducted; it was embellished by a trained choir accompanied by an organ, despite the strict Sabbath laws precluding any manual activity. The chief feature of this service was the courage with which educated Jews dared attack age-old traditions, although retaining and remodeling those parts of the liturgy which still appealed to them. It was the beginning of a synthesis between the old and the new, yet for the time being the emphasis was on dignified external forms, on excluding all references to the continuation of Jewish spiritual independence, on a service claimed to be that of a "persuasion" and nothing more. But for those very reasons it had the effect of maintaining the internal balance of those who might otherwise have drifted away altogether.

The Prussian government, now conservative in all respects, supported the fierce protests of the orthodox Jews and forbade the continued use of the new service, but a new home was found in Hamburg where a "Temple" was solemnly inaugurated in 1817. Memoranda prepared by well-known German, Austrian, and Italian rabbis were used in vain to oppose its establishment; their arguments were all based on Talmudic legislation, the validity of which had itself become a matter of contention. To the protests from within the Hamburg congregation, the "Temple" replied that they did not differ from any of the accepted Jewish *doctrines*. Here was indeed the significant shift of emphasis, the insistence on Judaism as a religion of positive *ideas,* of universal significance, as against a way of life in which ceremonial practice was the distinguishing feature. It was a reversal of Mendelssohn's position which had regarded the religious ideas of Judaism as common to mankind and reserved Jewish independence to religious observance, claiming "a solid philosophical background" for its concrete demands. Yet the Reformers were able to refer to Mendelssohn's description of Judaism as a religion of reason and they could therefore feel that their endeavors were in line with his own trend. They wished first and foremost to be citizens of their country and thus to remove the "fence round the Torah" that had shielded and secluded Jews from the surrounding world since the destruction of the ancient Temple. At the same time, they wished to remain Jews. This transformation of a distinctive way of conduct into a distinctive set of ideas, while severely limiting the range of traditional Judaism, was a novel and creative response to a dangerous situation. It prevented a spiritual catastrophe at the sudden collapse of a meaningful way of life by expressing the continuity and dignity of Judaism in a modern medium.

The transformation went in fact far deeper, so much so that the continuing label of a "religion of reason" was almost a paradox. For the loving care in the maintenance of the age-old minutiae of religious observance as the most intimate link between man and God's command now came to warm and to illuminate those convictions that had given rise to the rules of observance themselves. While discarding the latter as externals, their spirit was maintained all the more scrupulously. Two generations previously, until Mendelssohn's example brought about a change, the probity of Jews had been suspect, and not always without good reason. Emancipated Jews, without stressing the religious basis, quietly established a reputation for probity, helpfulness, undenominational charity, active interest in communal affairs, and patriotism. They justified the old view that the segregating effects of observance could be dispensed with in the Messianic Age or, put differently, as the accent on external forms receded before their inner significance, the effect was the same as it had been before: the piety of medieval German Jews reappeared with a new turn of the spiral, in the period of emancipation. This time, however, piety took the form of a mixture of fulfillment and dissent.

The Science of Judaism

As a "religion of reason," Judaism was dangerously devoid of any specific content of its own, and the more the supporting framework of ritual was removed, the more it had to go in search of new means of self-understanding.

In Germany the retrograde longing of the romantic age for the spiritual unity of the Middle Ages fostered reaction in the political field, whereas science and philosophy under such romantic influence evolved a new vision of great constructive strength. The mechanistic view of the eighteenth century, whereby any branch of science, society, or state could be taken to pieces and reassembled according to rational principles, was opposed by the conception of a living organism. Language, laws, nations, and religions were accepted as having grown like a flower, expressing their own innate rules of being, independent in their own right, explorable but not interchangeable. A flower grows, blooms, and wilts, but it never remains the same. In this sense, the former static view of immutable being was replaced by the dynamic conception of never-ceasing becoming—the discovery of the significance of *history* permeated and transformed every branch of human knowledge.

History and philosophy proved to be the keys to a new understanding by the Jews of their ancient heritage, thus engendering new confidence and increased resilience.

In 1819, while consternation was general at the anti-Jewish excesses, three young men, Eduard Gans, Leopold Zunz, and Moses Moser formed the "Society for the Culture and Science of Jews" in Berlin. They were of a new generation, educated in the schools that Mendelssohn had inspired, combining a solid grounding of Jewish knowledge with full academic training. The Society was joined by stalwarts of the older generation, such as David Friedländer and Lazarus Bendavid, as well as by contemporaries, in particular the budding poet and writer Heinrich Heine. The Society wanted to render Judaism conscious, "to give a center to what, in isolation, wilts and dies, a center to which its life should be directed and from which it can receive guidance." Lectures and meetings, but especially a "Periodical for the Science of Judaism," edited by Leopold Zunz, explored and represented Jewishness in terms of "the substance of all the circumstances, characteristics and achievements of Jews with regard to religion, philosophy, history, law, literature altogether, civic life and all human affairs." The Society established a library and archives. A widespread correspondence was initiated, among others with that fantastic character Major Mordecai Manuel Noah, who had attempted to found a city of refuge near Buffalo in America for the persecuted Jews of the world. Educated Jews undertook the teaching of the many youngsters from Eastern Europe who, attracted by the new light, arrived penniless in Berlin. Another feature of the Society's programme, the training of Jews to become artisans, met with only limited success, both because of its novelty and the still restricted opportunities. The direct aim of these activities was that of education in a double sense: by "the voluntary return" of those better placed to give a hand to those who still needed tuition in order to take their place in the fight for emancipation, and to strengthen educated Jews in their task "of merging into Western civilization without perishing within it."

The Science of Judaism, which for the first time appeared in the name and as the title of the Society's periodical and which formed the center of its program, had been outlined by Leopold Zunz a year before in his "Notes on Rabbinical Literature," and heralded what was to become the chief contribution of German Jews to modern Jewish life.

This Science was, first and foremost, strictly secular historical research in the service of a true representation of facts, viewing Jewish letters as the comprehensive totality of the spirit of Jewish history, yet keeping scientific distance as to the question of normative validity: "The whole literature of Jews in its widest extent is here set out as an object of research, without regard to whether its total should and can also form the norm of our own judgment." In this spirit of totality Zunz gave in the Society's periodical the programe of a "Statistics of Jews." The historical method he exemplified in a paper on Rashi, separating fact from legend with almost anatomical precision and not without the addition of caustic wit, appraising Rashi's commentaries with a critical scrutiny of the range of his knowledge, describing the work of his pupils, and so on.

The choice of this subject was not accidental. By presenting in its true perspectives the achievements of the greatest Jewish scholar of the Middle Ages—a period utterly scorned at the time because of its unforgotten horrors and its suppression of human rights—Zunz aimed at promoting a justified pride in Jews for their past and respect for it by the Gentiles. Yet what he had in mind was not merely an isolated instance or period. It was the history of Judaism as the expression of one particular aspect of the spirit of mankind, with all its widespread interconnected ramifications and its ever-present character of a living unity: "In order to have knowledge of literature, i.e., the coherence of the written monuments of the human spirit, this spirit both separates and connects freely all peculiarities after having recognized them all as emanations of a single original spirit. . . . Then the literature of the individual people appears as the product of formative forces, as a reflection of the divine spirit revealing itself in the particular which has also its share in the eternal, while its sum and apex allows us to survey what the most noble spirits have felt and desired, what they have sought, loved and conquered and for what they have given up their mortal portion."

Looked at in this spirit, the Science of Judaism could bridge the gulf between secular and religious education, link the past with the present and future, nullify the misleading distinctions between the particular and the universal, and provide a meaning for Jewish existence and guidance for its reform. Zunz was an avowed adherent of reform in this sense of "historical Judaism."

These ideas, however independently assembled and elaborated, owed much to Hegel, the dominant philosopher of the day. In his *Phenomenology of the Spirit* he had propounded his theory of the justification of history as demonstrating the ways of supreme rule in its gradual evolution of human freedom, of reason taken to be identical with reality. His famous sentence: "What is real, is rational, and what is rational, is real," could well be misapplied to the problem of Jewish reform by denying a basis of "reason, i.e., reality" for all the "particularities" of ritual no longer desired. Yet, in his description of the path of the "objective spirit," manifesting itself in individual national civilizations, Hegel had vindicated for Judaism the character of true religion as a revolution against the ancient orient. Though he held his own philosophy to represent the totality of philosophy as such, Hegel insisted that "in the true system of philosophy every stage has its own form, nothing is lost, all principles are retained, for the last philosophy is the totality of forms." Hence the Science of Judaism was fully justified in referring to Hegel's philosophy as implying and justifying the survival of Judaism as a primary expression of the "world spirit."

The demands of the Society for the Culture and Science of Jews, despite the enthusiasm it engendered, were too great to allow it to arouse popular appeal, and its life was short. When the right of Jews in Prussia to admission to academic careers, which had been granted by the decree of 1812, was withdrawn in the period of political reaction in 1832, Eduard Gans, the president of the Society, could secure his professional future as a historian of jurisprudence only by accepting conversion to Protestantism. To the members of the Society who had sworn to retain their Jewish faith, this defection of their president seemed like an act of treason. The Society did not survive this blow. In a disappointment bordering on despair, Leopold Zunz remained almost single-handed to continue his work for the Science of Judaism. Only his fellow-student Isaac Marcus Jost continued his pioneering *History of the Jews,* of which publication had just begun.

Neo-orthodoxy

Not only in Prussia but also in the Free City of Hamburg, most of the community reacted against the reform service in the "Temple." In 1821 Isaac Bernays was appointed Chief Rabbi of Hamburg, a post that had been left vacant for over twenty years after the repercussions of the fight about E. Eybeschütz's Sabbatianism. Who was this man Bernays?

Born in 1792 at Mayence, then under French occupation, the son of an innkeeper, Bernays had been regarded as an infant prodigy, knowing a whole tractate of the Talmud by heart at the age of seven. After his father's early death, his mother took it upon herself to send him to the Talmudic College or Yeshivah of R. Abraham Bing at Würzburg. There he received a thorough training in the traditional lore but at the same time, despite his strict orthodoxy, he was allowed to attend lectures at the University on oriental languages and Greek philology. This was not so contradictory as it appeared, for at the University Bernays met H. Kanne and J. J. Wagner, pupils of Schelling, who earnestly tried to prove that Hebrew had been the primeval language of mankind. By daring etymological interpretations they derived the names of ancient pagan deities from Hebrew roots, applying to the field of linguistics the rationalist and romantic theory that mankind had sprung from one primeval people.

Having to earn his living, Bernays became secretary to Baron von Hirsch, the ennobled Jewish banker, landowner, and philanthropist. Schelling himself, whose lectures at the Academy of Science of Munich Bernays went on to attend, became a decisive influence on his development. Schelling, personally a friend of Hegel, was also his philosophical counterpart. In Schelling's system the soul or feeling was given central significance, whereas in Hegel's system the spirit or logos took the central place. These conceptions were reflected and paralleled in the dominant interests of the two philosophers, Schelling being concerned with the living community of a people, Hegel with the state as a temporal embodiment of the eternal spirit. Both philosophers had a strong and lasting influence on Jewish thought, Hegel on the Jewish Reform movement, Schelling on Jewish neoorthodoxy. Having begun as a pantheistic follower of Spinoza, seeking the revelation of the infinite in finite nature and history, Schelling in his Munich years came to see the contrast between nature and ethics and to bridge the gap in his *Philosophy of Mythology* leading on to the *Philosophy of Revelation*. From Schelling (whose lectures were published only some thirty years later), Bernays learned to visualise the Pentateuch as reflecting the gradual evolution of religion from myth, its figures as prototypes of humanity, its rites as symbolic expressions of age-old wisdom.

On these ideas Isaac Bernays based his own conception of a "reform," or rather restoration, of Judaism. The title of a work in which he outlined this conception, *The Biblical Orient* (1820), was quite fashionable. For in the course of two generations the orient had yielded its secrets, the religion of Zoroaster from Persian manuscripts, the Indian Vedas accessible to those with a knowledge of Sanskrit, the Egyptian hieroglyphs deciphered by Champollion. Instead of the uniqueness of one single sacred text, a complex variety of conflicting and interacting religious traditions had emerged, giving rise to the new sciences of comparative religion and comparative linguistics and also to historical criticism of the Bible. Purporting to describe the "oriental significance," the "spirit of those sacred books in its purity and clarity" as the way of mankind from idolatry to monotheism, Bernays aimed at the same time to regain for the Bible its central place in the religious history of the world as the revelation of a personal God. Demonstrating scientific views of remarkable independence—as, for instance, that one day the analysis of the names mentioned in Genesis would reveal the spiritual trends of all early civilizations—and indulging in sometimes amateurish etymology, its author kept this aim firmly in view. Moreover, he continued his survey beyond biblical times throughout Jewish history to show how this tradition had been kept alive up to this time. The great learning of Bernays's philosophy of history was clouded by his florid language, yet despite his involved method of expression, the outlines of his conception were clear enough. With the significant exception that Judaism was no longer understood as a "religion of reason," his position was practically identical with that of Mendelssohn. Scientific thinking was left quite as free, ritual observance made quite as binding. To Isaac Bernays, Israel was "the spiritual and ethical Atlas," the carrier of world history through its religious law, this law being understood to be "universally significant, nay world-carrying" as the symbolic representation of divine manifestation. At the same time, the law to him contained "the body of Judaism," for "as long as His Law reigns among them, God has set this people as representing mankind."

In Hamburg, Bernays demonstrated his method of reforming Jewish life. He was far from denying the need for reform. On the contrary, the traditional title of rabbi was in his opinion so discredited that he preferred that of Haham, the title used by the Sephardic congregations, while for external purposes simply calling himself "ecclesiastical officer." In a congregation composed of a poor, uneducated, and even superstitious majority, and an upper stratum of wealthy, proud, self-made export merchants and bankers, he secured his independence by stipulating that he should be paid a lump sum instead of individual fees for attending marriages and funerals and that he should have the right to appeal to the state authority, the Senate of the Free City, if need be, against any decision of the representatives of the Jewish community. He never had to use this right, for the congregation became very proud of its Haham, the first orthodox rabbi to give a regular sermon every

Sabbath, to represent Jewish theology in the municipal ecclesiastical association, and to hold public lectures on the Psalms. But above all, he put the Jewish education of the poor on a new footing. Up till then the method of teaching at the Talmud-Torah school had consisted in the mechanical learning by heart of long passages of the Talmud, followed by an equally mechanical treatment of the translation. Bernays replaced the whole Talmudic training up to the age of thirteen, when the majority of pupils left school, by Bible lessons, Hebrew grammar, German, arithmetic, geography, and a little history, hoping to build up an advanced class into a theological seminary.

These innovations seemed trivial compared with the achievements of "enlightened" Jewish schools, which had reached the standard of the best German schools. Yet Bernays's introduction of the first wall map into an orthodox school, where anything but Talmudic studies was unheard of, caused quite a stir. Viewed as a whole, Bernays's activities demonstrated that there was a way of combining modern education with the traditional Jewish way of life.

He confined his activities to Hamburg, leaving the imprint of his personality on the congregation far beyond his own lifetime. He did not even publish his later writings, on the Psalms, on Jehudah Halevi's *Kusari,* the chief work of Jewish apologetics of the Middle Ages, on the Church fathers, on Spinoza, and on Greek philosophy. Despite this reticence he was the spiritual founder of neo-orthodoxy, although it was left to his pupil and friend Samson Raphael Hirsch to give it the shape of a movement and a program.

The two main lines of development, Reform and Neo-orthodoxy, which became the twin centers of gravity from the age of emancipation until the emergence of Zionism at the end of the century, were thus apparent as early as the eighteen-twenties. Both sides were in agreement in understanding Judaism as a historical religion and as being justified in its claim for survival on this ground, however much they differed as to its interpretation. Both sides were equally unanimous in desiring political emancipation as a fundamental condition for the survival of Jews, and thus of Judaism. The movement of religious Reform was willing and, indeed, determined to sacrifice to this aim all nonessential forms of religious observance and even the national and Messianic aspects of Judaism, in order to maintain the spirit of their religion as a coherent, rational system of ideas of universal significance. These ideals, lofty as they were, and tending to be stylized into near-dogmatic absoluteness, yet gave guidance to an increasingly assimilated daily life, expressing inner piety in social conduct.

The new orthodoxy, on the other hand, concentrating on religious law and ritual as the symbolic expression of man's relationship to God, as the body and soul of Judaism, left the realm of thought open to the inflow of Western ideas. Under the impact of the French Revolution and the influence of German philosophy, the totality of Jewish life in spirit, body, and soul seemed to have been split into complementary yet incompatible halves.

Liberalism

These two trends of development had by no means equal prospects. Characteristically, neoorthodoxy was for the time being restricted to the city of Hamburg, although in fact, albeit without any ideology, most German Jews still adhered to the traditional way of life, whereas the Reform Movement spread among wealthy and educated Jews throughout Germany and far beyond its frontiers. For orthodoxy had to rely on conservative governments which, although inclined to resist innovations, were certainly not prepared to contradict their general policy of dissolving the internal bonds of Judaism, let alone to strengthen such bonds. Reform, on the other hand, had a powerful political ally in the growth of the Liberal movement in Germany. This movement combined the struggle of commoners for their place in a feudal state, of industrialists against the restrictive practices of the guilds, of merchants for the freedom of trade, of individuals for the limitation of the functions of the state to the maintenance of order and to external protection, with a demand for freedom of thought, of conscience, and of the press—in one word, progress as against romantic hankering after the past.

The great bankers, such as the House of Rothschild with its five brothers settled in Frankfurt, London, Paris, Vienna, and Naples, which had become the Sixth Great Power of Europe, were in an easy relationship with the powers-that-be, however reactionary. Yet the sons of peddlers, who had learned a craft in the first enthusiasm of the emancipation but then found the exercise of their new occupation blocked by the guild system, installed machines and set up as manufacturers, only too glad to find support in a popular movement that represented their interests. Above all, the Jewish members of the professions, such as lawyers, journalists, and writers, who found their careers blocked because they were Jews, joined the ranks of the Radicals, the only party to make their cause part of its own.

Even Leopold Zunz did not disdain writing and speaking for the Liberal party in electoral assemblies. Where the fight for emancipation also implied the cause of Jewish Reform, he was ready to put the whole weight of his learning at its disposal. When the Prussian government tried to suppress the "innovation" of vernacular sermons in the synagogue, he published his work *The Liturgical Addresses of the Jews, Historically Elucidated* (1832), showing that the homiletical address in the language of the country was of immemorial antiquity. A pioneering effort in response to an external occasion, the volume became the standard work on the subject and still remains so, having been translated as recently as 1947. Similarly, in reply to a royal decree forbidding Jews to assume German "Christian" names, Zunz wrote a booklet on *Names of the Jews* (1836), analyzing some 8,000 names borne by Jews throughout the ages and demonstrating their Babylonian, Greek, Roman, Persian, Arabic, Spanish, Gallic, German, and other origins, and also giving the Jewish origins of certain supposedly Christian names. This publication caused sufficient sensation to bring about a modification of the decree.

It was against the same background that, with two pamphlets in 1831, and by founding the periodical *The Jew* in 1832, Gabriel Riesser renewed the fight for the emancipation of Jews, as a fight for "the holy spirit" of truth, justice, and humanity. He fought for his own rights as well as those of his coreligionists. His father, who had settled at Lübeck, had been expelled after the Napoleonic Wars. He himself had tried in vain to be admitted to an academic career at Heidelberg and Jena, and as a solicitor in his home town of Hamburg. Yet he expressed neither resentment nor complaint but a proud, deep-seated conviction of justice: "We are not immigrants, we are born in Germany and, therefore, have no other claim to a home: we are either Germans or homeless." This tone had not been heard since Joselman of Rosheim. Again there was a man "standing on the watch-tower of Israel," but he spoke as a German patriot: "The success of our endeavour will have to show that it would be a scandalous libel to say that in Germany right and truth are powerless and only force is of any avail." Yet, subtly blended with this fight for a particular cause as exemplifying absolute right and truth, was the religious motive of prophetic justice, which gave it its penetrating moral fervor: "The belief in the power and the final victory of Right and Good is our Messianic faith. Let us hold fast to it." A letter of congratulation from another leading Jewish Liberal, Johann Jacoby of Königsberg, echoed this passage: "Our Messiah is the passage of time that shakes ever more powerfully the shackles of old prejudices, and turns out, sooner or later, to our best as the voice of truth and right must prevail."

This belief, expressing the faith of German Jews of the time and of decades to come, meant a slight but decisive change from what it had been thirty years before. The expectation of Messianic liberation and redemption was still secularized and linked up with the concrete political aim of emancipation, still—and even more so—indissolubly connected with the spiritual salvation of mankind by prophetic justice. But the static belief in emancipation as one sudden event had now given way to the more fluid, dynamic theory of "the passage of time," of progress in time that could be confidently expected, worked for step by step, and shared not only with men and women of one's own nation but with those of many modern nations. Here the age-old belief of Jews in the idea of the future tendering its redeeming hands to the present, had after all found an adequate new expression. Messianic expectation came to be seen in terms of victory of the Liberal movement, fanned by the French July Revolution of 1830.

The common ground of this movement made it understandable that some of its outstanding writers, such as Ludwig Börne and Heinrich Heine, could continue to feel themselves to be Jews and to defend the Jewish cause although they had left the Jewish religion. "Riesser, it seems, would like to see the nationality of Jews retained," wrote Börne on the publication of the journal *The Jew*, "but Jewish nationality has perished in a fine and enviable way: it has become universality"—and now Jews should be "the teachers of cosmopolitanism" rather than pleading their own cause. Nevertheless, Börne himself, fighting with his brilliant epigrammatical wit for freedom and justice as the celebrated Paris correspondent of Cotta's journals, castigating the sleepiness of reactionary conditions in Germany with "scent-bottles of sharply satirical vinegar," appreciated "the undeserved good fortune to be a German and a Jew at the same time, to be able to strive for all the German virtues without sharing any of their faults."

Heinrich Heine, unlike Börne, was a divided character. In the first place he was a poet, undisputed in his time as the greatest lyricist after Goethe, hailed as a writer of European rank a century after his death, with some of his verses achieving the anonymous immortality of folksongs. The "spoilt pet-child of the Muses" was true to his own artistic sensitivity, to the hard-won nonchalance of his lines, rather than to any cause. Romantic in his poetic work, he was as attracted to Jewish subjects of the Middle Ages—for example, "Rabbi of Bacharach" or his *Hebrew Melodies*—as to Christian legends and lore. Being, however, a Liberal rebel at the same time and striving for social justice and freedom meant the opposite of glorifying the past. Thus Heine was forever torn between two poles, between feeling and sarcasm, realism and world woe, like a musician achieving totality by ambivalent contrasts. "I who like nothing better than to observe the drift of clouds," he confessed, "to subtilize rhythmical charms of words, to overhear the secrets of the elemental spirits and to delve into the wonders of old fairy tales—I had to publish political annals, lecture on contemporary interests, contrive revolutionary appetites, raise passions, pull poor German Michel continually by the nose so as to make him wake up from his sound giant's sleep. . . ."

In 1835 an edict was issued forbidding the future, as well as suppressing the past, writings of the harmless literary clique that called itself Young Germany, mistakenly construed as forming part of the Italian democrat Mazzini's revolutionary secret society, Young Europe. Heine, one of its chief members, went to Paris together with a host of lesser lights, many of them of Jewish descent. In Paris too Heine never tired of his concern for freedom in Germany and justice for the cause of the Jews. In these years, however, he also posed as a pantheist and libertinist, praising the gay sensuality of Greek antiquity (or rather of the Parisian Boulevards) and contrasting it with what he called the "dark, nazarenic" moral spirit of Judaism and Christianity alike. This black-and-white picture seemed quite plausible when presented in his sparkling style. Yet his playful paganism, with its antithesis of fair Greeks and dark "Nazarenes," intended more for entertainment than as a fully considered conviction, nevertheless evoked the powers of the deeply buried pagan past slumbering below the Christian surface. Heine's antithesis was to appear rather sinister a generation later, when Count de Gobineau substituted "race" for "spirit" and thus came to an equally black-and-white, and equally false, antagonism between "Aryans" and "Semites." After the revolution of 1848, Heine clearly foresaw where this much more elementary revolution was to lead; he could recant, but he could not undo what he had written.

Ideologies and Parties

From the mid-thirties of the nineteenth century onward, the two conflicting tendencies in Jewish life, Liberal Reform and Orthodox restoration, became stabilized in ideologies and soon led to the formation of parties. The formulation of these ideologies was chiefly due to two young rabbis who had been close friends as students at Bonn, Abraham Geiger and Samson Raphael Hirsch.

Abraham Geiger was deeply convinced that "universal humanity has its roots in Israel." These roots he saw in the biblical revelation of the

One God, unified and holy, manifested in its moral and social message through the "winged word" of the prophets. He felt it to be the mission of Israel to profess and propagate this message, to verify it in the daily life of every Jew. This mission demanded the permanent preservation of the Jewish community. Geiger held that its original limitation to the single nation of ancient Israel had been indispensable in order to evolve its universal meaning for humanity, and that a "rigid" religious law had been required to protect it through the ages. The particularity of ancient Jewish national existence needed, however, to be broken by the destruction of the Temple in order to release its universal meaning, and the segregating effect of the ceremonial law had now come to obscure its very purpose. The task of religious reform, therefore, was to define the spirit of Judaism in its true splendor and purity, to simplify and ennoble its ceremonial expression so as to render this spirit in its full and undimmed significance. Both these tasks, if undertaken by scientific investigation rather than by subjective assertions of faith and haphazard reforms, could be effected by the Science of Judaism: "This Science has above all undertaken the task of scrutinizing in a critical and unbiased sense the documents of Judaism, to follow their historical sequence, so as to ascertain on the one hand their genuine and essential content and, on the other, to prove the modifications produced by historical development. The practical religious interest, however, lies in utilizing the results of these investigations for the present, in consciously and diligently developing, along the present lines of history, what the past has developed according to its historical features and has handed down to us, and to make it come alive in the present and under present-day conditions."

The Science of Judaism, under Geiger's hands, acquired a new meaning. Never before had the universal significance of Judaism been placed in the focal center of belief with a conviction as glowing as that of this enrapturing preacher. Yet at the same time his historical analysis became a battering-ram against Jewish fundamentalism. He demonstrated that the Bible itself, let alone customs and ceremonial, was the product of specific periods and conditions of human history—the work of genius, yet not above further evolution and change. In his *Scientific Journal for Jewish Theology* (1835–39) he established the modern theology of Judaism. His book *The Original Book and its Translations* (1857) was the principal Jewish contribution to the scientific investigation of the history of Judaism in biblical times, which had otherwise been mainly left to Protestant theologians. His book *Judaism and its History* (1864) established the new view of historical Judaism as the religion of the prophets. Altogether, Abraham Geiger's work revolutionised almost every branch of Jewish learning.

As a critic, Geiger was at heart a rationalist, with a philological flair amounting almost to genius, with an acute sense of historical circumstance, but with little understanding of the irrational side of religious life, its matrix in myth or its flowering in poetry and mystical lore. He was fascinated by historical facts and intimidated by the advance of mythological investigations, which showed that many of the biblical beliefs and institutions were common to most peoples of antiquity. Thus he shyly recoiled from acclaiming the patriarchal period as the cradle of civilization, the model of human conduct—an appeal accorded to it by all previous ages. His understanding of Judaism reduced its range yet emphasized the moral and social aspects dearest to his heart and to the hearts of his contemporaries. Though at considerable cost, his interpretation restored the then needed capacity for development to a religion long devoid of important developments. Yet, sharply critical as was his theoretical approach, his practical attitude to concrete reform was guided by a rabbi's careful consideration of what his congregation could stand. The ensuing pruning of expressions of ceremonial observance thus had the saving grace of inconsequentiality compared with his theory, for it was merely a quantitative reduction of existing forms without any attempt at finding new ways of expressing a modified religious feeling. An age that had withdrawn from an overgrowth of ceremonial into an inner feeling of religious truth and its verification in daily conduct could hardly have acted otherwise.

Having characterized the party of Historical Reform through Abraham Geiger, let us turn to their opponents, the neoorthodox party. Geiger's fellow student, Samson Raphael Hirsch, formulated its position in his *Nineteen Letters on Judaism* (1836) and *Horeb, or Essays on Israel's Duties in Dispersion* (1837). If Geiger saw the goal of development as the promotion of a universal humanity that had its "roots," but not necessarily its crown, in Judaism, Hirsch held that ideal humanity was represented by strictly traditional Jewish life. The Jew educated in the true spirit of the Torah as the divine word, the "Israel-man," he said, is "at the same time the most universal cosmopolitan"—the spirit of the Torah being the goal of education for mankind. Thus he refused to distinguish between religion as faith and as an established observance. All his enthusiasm and superb eloquence were put to the defense of ritual ceremonies as symbols of eternal truth. He condemned any reform in this direction as heresy: the greater the burden of strict observance, he held, the greater the merit of sacrifice to God. In making his congregation at Frankfurt a kind of island fortress, Samson Raphael Hirsch succeeded in giving it a prestige far greater than its actual size.

Yet, strict as was the external appearance of this orthodoxy, which regarded all written and oral tradition as divinely revealed, its spirit was flexible and adaptable. Hirsch praised Mendelssohn for demonstrating that "one can be scrupulous in religious observance but be nonetheless a highly esteemed man and shine out as a German Plato." In this sense the content of symbolic ritual forms was interpreted in terms of rational morality. The national aspects of Judaism, as "mere means of its spiritual vocation," were held to be no obstacle to the sincere allegiance of Jews to other nations, to a combination of "Torah with *Derech Eretz*," the custom of the land. Hirsch referred to Jeremiah 29:7: "Further the welfare of the town whereto I have carried you away, pray for her to the Lord, for with her welfare you will prosper too." The emancipation of Jews was no less desirable to him than to his opponents, though he emphasized that its bestowal was rather the expression of a new spirit on the part of the Western nations redeeming an old injustice, and would enable Jews to live a fuller Jewish life. There was a sturdy toughness in Hirsch's advice that his followers should disregard the confusing results of modern historical research, as he himself had done or at least appeared to have done, in his translation of the Bible and in his commentaries on the Psalms and on the prayers: "There is but *one* way to salvation: to forget opinions or non-opinions on Judaism, and return to the sources of Judaism. . . ." Yet while higher criticism of the Bible remained uninfluenced by his disregard, and needed study and discussion, his spiritual island fortress provided an approach to a gradual transition to modern life for the many thousands of Jews for whom the pace of progress, not excluding religious reform, went too fast.

Ideological Fights and Stabilization of Reform

Moderate reform, in Geiger's sense, spread fast among educated Jews, supported since 1837 by Ludwig Philippson's first Jewish newspaper, the *Allgemeine Zeitung des Judentums,* which appealed to educated and uneducated alike by its combination of news, entertainment, and instruction. Striving to represent all Jewish interests, it was read wherever Jews lived and it survived until 1921. The movement of reform was not confined to Germany; a Reform Congregation was founded in London in 1840 and in Manchester in 1856, and by the middle of the century German immigration had led to the establishment of strong congregations in America. Yet not only Reform rabbis but also the learned among the orthodox ones, such as Nathan Marcus Adler, the founder of Jews' College in London and of the United Synagogue, continued to fill renowned posts outside Germany.

The advance of the Reform movement did not proceed unchecked or indeed without determined opposition either in Germany or abroad. Geiger's appointment as rabbi split the Breslau congregation into two hostile camps. He was refused a seat on the rabbinical board on the grounds that, "having attended a university, he was unfit to be a rabbi." In Hamburg the Reform Temple Association intended to build a larger synagogue and issued a revised prayer book, whereupon Haham Bernays, by publicly forbidding its use, tried to revive the old rabbinical ban of excommunication—the last time in Germany that rabbinical authority was used to force a spiritual issue. Both cases became the subject of heated controversy and learned memoranda, showing that orthodoxy, both old and new, had overplayed its hand. The new movement could no longer be stamped out by force, spiritual or political; even Gabriel Riesser, the political protagonist of emancipation, emerged from his religious neutrality and came down on the side of progress, if only for the sake of toleration.

This ideological fight was affected by the Damascus Affair of 1840, a renewal of the charge of ritual murder, which deeply stirred all Jews at the time. It was far away, but the reappearance of medieval barbarity had been held to be no longer possible under modern conditions. A delegation composed of Sir Moses Montefiore of London, Adolphe Crémieux and Salomon Munk of Paris—the latter one of the German-Jewish pioneers of the Science of Judaism, as well as an Arabist and Hebraist of high repute—successfully dealt with the calamity. In Germany the incident prompted further strivings for reform as well as thoughtful meditation, and even faint stirrings of Jewish national feeling.

At Frankfurt an Association of Friends of Jewish Reform proclaimed "the Mosaic Religion" to be "capable of unlimited evolution." It denied the Talmud any authority "in a dogmatic as well as in the practical sense"; it abrogated belief in a Messiah to lead the Israelites back to Zion, and did not recognize "any fatherland but that to which they belonged by birth or civil condition." The Association tried to abolish circumcision, the ritual connected in the Bible with Abraham, and thus with the first beginnings of belief in the One God. These proposals represented a type that was Jewish in little more than name and imponderable feelings of reverence. On the question of circumcision, general opinion, including that of Leopold Zunz, was practically unanimous in favor of retaining the binding force of that ritual.

Even more drastic views of extreme reform were voiced in Berlin. Lecturing "On the Task of Judaism and of Jews in the Present," Sigismund Stern advocated a Jewish Church within the Prussian or German, national Christian Church. Samuel Holdheim applied his Talmudic training in his book *The Autonomy of the Rabbis* to advocate the most uncompromising theological separation of a "pure biblical belief in positive revelation" from any trace of Jewish communal feelings or ritual; he also defended a transfer of the Sabbath day to Sunday, on the grounds that national authority had now been vested in the host state.

Views such as these, reforms that were but steps toward a dissolution of Jewish life, were abhorrent to men like Zunz. His defense of a reform of the synagogue service aimed at restoring the true meaning of Jewish worship by enhancing the dignity of the service and by removing a number of usages that, though customary, were without traditional foundation or, indeed, meaning. This situation would have called for a generally recognized religious authority. There could, however, not be any such authority even in the limited sense of administrative representation. For the governments of the day, with the sole exception of Württemberg and Baden, still maintained the formula of the French Revolution and denied the Jewish congregations any right of association or common representation.

In the circumstances, Ludwig Philippson's newspaper put forward the suggestion of a rabbinical conference, representing all schools of thought, with the task of working out a common platform. In fact, three such conferences were held, at Brunswick, Frankfurt, and Breslau (1844–46). The scholarly level of their deliberations enhanced the reputation of the rabbinical profession. At the first conference the radical group dominated the proceedings and moved Holdheim's extreme alterations of the liturgy and marriage laws. The second conference took a dramatic turn. Salomon Judah Rapoport, chief rabbi of Prague and one of the pioneers of the Science of Judaism, had sent a solemn warning. This would hardly have deterred the radical reformers, yet Zacharias Frankel, rabbi at Dresden, attended the conference and demanded that principles of reform should be worked out before entering into a discussion of details. Geiger objected, and the meeting sided with him. Nevertheless, matters of principle were again at stake in deciding the extent to which Hebrew prayers should be retained in the service. Sermons in the vernacular were sanctioned by tradition. The controversy thus was not one of plain affirmation or denial but over a question of degree, namely, whether the retention of Hebrew in the service was merely a concession to the past, to be recommended for a transitional period, or a necessity of Jewish religious life for all time. Geiger emphasized that, by remaining tied to the Hebrew language, Jewish religion would depend on a national element. Frankel replied that if nationality were indeed part of religion it should be honestly admitted.

He went farther by questioning the validity of Geiger's application of the results of historical criticism to liturgical reforms. He sharply distinguished between the right and even the duty of every individual to unbiased and independent investigaton and the utilization of the results of such studies. Instead of the rational conviction of any individual, Frankel established the living feeling of the community of Israel as the final authority for decisions on changes: "Everyone is allowed, is enjoined to *think* independently, to conduct his scientific studies with an independent mind; yet to *act* differently in religious matters, that is a decision to be left to the whole of Israel as the tribunal. Popular practices that have attained the form of a statute are historically endorsed, they are holy; mature consideration is required before they may be touched."

Here was the program of a new understanding of historical Judaism in a conservative sense, responsible both to tradition and to the demands of present life. The invocation of *klal Israel,* the community of Israel, as the final tribunal in deciding on any religious changes was true to the oldest of Jewish traditions. At the same time it was in tune with the Prussian legal historian Savigny's view that each system of law should be regarded as an individual organism, and should be developed only in relation to its totality.

The critical point was whether Geiger's more radical view or Frankel's conservative attitude would prevail. The majority vote of the conference was cast in favor of Geiger. Frankel withdrew from the conference, protesting against its decision because he held that it would not gain the confidence of the congregations nor fulfill its function of mediating between the opposing opinions.

As a result of the conference a Reform Congregation was established in Berlin, with Holdheim as its minister. The service, for lack of attendance on Sabbaths, was transferred to Sunday; separation of men and women was abolished as well as praying with a covered head; a new liturgy, almost entirely in German, was adopted, and there were other important alterations of tradition. This service became the model for American congregations, which had to begin without any local tradition.

On the whole, however, Frankel's stand decided the issue. The outcome of this Frankfurt conference throughout Germany was a stabilization of the reform of the synagogue service at the point it had reached, as a modernized form of worship yet without breaking with the past. The voice of faith that wished to be neither out of touch with modern development nor swamped by reason had been expressed by Frankel. The feeling of community on which he relied was stronger than all divergent opinions.

Liberal enthusiasm and propaganda had its effect. In 1847 the Combined Prussian Diet passed a law that, still far short of full emancipation and in some respects a retrogressive step from the decree of 1812, abolished a number of irksome restrictions and granted recognition to individual Jewish congregations. As the first measure of its kind it implied the levying of taxes for their maintenance by the state and a semi-official status for rabbis. At the same time, this law still prevented any collective representation of Jewish interests. The Jewish congregations thus established, ranging from strictest orthodoxy to extreme reform, achieved the feat, unparalleled by any other Jewry, of maintaining full internal and administrative unity, taking care of all sectional interests with sympathetic impartiality. This internal unity, an expression of common sense and a source of pride, was for nearly a century broken only by Samson Raphael Hirsch's separate orthodox congregation at Frankfurt and by a sister congregation at Berlin, for which, in the name of tolerance, a Liberal Jewish representative, Ludwig Bamberger, tabled a special law that was passed in 1876, enabling them to contract out of the total community.

Religious Philosophy, History, and Science of Judaism

In the Jewish sphere the unbounded optimism of the eighteen-forties, stirred up by the visible advances of science and technology, found its expression in a series of creative achievements in religious philosophy and in the history and science of Judaism.

Samson Hirsch, then rabbi at Dessau, Mendelssohn's birthplace, and Salomon Formstecher, later Grand Rabbin of Luxemburg, and finally, at Philadelphia, one of the leaders of Reform Judaism, each published philosophies of religion almost simultaneously, in 1841 and 1842. Formstecher based his work on Schelling's earlier idea, Hirsch on Hegel's system. Yet both, although accepting these systems as their point of departure, nevertheless tried to establish within them the universal content and the continuing significance of Judaism, viewed by both of them in the main as an ethical system of ideas with its foundation in a personal God. Hegel's and Schelling's systems were too solidly constructed to be easily twisted off their own framework from within. Yet these detailed philosophies of history, in which both Jewish authors arrived at remarkably similar conceptions regarding Judaism as opposed to paganism and Christianity, contained thoughts and observations of permanent value. While at the time Hirsch was the more conservative, both writers agreed in their wish to further the cause of emancipation by stressing the inherent values of Judaism as well as its capability of evolution.

The work of Salomon Ludwig Steinheim, medical practitioner at Altona, on *Revelation according to the Doctrine of the Synagogue* was on quite a different level, that of profound personal experience rather than theoretical reasoning. Published in four volumes from 1835 to 1865, this work varies and repeats one single idea—that revelation manifests truth that human reason could never have constructed by itself, but that, once revealed, critical reason can test and has to admit almost despite itself. Judaism, as revelation, was here established on a nonrational, nonhistorical basis of its own, as necessary, timeless truth of universal validity. At the same time, revelation was held to be the chief cause of the formation of a Jewish community and, rather than history, language, or race, the dominant factor in its miraculous survival after the loss of national independence and sovereignty: "Every member of this people participates in its great mission in dispersion, forms by his existence part of that age-old great missionary institution that still persists under the immediate direction of the same invisible Head . . . the first priest and missionary of which was Abraham."

Religion, understood as a reality in its own right, was no longer, as Mendelssohn had held, identical with the findings of natural reason; yet Steinheim's basic ideas of this religion—God, Freedom, and Immortality—coincided with Kant's postulates of Practical Reason. On the other hand, positing Creation *ex nihilo,* Steinheim opposed any theory of evolution. His position equally enabled him to fight Hegel's identification of God with a "world spirit" and Schelling's pantheism. In the Jewish sphere Steinheim could take Samson Raphael Hirsch to task for trying to establish religious law as the basis of Jewish life without first establishing its source in the living God.

Yet, for all his apparent irrationalism, Steinheim, touched by deeper insight but unmoved by the romantic wave, had passed from the age of enlightenment discreetly to modern scientific methods. Indeed, he claimed that religion, as a feature of reality, held a secret in the same

way as any flower or stone, being subject to the same divergence
between the mathematical basis of experience and its empirical contents, and in its demonstration capable of the same degree of certainty.
He therefore called the second volume of his work *The Doctrine of the
Synagogue as Exact Science.* For all its originality as the outstanding
work of Jewish philosophy in the nineteenth century prior to Hermann
Cohen, its tendencies were in opposition to the prevailing idealistic,
rational optimism of the time; it was almost regarded as a curiosity.

These were the great years of the Science of Judaism. In 1845
Leopold Zunz published his *Contributions to History and Literature,*
the first scientific survey of the work of the medieval Tosafists, or
Talmudic casuists, in Germany and France, followed from 1855 to 1865
by *Synagogue Poetry of the Middle Ages, The Rites of the Synagogue
Service,* and *Literary History of the Poetry of the Synagogue.* This was
historical research of the first order, incorporating the results of tireless
spade work on manuscripts preserved at Hamburg, Oxford, Paris,
Parma, and Rome. The presentation of this research had a touch of
luminous greatness, brought about by a combination of almost heterogeneous qualities: a powerful, critical, and disciplined mind capable of
arranging masses of remote material, deep poetic feeling, minute observation, and a gift of intuiting the spiritual life of Jews throughout the
ages, both as a totality and as but one ray in the prism of the human
spirit.

Zunz's younger friend Moritz Steinschneider, "the prince of Hebrew
bibliographers," had begun to explore the libraries of Europe for their
treasures in Hebrew manuscripts. In Galicia, Nachman Krochmal,
"The Galician Mendelssohn," worked on his philosophy of Jewish history, interpreting it as wave after wave of growth, flowering, and de-
clining. As his literary executor, Zunz edited this work in 1851 and
published it under the title of *Modern Guide of the Perplexed (More
Nebuke ha-Zeman).*

The Science of Judaism spread in Germany and beyond. Jost revised
his *History of the Jews,* and Heinrich Graetz published the first outline
of his monumental work on the subject. Michael Sachs described *The
Religious Poetry of the Jews in Spain* with the same warmth, eloquence, and conservative fervor that characterized his sermons at Berlin. In Prague, Salomon Judah Rapoport wrote penetrating essays on
personalities of the Talmudic and post-Talmudic epoch and on religious poets such as Elasar Kalir. Salomon Munk in Paris, Samuel
David Luzzatto at Padua, and Isaac Samuel Reggio at Gorizia ex-
changed letters and manuscripts, and gave mutual advice, all forming
part of a common endeavor to explore and investigate Jewish history

and literature by modern standards. Zunz expressed the aim of all this hard and devoted work: "One should concede the spirit its right; the recognition of the spirit will be followed by that of the person. . . . The equality of the Jews in custom and life will result from the equality of the Science of Judaism."

Zunz tried to translate this conviction into academic practice by applying to the University of Berlin for the establishment of a professorship in the Science of Judaism. The main branches of this science had, however, been neatly separated and distributed: biblical science and history of Judaism in biblical times formed part of Protestant theology as a necessary introduction to the New Testament; the civilization of Jews in antiquity was handed over to Comparative History; the remainder, the whole of postbiblical, Talmudic, and medieval Jewish history and literature, was felt to lack sufficient general interest and was excluded. The application was turned down without malice—the great historian Ranke, and Boeckh, a pioneer of linguistics, were members of the committee that investigated it—but purely on the grounds of academic "coverage." Hence it was only natural for Jewish scholars, working single-handed without state posts, institutes, or grants, to concentrate on the neglected branch.

Yet within the Jewish sphere their handicap was hardly less great. The dedication of Jews to matters spiritual had not died out but had been transferred to culture, to general literature, and to art. The way of assimilated life was still too new; memories of the ghetto were still too vivid to kindle any particular interest, let alone enthusiasm, for anything but the biblical prophets, and certainly not for the Talmud and Middle Ages. And as for the thesis that respect for Judaism would pave the way to emancipation, political support for the Liberal movement was felt to hold out better hope of success than the slow, long, uphill struggle of Jewish historical science for recognition. On a short-term view this calculation was even correct. The scholars of the Science of Judaism, seeking the soul of Judaism in the glories of the past, were pioneers of the future rather than leaders of the present.

Revolution and Reaction

All the Liberal hopes, culminating in the political unification of Germany and in constitutional government, seemed to be fulfilled by the victorious revolution of 1848. The German National Assembly at Frankfurt had among its deputies the flower of mind and character in Germany. Eduard Simson, cousin of David Friedländer and a convert, was its president; Gabriel Riesser was elected as one of its vice-presidents. In the discussion on a draft constitution containing "Fundamental Rights of the German People" there was an attempt to make "the peculiar conditions of the Israelitish race" the object of special legislation, after the provision that "enjoyment of civic rights will not be conditioned or limited by religious faith" had already been carried. In a passionate speech Riesser opposed any disabilities on national grounds, pointing out that any legal exception would mean a disruptive cleavage in the principle of freedom and that Jews were not conscious of a national difference, whereas the nationality of groups who were so conscious, such as the Danes, Poles, and Czechs, had already been recognized as not constituting a disability. The proposal was rejected. The Constitutions of the German Federal States, conceded under the impact of the revolution, all recognized the full emancipation of Jews.

The members of the Assembly, men of the highest ideals, relied on the moral authority of the national will to carry through its designs. Not being backed by military power, however, the Assembly had to yield to Prussian bayonets. The revolution was a short dream with a bitter end.

A long period of reaction set in once more. The prevailing official attitude was largely due to the strengthening of the conservative view, which F. J. Stahl (1802–61), of Jewish descent, had brought about by founding the legitimist Christian Conservative Party and by providing it with an ideology. Since 1840 he had been professor of public law at the University of Berlin. While supporting capitalist economic expansion, he held the romantic conception of a "totally Christian-Germanic State" of medieval structure to be "a true expression of progress," because it could maintain harmony between opposed interests and layers. This ideology, which presented Protestantism as the only alter-

106

native to religious indifference, continued to exert a strong influence well into the twentieth century.

The new constitutions were either withdrawn or severely circumscribed. Even so, the Prussian constitution of 1850 was an enormous advance, since it recognized no differences of class or birth, granted franchise to Jews and—though only in theory for the time being—the right to hold public office. In Austria the old disabilities returned in full force. In most of the other states, civic equality of Jews remained at least on paper, whatever administrative obstacles were put in the way of turning it into reality. Yet the demand for its fulfillment was kept open by the essential fairmindedness of large groups of liberal Germans.

The Industrial Revolution

In the age of railways, gas light, the fast printing press, and the stock exchange, a revolution got underway, far more powerful than that of 1848—the industrial revolution. The use of machines led to an undreamed-of expansion of production, and production created demand. Whoever was capable of holding his own in economic competition could win respect and gain wealth, regardless of his origin. The coal and coke industry of Upper Silesia, the second largest in Germany, was predominantly created by Jews such as Moritz Friedländer and the Caro brothers. Jews who had seen no other way of making a livelihood than dealing in old clothes, revolutionized the clothing industry, timber dealers opened up the furniture industry, while others developed the production of textiles, fancy goods, and jewelry. In an age of expansion Jewish merchants dealing in grain, wool, hides, and metals saw their businesses grow by leaps and bounds. The trade in furs, centered on Leipzig, became a Jewish monopoly. Family and business connections led to the setting up of export industries.

Though the House of Rothschild could no longer retain its practical monopoly of the money market, the Rothschilds of Vienna and Paris, the Oppenheims of Cologne, and later Maurice de Hirsch at Brussels, the son of the Bavarian court banker, became pioneers of private-enterprise railway construction. Jewish bankers in poor Silesia as well as in the rich Rhineland were instrumental in the process of industrialization. The Telegraphic News Agencies founded in 1851 by Paul Julius Reuter and in 1848 by Bernhard Wolff, came to attain international and even worldwide importance. Indigent students became influential publishers and booksellers. Ready wit could make a name in journalism. The flow to the medical profession continued unabated; to the legal it was barred until 1859; there was merely a trickle of musicians and actors. Felix Mendelssohn, however, Moses' grandson who was brought up in the Protestant faith, won the lasting gratitude of his own time and of posterity by his rediscovery of Johann Sebastian Bach, then totally forgotten. As a composer and conductor he occupied one of the most respected positions in the musical life of Germany and England. The fame won in Paris by Giacomo Mayerbeer as an operatic composer prevailed upon the Prussian king to make him director of the Berlin opera house despite the fact that he was not converted.

The new opportunities drew Jews from villages to towns, from towns to cities. In 1840 about 6,500 Jews lived in each of the cities of Hamburg, Berlin, and Posen, and about 5,000 in Frankfurt. By 1871 there were 36,000 Jews in Berlin, whereas the province of Posen saw its Jewish population reduced by 30%, from 80,000 to 55,000. Cologne grew from 615 to over 3,000 souls in this period. In Vienna the movement of concentration was even more rapid, from under 4,000 Jews in 1846 to over 14,000 in 1854, while the communities upon which it drew, such as Pressburg or Prossnitz, were in turn replenished from their Eastern hinterland. Yet many were attracted even farther afield than the nearest town or the distant city. Emigration, above all to America but to a smaller extent also to England, had begun in the period of political reaction in the eighteen-thirties and reached large dimensions in that following 1848.

It was no accident that the industrial revolution succeeded where the political had failed. Capitalist production provided work, accumulated national as well as individual wealth, and thus meant power. The failure of 1848 had discredited the high-minded idealism of the preceding period. Idealism was not indeed discarded but rather left on one side for lofty addresses on festival occasions, however much selfless devotion to humanitarian or social causes there still remained in actual life. Liberalism entered into an informal but very effective alliance with advancing science and technology; the idea of "progress" imperceptibly shed its idealistic connotations of truth and social justice and acquired the material meaning of new methods, speedier production, and increased personal comfort. Views of the English philosophers, such as John Stuart Mill's that experience was the sole source of knowledge, or Thomas Huxley's agnosticism, holding truth and reality to be unknowable and only phenomena to be observable, became the dominant convictions of the time. Its characteristic expression was Comte's positivism, declaring first causes and final purposes to be unexplorable, and hard-and-fast facts, graspable matter, to be the only "positive reality." How could this shrinking of the sense of reality come about, which by implication made every immaterial truth, religion, art, and even intuitive aspects of science appear "negative"?

Heinrich Heine, suffering for the last eight years of his life on his "mattress grave" in Paris, but strongly denying that his return to belief in a personal God and his rediscovery of the meaning of life in the Bible had anything to do with his illness, gave a penetrating and even prophetic answer to this question. He had seen that atheist philosophy, far from being a mere diverting play of wit, would lead to a social revolution shattering the whole fabric of western civilization; Marx's and Engels's Communist Manifesto of 1848 had envisaged that even marriage would have to give way to promiscuity.

"Truth to tell" Heine wrote, "it might well be not merely disgust that made me sick of the principles of the godless and prompted my withdrawal. There was also a certain worldly apprehension I could not overcome. For I saw that atheism had entered into a more or less secret alliance with the horridly naked, quite fig-leafless, vulgar Communism. My dread of the latter certainly has nothing in common with the fear of the upstart who trembles for his capital or with the annoyance of wealthy merchants afraid to be hampered in their deals of exploitation. No, I am rather oppressed by the secret fear of the artists and scholars who, all of us, see the whole of our modern civilisation, the achievements of so many centuries of toil, the fruit of the noblest work of our predecessors, endangered by the victory of Communism. Carried along by the tide of a generous mood, we might well sacrifice the concerns of art and science to the interests of the oppressed and the suffering. Yet we can never hide from ourselves what we would have to expect as soon as this great, crude mass called the people by some, the rabble by others, would really take charge—their legitimate sovereignty has long been proclaimed. The poet above all feels an eery shudder at the accession of this awkward sovereign." In short, Heine saw that what at first had seemed to be an open road led but to an abyss. Others did not see this so clearly, but for all the rational optimism, for all the continuing hope of moral progress and social betterment together with material improvements, the clinging of the age to the "positive," to the material side of life, hid an underlying anxiety.

The Fabric of Jewish Life

Jews then, like everyone else, directed their energies and cast their glances outward. Opportunities now outweighed restrictions, and work, politics, and reception by society became their dominant interests. The old simple way of living, even among the wealthy, now occasionally gave way to ostentatious display of riches and greater comfort, though still frowned upon by the more settled and educated. Yet charity without regard to race or creed to those in need was widespread, and not only money but also experience, time, and work were readily put at the disposal of many a deserving cause. Jews devoted unobtrusive work to the municipal services of their German home towns, and many gained satisfaction, earning sincere respect and gratitude by such activities in a wider yet still limited sphere. Young talent in literature, in art, in science could always find support from Jewish patrons.

Within the Jewish sphere, too, the signs of prosperity became visible. Stately synagogues were built in the then modern, oriental style. An imposing network of charitable foundations was built up, inspired by the growing congregations, maintained by private generosity. Old-age homes and orphanages, foundations for the poor, sick, deaf, and blind, large hospitals with up-to-date equipment that not infrequently came to be run by Jewish doctors of worldwide reputation, and well-stocked libraries were the outward signs of a communal spirit second to none among the Jewries of the world, in their totality an amazing achievement for a comparatively small sector of the population.

The Jewish Theological Seminary

An outstanding example in the spiritual field of this Jewish generosity was the establishment of the Jewish Theological Seminary at Breslau in 1854, a foundation bequeathed by Kommerzienrat Frankel of that town; his courtesy title of Economic Counsellor, much coveted both then and later, was an official recognition of his munificence to charitable causes.

The Seminary was the first modern institution for the training of rabbis. As long as thirty years before, such an aim had been envisaged by Haham Bernays of Hamburg, and it was more and more urgently demanded by Abraham Geiger who, as rabbi at Breslau, had introduced theology as a branch of Jewish learning. It was a bitter disappointment to the spiritual leader of the reform movement when the trustees of the foundation chose Zacharias Frankel instead of him as director, determining thereby a conservative tendency for the Seminary. In another respect, however, Geiger got his revenge. In the same town where, scarcely fifteen years before, he had been refused a seat on the rabbinical board for being academically trained, academic as well as Jewish training now become the standard practice for future rabbis. The alumni of the Seminary were expected to study and take a degree at the university alongside their Jewish studies.

The teachers of the Seminary themselves set and maintained a distinguished level of scholarship. Zacharias Frankel investigated the history of the Mishnah, the Oral Law which, having evolved for several centuries, reached its final form c.200 CE. Heinrich Graetz worked on his *History of the Jewish People*. Jacob Bernays, the son of the Hamburg Haham and one of the leading Greek and Latin philologists of the century, was at the same time a lecturer at the university, a colleague and friend of the historian Theodor Mommsen. He gave advice to Mommsen on his *Roman History* that was to make him famous, and read its proofs.

The combination of Jewish with academic training of the high standard then prevailing became the hallmark for a new generation of rabbis. The reputation of the Seminary spread fast throughout the Jewries of the world. Rabbis who had received their training there came to occupy the pulpits of congregations in many countries. They retained for life the love of scientific studies that had been imparted to them in their student days. This was important for two reasons. On the one hand, their scientific standing secured them the respect of their congregations and gave them a wider outlook beyond the Jewish sphere; many of them also came to play a distinguished part in the life of their town, in learned and charitable societies and associations.

On the other hand, the academic bent of these young rabbis gave a wider basis to, and provided new workers for, the Science of Judaism. Historical as well as philological, theological, and other studies set a new and lasting standard of Jewish scholarship, exemplary in its scientific thoroughness and breadth. In 1851 Zacharias Frankel founded the *Monatsschrift für Geschichte und Wissenschaft des Judentums*, which became, and until 1939 remained, the most distinguished academic periodical devoted to Jewish studies. An impressive array of publications complemented this periodical. Other journals served more specialized fields, such as S. R. Hirsch's *Jeschurun*, devoted to stating and defending the position of orthodox Jews in its spiritual and communal aspects.

The Inner Life of Jewish Communities from 1850 to 1870

The Jewish congregations liked their rabbis to be educated and scholarly. These congregations were led, however, by lay members, mostly businessmen successful in their own field, of great integrity and more often than not of great personal generosity, yet devoid of vision and inclined to conduct communal affairs on the pattern of a joint stock company.

This divergence of outlook between rabbis and congregation was characteristic of an increasing secularisation. The members of the congregation were proud of being good Jews, but the passionate concern of the first half of the century for the Jewish faith and its compatibility with modern life belonged to the past. In the age of positivism, religion as a whole was suspected of clashing with the hard-and-fast certainties of science, and belief in science increasingly became the dominant faith of both Gentiles and Jews. Thus it was as well to hold Judaism to be a historical and rational religion that implied optimistic belief in moral progress and social improvement, yet otherwise permitted great latitude of opinion, and to leave it at that.

The stream of Jewish life, now past the rapids, became broader and more leisurely. In the large towns and cities of the machine age, bustling with activity, personal friendships and contact were more difficult to maintain than in the small, closely-knit communities where many of the Jews had spent their youthful years. Though in reality none of them dreamed of retracing their steps, in retrospect the warm, cosy old ways of traditional piety in these small communities attained a golden glow. In the broader field much the same feeling had made Berthold Auerbach's *Village Tales from the Black Forest* famous in German literature. Leopold Kompert, Aron Bernstein, and later Karl Emil Franzos glorified the Jewish ghetto in careful, idyllic sentimentality. Aron Bernstein, characteristically enough, combined this romanticism with great realism by editing a Radical newspaper in Berlin, being one of the leading spirits of the Jewish Reform Congregation, and at the same time writing popular books on natural science.

Similar in tone and content to these ghetto novels, a whole literature of almanacs and devotional works found readers far beyond the confines of Germany: German had become the lingua franca of the Jews as a result of the pioneering work undertaken by German Jews since Mendelssohn in bridging the gulf between tradition and Western civilisation. It was through the medium of the German language that the large settlements of Eastern European Jews became familiar with Western ideas, and that those overseas felt included in the stream of Jewish life.

Heinrich Graetz's monumental *History of the Jewish People* (1853–76) became the most important factor in maintaining a spiritual union of Jews in an age of loosening religious bonds. Science and literature combined to give this work a resounding popular success such as no other Jewish work of the century had achieved. In its scientific aspect it was based on original sources in an amazing variety of languages, both old and modern; its notes presented pioneering work often not superseded to this day. Its artful exposition, a colorful style with a wealth of detail, vivid portraits, and warmth of feeling made it read almost like a novel—the canvas of the Jewish past on the grand scale. For in this work a modern, critical, and assimilated Western scholar had created the feeling of the unity and continuity of Jewish history throughout all its vagaries—a unity and continuity that past ages had by no means appreciated. Describing with woeful compassion the sufferings of Jews in the Middle Ages, he evoked a passionate pride in their martyrdom. Strict in rejecting the legendary aspects of biblical history, rationally interpreting its miracles, lightly gliding over the thorny problems of historical biblical criticism, he showed the unity of Jewish history in Jewish faith, and its continuity in the common fate of the Jewish people.

Graetz had learned from Hegel to seek in history the manifestation of an idea, and from Ranke's historical work to regard a people as a national individuality "immediate to God." Yet his comprehensive view of Jewish history effectively refuted the common view of his time that beyond the biblical age this history no longer held any values. And within the Jewish sphere, for all his lack of understanding of mystical movements, for all his sallies against religious reform, he communicated to his readers a pride in the past of their own people and a fervent belief in its future as a community. The strong national bias of his work openly conflicted with the tendency dominant among the Jews of his time to regard themselves as individuals with patriotic feelings for their German homeland, differing from other citizens only by their Jewish persuasion. Yet, while incurring strong opposition in respect of contemporary reality, the national pride imparted by Graetz's *History* was all the more acceptable as a unified view of the past, giving it that golden glow with which the ghetto novels glorified a state which was no longer desired in reality. Graetz's work, however, was not a sentimental story; for all its shortcomings it reflected true history. The pride that Graetz imparted was based on genuine achievements. The conservative national feeling he engendered attained an immediate and lasting effect. It gave many an individual Jew a sense of belonging to his community that he would no longer have felt on religious grounds. Graetz's history of the past built a bridge into the future.

Gradually, by slow and almost imperceptible stages, the positivism and materialism of the age corroded religious feeling in Jews and Christians alike. The increasingly materialistic interpretation given to the idea of "progress" in Liberal circles did not indeed make Jews lose the Messianic hopes that they had invested in this idea but it blunted their edge. The dominant belief in science referred to impersonal, mechanical, or mathematical laws of nature. Belief in a personal God seemed to be incompatible with these laws, and religion altogether superfluous and obsolete, once man had begun to explore the laws of nature and, by using his newly acquired knowledge, to fashion the world according to his own image. In Jews this loss of belief in a personal God rendered the whole body of religious ceremonial meaningless, except as a formal expression of adherence to the Jewish community, as pious reverence without inner meaning or reality. Even worse, this loss of belief in a personal God barred access to the deepest hidden resources, the mainsprings of creativity that are reached through prayer.

The social consequences of this loss of active, conscious religious belief among educated Jews, particularly in the cities and towns, were clearly marked. Swayed by the pressure of business or office, they made the Sabbath a day of work instead of one of worship and meditation. The synagogues became emptier and emptier throughout the year, although overflowing on the days of the High Festivals. Zest for religious reform waned—congregations indeed perferred their rabbis to be conservative and pious, by proxy. The rabbis themselves tried their utmost to attract larger audiences: the nineteenth century was perhaps the zenith of Jewish pulpit eloquence. Yet, with secular interests absorbing more and more of the congregations' attention, sermons sometimes tended to become lectures, which exhibited the rabbi's general learning but diluted the message of religion. Surprisingly enough, the volume of Jewish communal life did not decrease. This was partly because the loss of educated groups in the large cities was more than balanced by the continuous inflow from smaller towns of Jews who held on more tenaciously to the traditional ways, and partly due to the fact that the cultured elements still maintained their connections although their general interests were far more diversified.

Despite the externalization of Jewish interests, there were valid inner reasons why not all the bonds linking them with their religion were severed. The optimistic belief in the advance of goodness, truth, and beauty, and the conviction of a slow but continuous progress of civilization and of social justice made any regress seem but a temporary setback, soon to be made good and overtaken. The laws of nature yielded no guidance in human conduct. The heavy emphasis of the time on the rational and abstract moralistic contents of religion, which attempted to fill this gap, left no space for a consideration of the irrational, the less moral side of human nature. There were but few who, like Jacob Bernays, stopped to ponder the function of evil in life and in the world. The loss of long-established religious ceremonial was especially grave. Embodying the accumulated experience of past generations with its balancing effect on life, it comprised both its dark and its bright sides, expressing them in the synthesis of a visible way. Jews could secularize their love of God in daily conduct. The awe of God was largely lost in Western life, to reappear in due course in the demonic aspects of nature, in the terrors of war, and in the fear of hydrogen bombs. By the slenderest of threads Jews did not lose this awe entirely. If only on the two days of the New Year festival, they still worshipped the God who holds command over life and death. If only on the Day of Atonement, in confessing their sins they partook in the expression of collective responsibility to the Deity of the People of Israel. The Day of Atonement saved the spiritual existence of many thousands of Jews.

Expansion and Secularization of Jewish Ideas

From the eighteen-sixties onwards, political reaction in Germany gave place to a more liberal policy. After the defeat of Austria in 1866, Bismarck, the Prime Minister of Prussia, entered into an alliance with the National Liberal Party that lasted until 1879. The Liberal movement gained the full support of the state for industrial expansion, greater freedom for the individual, and increased political rights in return for surrendering its own republican ideals and supporting the feudal framework of the Prussian state. With the victorious outcome of the Franco-Prussian War of 1870–71 Bismarck achieved the unification of Germany in the second German Reich under Prussian predominance.

In this setting the full emancipation of Jews, long overdue, was granted as a matter of course, in southern Germany after 1862, in the North German Federation in 1869, and throughout the Reich by its constitution of 1871.

This fulfillment of patient hopes gave a temporary boost to long-shelved aims within the Jewish field as well as opening up new and external avenues to individual Jews. In 1869 an Association of German Israelite Congregations could be founded. In the same year an international conference of rabbis and laymen was held at Leipzig with the aim of defining and extending religious reform, carrying on the work of the rabbinical synods of the mid-century. Despite the brilliant chairing of the conference by Moritz Lazarus, professor of philosophy in Berlin, its liturgical and theological recommendations found but lukewarm response. Another suggestion put forward by the conference, however, was carried out—the establishment of the academic representation of the Science of Judaism. The *Hochschule für die Wissenschaft des Judentums* was founded in Berlin after the Franco-Prussian war. Abraham Geiger, the chief scientific and organizational representative of the reform movement, had in 1870 accepted the post of rabbi in this greatly expanding community. Since 1836 he had pro-

116

claimed the necessity of establishing the academic standing of Judaism, but neither his appeal nor Zunz's application to the University of Berlin in 1848 had succeeded. Now Geiger could carry out the dream of his youth. Apart from training rabbis, in which it achieved as widespread a reputation as the Breslau Theological Seminary, this Academy opened its courses to Christians and Jews, to men and women alike. It also extended the range of theology and history by including in its syllabus the comparative history of religions, the philosophy of religion, the history of Jews, and present-day tasks of Judaism. Abraham Geiger's death in 1874 meant a great loss to the young institution, but in spite of an uphill struggle in the difficult times to come, the Academy established itself as the most respected Jewish institution, the spiritual center of Jewish learning in Germany and far beyond.

Almost at the same time, in 1873, Esriel Hildesheimer founded in Berlin a Rabbinical Seminary for Orthodox Judaism. Unlike Samson Raphael Hirsch at Frankfurt, Hildesheimer did not isolate himself. He combined a full academic training, leaning toward philosophy and mathematics, with strict orthodoxy: despite some initial resistance among his congregation, for fear that worldly knowledge might weaken their uncompromising attitude he maintained a high academic standard among his own scientific staff and included the external academic training of rabbinical candidates as part of the syllabus. Orthodoxy as represented by Hildesheimer won sincere respect though only limited influence in Germany. The rabbis trained in his Seminary spread its reputation far and wide.

Individual Jews too were no longer debarred on principle from holding official, administrative, academic, and legal posts. The Berlin banker Gerson Bleichröder—his grandfather was the youngster who had been expelled from Berlin for fetching a German book for Moses Mendelssohn—was the German financial adviser on the Peace Treaty with France. Ludwig Bamberger, one of the leaders of the Liberal party who, during the revolution of 1848, had fled with a price on his head, was operative in founding the German *Reichsbank* in 1875. In Baden, Moritz Ellstätter became Minister of Finance and remained in office for twenty-five years. Gabriel Riesser, who had fought for the emancipation of Jews since 1830, became in 1861 the first Jewish judge in the High Court of his home town, Hamburg. The struggle for the admission of Jews to academic posts had for fifteen years centered around Jacob Bernays in the Prussian Diet; in 1866 he left the Breslau Jewish Seminary for a professorship of philology at the university of Bonn.

The mental and emotional energies formerly devoted to religious pursuits and now released by the process of secularization among Jews, often led to the opening up of new fields of science or to new lines of work in existing ones. While such work naturally took its proper place in the particular scientific setting to which it belonged, the inner motives that inspired it quite often—and particularly so in outstanding work—constituted a transformation of Jewish problems or attitudes into a secular field. A few examples may illustrate this trend.

In 1860 Moritz Lazarus and his brother-in-law, Heymann Steinthal, both professors at the university of Berlin, founded the science, and a journal, of *Völkerpsychologie,* the psychology of peoples or civilizations as groups, as distinct from the psychology of the individual. In its scientific aim the founding of this discipline meant a determined opposition to the then prevailing tendency to regard human groups as mechanisms explainable in terms of forces and processes without any recourse to ideas. On the basis of a renewed evaluation of Kant's philosophy, Lazarus stressed the importance of ideas in the formation of peoples: "In the natural distribution of the human species—according to space, smaller or larger family groups and tribes—spirit, freedom and history intercede, separating what by nature belongs together, unifying or assimilating what is different in its natural state. The effect of spiritual and historical conditions upon naturally given differences gives rise to the notion of a people." This idealistic opposition to a purely mechanistic interpretation of social conditions and movements was in tune with academic and official policy and gained the attention it deserved. Yet the deeper, personal motives that, in an age of growing nationalism, had made the conditions of inner cohesion of peoples and nations a problem to be investigated scientifically was the malaise of Jews, the denial of their rights as a community.

Lazarus and Steinthal combined their academic activities with a leading position and a warm interest in Jewish communal life. Yet Lazarus did not even attempt to elucidate, let alone alter, the abnormal structure of Jews as a group that had been established by the formula of emancipation, so much was it accepted as final and unalterable by his time.

Reapplying and relating new scientific work to problems of Judaism or Jewish life became an exception. As a rule such work was visualized only in its external setting. Sometimes to his embarrassment, the author was claimed by apologists as a Jew. But the results of such work did not flow back into the Jewish sector. The tradition of Judaism was therefore not maintained in accordance with the standard of the age, let alone extended. While Jews as individuals did pioneering work in many new fields, scientifically and spiritually the Jewish community shrank and became impoverished.

This was particularly so in natural sciences, medicine, and mathematics, in which, up to Albert Einstein, many Jews had won high distinction—far too many, indeed, to mention here. A few examples from medicine may be given by way of illustration. Among the Jewish research workers in medicine was the anatomist Jacob Herz (1816–71), the first to attribute infectious diseases to microscopic parasites; he was honored with a monument by his home town, Erlangen. In Berlin, Ludwig Traube (1816–76), outstanding as a teacher as well as a research worker, founded modern experimental pathology, introducing digitalis for the treatment of heart diseases. Robert Remak (1815–65), also in Berlin, was equally distinguished as an embryologist.

Reasons why natural scientists in particular were usually led away from contact with their religion, and not back to it, may be seen in the characteristic individual development of Ferdinand Cohn of Breslau. His diary from his student days records a discussion with a Christian theologian in which he held that "1. Not everything in the Bible was literally true, 2. Truth was only what was revealed about God, 3. The relationship of God to Nature was not revealed." The note ends with the enigmatic sentence: "what is still to come about, belongs to the God of Truth." Its meaning, however, becomes clearer when we understand "the God of Truth" to be the God who has given man reason to apply to research and has imparted to him a sense of truth as his chief guidance in that research, without regard to past tradition. Thus, on the lines of Spinoza's philosophy, Cohn came to identify nature with God. In a poem he praised nature in her mysterious majesty as the "eternally One," unifying sun and planets, man, plant, and animal, and declared it to be man's task to try and elucidate from the "hieroglyphs" of nature the "creation that once has been." Devoting himself to this task, Ferdinand Cohn became a botanist. Bent over his microscope, he searched for the unity of nature in the living cells of plants and animals with the same single-minded devotion that the mystics of old had given to prayer and meditation in the hope of beholding the unity of the invisible God.

With great difficulty, but by shrewdly enlisting the support of the Ministry of Agriculture for his work because of its bearing on agricultural and forestry pests, Cohn secured the foundation of an Institute of Plant Physiology at Breslau, his home town, in 1866. In his research he went on to smaller and smaller units of nature, examining chlorophyll and algae which, living in hot mineral and sulphurous springs, he discovered to be the first signs of life on earth. Investigating the red spots formed by microorganisms that in the Middle Ages were called "blood rain" and that, when found on sacramental wafers, had caused Jews to be charged with desecration of the Host, Ferdinand Cohn discovered their bacteriological nature and became the founder of systematic bacteriology. It was to him that Robert Koch submitted his discovery of the bacillus anthrax, which started his scientific career.

While in men like Ferdinand Cohn the age-old concentration of Jews on beholding or understanding the unity of God was almost unconsciously transformed into pioneering work in natural science, we find a far more direct and immediate way of transferring old Jewish impulses to the outer world in the political activities of Ferdinand Lassalle (1825–64). In 1840 the fourteen-year-old boy confessed: "I think I am one of the best Jews there are, if the ceremonial law not be taken into account. Like the Jew in Bulwer's 'Leila' I could risk my life to free the Jews from their present depressed condition. Even the scaffold I would not dread, could I make them an honoured people again. If I indulge in childish dreams it is always my favourite idea to be at the head of the Jews, weapons in hand, to win their independence."

Philosophical, philological, and legal studies seemed at times to lead him to a scholar's career rather than into politics. Yet Heinrich Heine, whom he met in Paris, clearly saw that the brilliant intellectual gifts of this young man, his burning ambition, and his aristocratic manners would not be confined to academic fields: "This new generation is determined to enjoy life and to assert itself in visible reality; we in our time bowed meekly before the invisible, we snatched at shadowy kisses and blue scents of flowers, resigned ourselves and wept. And yet our lot perhaps was happier than that of these stern young gladiators who so proudly march towards their doom." Returning from Paris to Berlin in 1863, Lassalle founded the trade union movement of German workers and artisans. Taking over the Radical trends of the Liberal movement that had come to be dimmed by their political success, he formed these workers into a socialist organization with national aims, much against Karl Marx's insistence on the international character of his revolutionary movement. Not without success Lassalle tried to persuade Bismarck to adopt equal and direct suffrage. Thus he went far to realize his childhood dream, though its object had shifted from Jews, no longer oppressed, to exploited workers. The burning zeal for social justice that inspired him, the legacy of the prophets of old Israel, remained the same. He did indeed die a fighter's death, though not at the head of a mass movement but, scorned as a Jew, in an aristocratic duel over a blonde and tall noblewoman.

The increasing momentum toward a secularization of the spiritual content of Judaism meant that its values were given new and creative applications. Their origin in Judaism, however, was hardly ever realized, in contrast to established expressions of Jewish faith within daily life—as, for instance, charity. The new applications were neither seriously claimed to be, nor appreciated as, values of Judaism transferred to a new medium, but at best as individual contributions by Jews to German science, culture, and life. Whereas every conscious act of faith increased the Jewish feeling of basic security, the displacement of unidentified spiritual values reinforced the feeling in Jews of the superiority of the surrounding civilization, and thus their dependence and vulnerability. For, once this feeling of basic security, formerly firmly anchored in their relationship to God, had also been imbued with the hope of redemption from without, Jews had to rely more and more on external recognition and approval. Antagonism, formerly taken for granted, began to hurt once the protective shell of a tightly knit and closed community had been broken by the civil equality granted to individual Jews in a new fatherland.

Nevertheless, Jewish communal feeling was not only maintained by internal cohesion but came to be reinforced by external pressure. In an increasingly materialistic age, the spiritual qualities of the Deity had come to be displaced by the visible world. But while Jews lost much of the inspiring force of being a Chosen People, they could not accept as God's voice the voice of the host nation that, in an age of nationalism replacing and correcting the individualism of the preceding century, idolized herself to the detriment of the Jews.

Nationalism and Anti-Semitism in the New German Empire

The unification of Germany, the goal of hearts and minds throughout the century for Jews as well as Gentiles, was finally achieved by Bismarck, the Prussian Chancellor. It appeared that the forces of "blood and iron," combined with "empirical" politics, had succeeded where the idealistic enthusiasm of the Liberals of 1848 had failed. The second Reich, however, lacked the all-embracing spiritual basis of the first German Empire of the Middle Ages, as well as its universal outlook. Divergences, sometimes almost amounting to a centrifugal force, remained between Protestant Prussia and Catholic Bavaria, between the more liberal and democratic attitude of the South and West and the feudal and militaristic Prussian tradition. It was an accepted political device to foster a strong national spirit as a uniting force. Fervent nationalism, in any case widespread throughout Europe, came in Germany not only to permeate the scientific and industrial field but even the Protestant Church.

National self-consciousness, to be sufficiently vivid, needed some contrasts to define itself. Such a contrast could be found either externally or internally. Externally, national differences between Germany and France were stressed but, with France brooding over revenge for the defeat of 1870–71, had to be soft-pedaled. Internally, the established differences between the federal states needed to be bridged in the interest of the Reich. Minorities, such as the Danes or Poles, were too small to serve as effective contrasts and their homelands too near, so they had to be treated with caution. Only one minority, just sufficiently different to be recognizable, unprotected and widely enough scattered throughout Germany, did fill this need for a contrasting "shadow function"—the Jews.

During the whole of the Middle Ages the Jews, being outside the ordered structure of Christianity, had had much the same function of a contrasting shadow, in the religious as in the economic sphere of the host nations. In the age of nationalism, the old antagonism, never quite

122

dissolved and above all always dormant in the lower middle classes among the artisans and peasants, could only too easily be revived and utilized. Jew-baiting still maintained its medieval characteristics: it indicated with precision the unresolved internal aggression within a given community, and offered a safety-valve for its release, a target for its deflection from its real objective. Although, until the mid-twentieth century, the religious education of Christian children from the earliest age upward tended to perpetuate the religious basis of anti-Jewish feeling in each subsequent generation, anti-Semitism, as it came to be called, was more and more severed from its original religious background. Its new significance was political, though not necessarily exclusively so. This political significance lay in the seeming unity that the vague and indistinct national characteristics of the Germans could be made to assume when "The Germans" were held up in contrast to "The Jews."

Anti-Jewish feelings adopted the most varied expressions. For example, during Bismarck's alliance with the Liberals, he resented the resistance of Catholics to his secular policy and started a *Kulturkampf* against the *Roman* Catholic Church. The Catholics countered this struggle of State versus Church with a press campaign against "The Jews," describing Bismarck's measures as a Jewish attack against the Christian religion—not without the hope of winning the sympathies of Protestants by this indirect countermovement.

Furthermore, in the industrial field, the national buoyancy, combined with the huge war indemnity paid by France to Germany after 1871, caused a boom of feverish industrial expansion, much of it sound and lasting but with the usual fringe of wild speculation on the seemingly limitless opportunities of getting rich quickly. When the inevitable economic crash came some years later, ruining the hopes and the fortunes of many small investors as well as those of overconfident bankers, it did not seem too fantastic to depict this crash as "the victory of Judaism over Germanism." It was regarded as sufficient proof to point to a few Jewish financiers who had swum with the tide but also suffered the consequences, and safe to ignore the fact that it had also been the Jewish Liberal deputy Lasker who had pricked this German equivalent of the English "South Sea Bubble."

Toward the end of the eighteen-seventies, the competitive expansion of national economies precipitated an economic crisis of international proportions. This crisis spread to trade and agriculture as well as industry. Bismarck countered it with a policy of protective tariffs. The National Liberals in Germany were unwilling to renounce their political program of free trade, and this put an end to Bismarck's alliance with the Party. A wave of propaganda, officially inspired or at least condoned, tried to discredit the Liberals—and to draw voters from their ranks—as the party of Jews or "slaves of Jews." The diversionary red herring of anti-Semitism could be introduced in almost any scene, with invariable success.

As an outcome of Bismarck's sharp turn from a liberal to a conservative policy, the Social Democrats were outlawed from 1878 to 1890 as an international movement and at the same time were made the object of an incessant campaign of moral denunciation as traitors to the national cause. The outlawing of the Social Democrats was, however, complemented and even preceded by an attempt to win over the workers to the conservative patriarchism of Church and State. The Protestant court preacher, Adolf Stöcker, founded the Christian-Social Workers Party for this purpose. Being a demagogic spellbinder with a flair for mass effects and well aware that his efforts found next to no response among the workers themselves, Stöcker used a whole array of anti-Semitic slogans as a means of drawing popular attention. He did not mind having a middle-class audience as long as it was a mass audience, and he succeeded in founding a widespread movement, based on and kept together by nothing more than nationalistic emotions and a program of anti-Semitism as an end in itself.

Stöcker's position gave an air of respectability to this anti-Semitic movement, although the liberal Crown Prince, Frederick William, tried to stigmatize anti-Semitism as "the shame of the century." The success of the movement, however, underlined the political value for the new creed of nationalism of even this formalized kind of Protestantism that did not dare to rely on its own spiritual values. It was significant as well as alarming that, in a series of articles in 1880, Heinrich von Treitschke, one of the leading German historians, reproached his Jewish compatriots with inadequate national fervor. Varying a phrase of Heine's—who had called his Jewish heritage "a misfortune" because of the persecutions it entailed—Treitschke declared the Jews to be "our misfortune" and justified Jew-baiting as a "natural reaction of German folk-feeling against an alien element." He was far from suggesting that the emancipation of Jews should be withdrawn and he admitted that if Jews, one and all, met the required standard of exclusive national feeling, "some one-sidedness in Germans might be wholesomely complemented by them." Yet, reproaching Jews for falling short of absolute identification with German nationalism, he took exception to the cosmopolitanism of Liberal Jewish journalists, attacked Graetz's *Jewish History* for its tinge of Jewish national feeling, complained about the dwindling number of mixed marriages, and indicated that, to be complete, conformity to the national cause required religious conversion as well.

German professors were regarded as the authoritative spokesmen on public as well as scientific matters. For this reason Treitschke's attack was as serious as it was unexpected. A number of Jewish replies were published, meekly protesting the sincere patriotism of Jews and trying to refute his charges as being grossly exaggerated. More trenchant was a quiet defense by Theodor Mommsen, world-famous for his *Roman History* and one of the leaders of Liberalism; yet he too held that "the entry into a great nation costs its price"—unconditional assimilation. The defense was almost worse than Treitschke's attack. For it seemed to mean nothing less than the end of the hope that Jews, while becoming Germans, could remain Jews. "Lived and worked in vain!" exclaimed Jacob Auerbach. Jacob Bernays had given a lifetime of devotion to the "European task" of bringing about a synthesis of the biblical and the Greek heritage. Treitschke had been his pupil; Mommsen was one of his dearest friends. When Graetz, his colleague in the first years of the Breslau Theological Seminary, invoked his Jewish feeling and international reputation for help against Treitschke's attack, Bernays, still only fifty-eight years old, had a cerebral stroke from which he died.

A wave of anti-Semitism swept not only over Germany but through the greater part of Europe. In 1879 disciples of Stöcker had formed a League of Anti-Semites, aiming at "Liberation of the German Fatherland from complete Judaisation and the preservation of a tolerable existence for the descendants of the original inhabitants," exhibiting a national inferiority complex of the first order. A whole literature exploited this rewarding subject. Parliamentary parties sprang up and were able to get candidates elected merely by whipping up agitation over the so-called Jewish Question, without even the pretense of concrete aims. For all the fervent nationalism characterizing this mass movement in every country, anti-Semites were quick to form international associations.

Yet, despite its extension, and for all the gravity of its charges against "The Jews," this movement was characterized by a strange unreality, vagueness, and elusiveness. In Russia sinister motives were ascribed to the Jews of Paris, in Berlin to those of London; the alleged danger was always somewhere else. Whenever pinned down by libel action by individual Jews, the anti-Semites with amazing regularity apologized and ate their words. Was it, as Jews were inclined to believe at the time, only a deep-seated though incomprehensible disease in those nations or mere envy of less successful competitors, or did this

very vagueness and elusiveness hide some other purpose beyond its
overt political significance of shifting the blame for any social unrest
away from those responsible?

The secret significance of anti-Semitism lay in a hidden spiritual
motive. It can best be demonstrated in the form of "racial" anti-
Semitism which, appearing in occasional utterances as early as the
eighteen-forties, from about 1880 onward increasingly replaced and
transformed the former religious antagonism without, however,
superseding it entirely.

"Racial" anti-Semitism was the outcome of a development combin-.
ing heterogeneous linguistic, anthropological, and biological theories
with a background of Christian theology reverting to pagan mythology.
The resulting ideology invested these original notions with values entirely alien to, and far remote from, their prime intention. For as
scientific theories they were means of describing complex observations, but were not concerned with their evaluation.

"Racial" anti-Semitism alleged a discrepancy and antagonism between so-called Aryan and Semitic *races*. It rested on no scientific
anthropological basis at all, its sole foundation being a *linguistic* hy-
pothesis. In 1833 Franz Bopp had observed basic similarities, such as a
number of common word-roots, in ancient languages, Indian, Persian,
Greek, Roman, Gothic, Celtic, Slavonic, and so on. From this observation arose the theory of an original "Aryan" group of languages, the
word being taken from Sanskrit, in which the Indians called themselves
Aryana. The existence of a common prehistoric civilization, to which
these similarities of languages may point, has not so far been supported
by any other evidence. Still less conclusive is the assumption that a
number of peoples sharing a given number of words must also have
originated from the same stock. At any rate, the intermingling of ancient tribes owing to migration, to intermarriages between conquerors
and conquered, and the like, did not leave any existing racial group
even comparatively pure. The racial character of prehistoric Aryans, if
ever they existed, is a matter of pure speculation, unsupported but also
unrestrained by exact knowledge.

The positivism of the later nineteenth century, however, seen for
instance in the philosopher Feuerbach's suggestion that theology ought
to be replaced by anthropology, made it rather attractive to transfer
conclusions from language to "race." Thus the mirage was evolved of
"Aryans" as being tall, fair, and blue-eyed, not unlike Germanic gods
of old, without any qualms about the short, dark-haired, and dark-eyed
Indians who provided the starting point for the linguistic theory.
Speculations about the hypothetical "Aryans" placed their homeland

almost everywhere between Central Asia and the North Sea. In Count de Gobineau's *Essay on the Inequality of Races* (1853–55) "everything great, noble and fruitful in the works of man" is ascribed to the "single starting point" of this "race," "one family, the different branches of which have reigned in all civilised countries of the globe." As pointed out above, Gobineau merely substituted the notion of "race" for Heine's romantic distinction of fair Greeks and dark "Nazarenes," yet the distinction between easy-going sensuality and moral earnestness that Heine had made between these two groups now took on the exclusive character of positive and negative. Ernest Renan, in his *Histoire des Langues Semitiques* (1855), indeed went so far as to ascribe to the Semitic race "an inferior composition of human nature" in comparison to the Indo-European—what a development, when only fifty years before all educated men had been agreed on regarding the Bible as the cradle and prototype of human civilization! It is, however, only fair to mention Renan's rider that "physically, the Semites and Aryans were but one race, the white race, and intellectually, they are but one family, the family of civilization."

"Racial" anti-Semitism took the basic pattern of its arguments from the lingering concepts of medieval Christianity about the Jews, although now the ideas were secularized almost beyond recognition. Above all, the idea of an exclusive truth, the alternative of either Christianity *or* Judaism, with the corollary that any weakening of Christian faith automatically meant the victory of Judaism, reappeared in the black-and-white opposition of "The" Aryan and "The" Semitic "race." The rejection by the Jews of Jesus as the Messiah had been held to exclude the Jews from divine favor for the duration of history, and had been extended into the view of a "rejection" of the Jews by God. Could a claim be based on this view that the People of God were now the Germans and no longer the Jews?

A transition of this view from the theological to the biological field could already be observed in the eighteen-forties. "The Jewish People," wrote Constantin Frantz in 1844, "has rejected the true Mediator, the promised Messiah, Jesus, and has thereby excluded itself from history for all future time, the Germans now having become the People of God instead of the Jews." At the same time, Theodor Rohner, a psychologist, explained "The Task of Germany" in that "The first Testament was given to one people only, the second to humans altogether, the third will be given to all peoples by one people, the Germans, who will found a new order," adding that whereas the Jews had indeed been favored by the "great fate" of divine calling, the Germans were not in need of this, having been "elected by the gifts of nature." It was only one step further to justify the Germans, by virtue of their "divine natural self," in executing God's "judgment" in rejecting the Jews.

But at the same time, some of the awe with which the Jews had been invested in the Middle Ages survived as a crude secularization in this kind of substitute theology. In the same way as the biblical tradition of a Chosen People was scorned as "arrogance," the Jews were credited with extraordinary sexual potency, enhanced by circumcision. The mystery of Jewish survival, formerly explained as their being "witnesses" of the Christian faith, could find no proper equivalent in the new conception. Demonized as uncanny, unnatural, and dirty, Jews were now regarded as "bastards who willfully oppose the laws of nature and mankind," as "underlings," "locusts," or "vermin." Their astounding success in the rapidly changing capitalist world could not, however, be explained in this way, especially to Protestants used to measuring godliness by the yardstick of worldly success. Yet the capitalist system itself was denounced as "the victory of Jewish usury," "the kingdom of the Antichrist." On the assumption that whatever changed the existing order, still held to be Christian, must lead to a predominance of Judaism, the idea of social justice, "the Jewish Messiah," was likewise equated with the kingdom of the Antichrist. Hence there was even a kind of wild logic, inconceivable to any sane outside observer, in the final trump card of this "racial" anti-Semitism whereby all Jews, capitalists and socialists alike, were charged with "plotting" to attain world domination, that world domination which, according to the Gospels, the devil usurped as his own and which was rejected by Christ. This world domination, however, was precisely the aim of both the Germans and the Russians of the time. As is well known, the Russian secret police took considerable trouble over faking a "proof" of this plot in 1905, in the infamous "Protocols of the Elders of Zion."

In spite of the almost desperate manner in which European peoples clung on to Christian tradition, the cult of nature underlying and permeating the outlook of the second half of the nineteenth century could not but activate the long-suppressed, never-integrated, pagan background of their origin. Criticizing Abraham Geiger's thesis that the Jews were merely a religious group, the publisher Otto Wigand had in 1858 referred to "the racial antagonism between the children of Jacob who are of Asiatic descent, and the descendants of Teut and Hermann who have inhabited Europe from time immemorial, between the proud and tall, blond Aryan and the short, black-eyed, dark-haired Jew," and he went on: "Races which differ to such degree, oppose each other instinctively and, against such opposition, reason and good sense are powerless." If such instinctive opposition between individual Germans and individual Jews did indeed exist, it would have been a sheer impossibility for Jews to settle in Germany for any length of time at all, let alone throughout the centuries. Feelings of this type were rather a rationalization—or should one say, irrationalization?—of the old, lingering, religious discriminations. Yet the reference to "the descendants of Teut," the mythological ancestor of the "Teutons," points to a revival of pagan mythology below the surface of Christian tradition. Seen in this light, the antagonism between "The Aryan" and "The Jew" recalls the mythical opposition between the fair and radiant hero Siegfried, and the dark and "sinister" Hagen—the antagonism of day and night, of good and evil. In this myth Hagen represents the dark side of Siegfried. Relieved of all things blameworthy, which are instead ascribed to Hagen, Siegfried can appear bright without blemish. In other words, Hagen is the scapegoat of Siegfried.

Here appears a glimpse of the function of this "racial" anti-Semitism. In the absence of any moral principle or guidance, which no positivism could provide, such a principle had to be found in nature, where it does not exist. The myth of an "Aryan race," however, seemed to provide both a mark of natural distinction and a convenient way of burdening a "scapegoat" with whatever character traits or actions were felt to be less creditable—in fact, a method of projecting shortcomings and feelings of guilt onto "The Semitic race." Similar projections on a collective scale exist in a comparatively mild form among all national and religious groups. As soon as the total amount of such projection exceeds a certain proportion, however, there is grave danger that they can no longer be reassimilated, and that these dark forces, unconscious like all projections, may prevail over the light of consciousness. Hence the constant fear of Germans who subscribed to this "racial" creed, of being "dominated" by a small group of Jews, invested with so many of their own less-desirable characteristics. Hence the urge to persecute Jews and with them those shortcomings, if only by proxy, so as to make them, as it were, disappear.

A further, and decisive, aspect of this "racial" anti-Semitism is derived from an unexpected source, Charles Darwin's dominant influence on the Continent in the later nineteenth century, the effect of which differed basically from influences in his own country. In order to show this, we must first briefly consider Darwin's theory of evolution.

Darwin's conception was expressed almost completely in the title of his chief work: *The Origin of Species by Means of Natural Selection, or the Preservation of Favoured Races in the Struggle for Life* (1859).

The theological concept of "Favored Races" in an epoch-making work of natural science came on the Continent to be accepted as one of its chief operative ideas.

The resounding and lasting success of Darwin's work was due to its presentation of life on earth as a hierarchy of living forms, interconnected and evolving from the primitive to the more differentiated, including man himself. The *fact* of such evolution he did indeed demonstrate with an impressive array of observation and induction. His *explanation* of these observed facts as brought about, mechanically, by "natural selection" according to fitness for survival, triumphantly succeeded in extending to the realm of living forms the common view of the time, namely, that nature is governed by unfailing, mechanically operating laws. "Natural selection" thus fitted far too well into the current pattern of thought to be recognized as the metaphysical principle that indeed it is—an article of faith capable neither of demonstration nor of refutation. Incidentally, Schopenhauer's explanation (*On Will in Nature,* 1835) of the formation of new organs as the expression of "a longing fixed in a species"—so that, say, the aggressiveness of bulls would, in the course of time, have led to the formation of horns—is at least as plausible.

Regarding the "survival of the fittest," however, Darwin adduced a second principle of explanation in addition to "natural selection," expressed by the phrase "the Preservation of *Favoured Races*"—namely, divine providence. This was a brave attempt—Darwin being a sincere Christian—to preserve at least part of a religious concept, though here more concerned with preservation than creation. On the scientific plane, the effect of these two different but concurrent principles was somehow confusing. For in Darwin's view, apart from, and in addition to, natural selection, it is Favor that results in survival; that is to say, survival proves Favor in addition to Fitness. Scientifically, therefore, the theological concept did not add anything to the principle of natural selection, which was held to give a comprehensive explanation of all observed phenomena, and in scientific discussions this part of Darwin's theory was simply disregarded.

The theory eliminated the special place assigned to man in the scriptural account of creation. It incorporated him, as descending from apes, in the hierarchy of biology, thus clashing with the accepted religious tradition at least in its literal understanding. In this respect, it caused a considerable stir, especially since its view of "struggle for life," reflecting the industrial cut-throat competition of the times, challenged the complacency of the Victorian age. The emphasis on this relatively superficial incompatibility tended to obscure the fact that

Darwin himself felt well able to combine religious and scientific points of view.

But there was an implication of Darwin's work that affected a really vital question of his time, namely, whether England, as a Favored Nation, would be able to maintain her position permanently. This implication might be taken to read: "There is no reason to believe that Providence will not preserve us—provided only we keep fit!" Nor was the comforting rather than disquieting moral of the lesson lost. Its effect in England was to raise sport from a pastime to a vital concern of national survival, to encourage open windows and cold baths, to make central heating popularly unacceptable, and to introduce a spirit of competition even into parlor games.

In Germany, Darwinism, popularized by Spencer's numerous works, tended first and foremost to discredit the Bible in the eyes of the educated, and thus religion altogether. Gradually, being truly educated came to be regarded as being incompatible with holding more than the vaguest religious beliefs. This development, affecting Gentiles and Jews alike, naturally deflected attention from the deep impact that Darwin's idea of a Favored Race made on German writers. Here was the notion of a spiritual *value* ascribed to the purely natural phenomenon of a group of people, regardless of what use they made of their inborn gifts for the sake of mankind, regardless of any obligation or responsibility on their own part, be it to God or to fellow-human groups. In this respect Darwin's concept basically contrasted with the biblical notion of a Chosen People that depended on the acceptance of responsibility toward both God and fellow man. It was only logical for Nietzsche, on the basis of Darwinism, to reject even Darwin's derivation of social consciousness from social instinct for the preservation of the species and to replace it by the "will to power" of a "super-man," subject to no moral restraint whatsoever—the extreme position of paganism fostered by the apodictic scientific authority of Darwin's work.

Darwin, not concerned with any application of his theory outside his own field of natural science, had spoken about a multitude of "favored races," in fact, all the species that did survive. Both the Christian and the pagan roots of the existing antithesis between "The Aryan Race" and "The Semitic Race" rendered it inconceivable that both "races," each in its own way and according to its own gifts, could be "favored." It had to be one *or* the other. Similarly, it was taken as self-evident that divine favor implied a claim to world domination, again in the strongest possible contrast to the Bible, where the notion of a Chosen People constitutes a free act of love on the part of God and confers responsibilities but no claim to domination over other nations whatsoever, let alone to world domination. Yet the fascination of the idea of a "favored race" lay precisely in its ability to open a positivistic back door to becoming a Favored Nation. Two conditions were required for this aim. The first was to establish "The Germans" as the chief representatives of the "Aryan" race, and German professors busied themselves with this aspect from every conceivable angle; the second, according to Darwin, the only valid and admissible test was survival in the struggle for life.

This second test, however, contained the rub of the problem. For however hard one might try to enhance the prestige of the "Aryan" race and lower and denigrate that of the "Semites"—and, apart from actual vilification of living Jews, the fight for "Aryan" supremacy extended into the far distant past with scientific "proofs" that Jesus had been of "Aryan" descent, that the chief parts of the Bible had been imitated from "Aryan" sources, and the like—one hard fact remained undeniable—the Jews' survival.

This was the reason, not consciously realized and thus never openly mentioned, why the spiritually insecure but all the more fervent nationalism of the second German Reich condoned or even implied anti-Semitism, and yet limited its aggression to those Jews who did not wish to give up their religion. Insistence on full conformity by "assimilation," including the adoption of the Christian faith, was paradoxical if "race," the biological substance unchangeable by religious conversion, had really been the point. However, every Jew who became a Christian seemed to diminish the number of "surviving" Jews and to reinforce the spiritual claim of the host nation to being "favored."

Such was the background of "racial" anti-Semitism, which in the last analysis regarded the mere continuation of the existence of Jews as Jews as a threat to its valid claim to world domination as the only "favored race"—invoking Charles Darwin's scientific authority for the validity of this ideology. German Jews were no longer shut off in inaccessible ghettos; they were living and working in the bright daylight of everyday life. They found it hard to believe that, in an age of such visible and tangible progress, a time of fulfillment for their dearest hopes, such a nighmarish fog of nonsense could descend. They felt it incomprehensible that, in plain contrast to all the visible facts, it could find any credence at all. Had not the very structure of emancipation led them to regard themselves as individuals, as German citizens retaining merely the slenderest thread of religious adherence? How could anyone ascribe any political intentions at all, let alone sinister plots aimed at dominating Germany, nay the world—plots that, had they existed, would have required a worldwide organization—to a community of faith, nonexistent as a political body, organized only for the limited purposes of religious service, instruction, and charity?

Still, there was more than mere nonsense behind this "racial" anti-Semitism of the 1880s, however irrational it seemed. Seen in retrospect, the fears of a "kingdom of Antichrist" were but an indication that the Christian faith of the time had failed to make itself felt in the economics and politics of capitalist expansion and national imperialism. Above all, however, a central value of Judaism, the belief of being a Chosen People, had assumed urgent actuality in the struggle of European nations for their own self-understanding, prestige, and position among the nations.

The Jews of the time who in their endeavor to be members of European nations were increasingly losing their inner certainty of being members of a Chosen People, remained unaware of this critical development. True, a very few Jews noticed this dynamic religious core of anti-Semitism, but they did not take it sufficiently seriously. Looking back, the safeguarding of the Jewish position would have implied a triple task: reinterpreting the meaning of this belief to the Jews themselves; making it clear to the surrounding world; and—realizing that this great experience enshrines a spiritual value of the first order—offering other nations such guidance as might enable them to find their own bearings in this realm.

Only the first of these tasks was visualized when, in 1890, H. Steinthal published an article on this rather delicate subject, significantly enough in the *Allgemeine Zeitung des Judentums* and not in a general periodical. He was a distinguished linguist, professor at the University of Berlin and, at the same time, lecturer at the Institute for Jewish Science in Berlin. Under the heading "The Chosen People, or Jews and Germans," Steinthal wrote:

> Are we the Chosen People? We believe it. And how much hatred, derision, and blame this belief has caused us. What presumption, it was called, what vanity and self-glorification! Yet there is no people on earth, not the smallest little nation that would not regard itself as the Chosen People of its own deity. Yea, travel round the world: whatever people will receive or maybe, reject you, they will expect you to hail them as a Chosen People, from Australia to South Africa. Glorious sun, thou shinest but on Chosen Peoples!
>
> Yet we were taught by our master, Moses (Deut. 7:7; 9:5): "Not because of your virtue or the uprightness of your heart nor because you were eminent among the peoples have you been chosen but

because God loved our fathers who, as the first on earth, had recognised the Holy One and who were to acquaint the world with this experience of God.

Thus it is inborn in us, a duty inherited with the blood, to think in the spirit of the prophets, to feel with their heart, to act according to their words. This is the duty imposed upon us as the "first-born among the peoples. . . ."

We call ourselves the Chosen People, not to indicate the height on which we would stand or would ever have stood, not to claim any superiority among our fellow human beings but to hold forever before our eyes the chasm separating our reality from the ideal task of morality, the chasm between our shortcomings and the model drawn up by the prophets. . . .

We are now no longer a Jewish people. This means much. It means that in all ways of ethical activity we are determined by the spirit of the people among which we dwell. The prophet who had suffered most painfully when Jewish nationhood perished, Jeremiah, called upon the exiles to promote the welfare of the state where God had led them; his words (Jer. 29:7) that "the welfare of this state is your welfare" enjoin us to promote with all our might the growth of all the moral and spiritual aims of the peoples among which we live, and to co-operate in their national task. It is our duty to co-operate in the strengthening, widening and heightening of their national spirit, and in attending to it we fulfil our mission.

Or do we still have a special mission, be it for ourselves or for mankind? This belongs to the "secrets" of God who rules over the history of the world (Deut. 29:28), yet what has been revealed to us by the prophets is simply and plainly the task to love God and to walk in His path—and this task applies to all peoples. . . .

There is no contradiction between being a Jew and being a German and being a human being—all three are so interwoven that we can be the one only by being the two others as well. The Jewish German can be among the best Germans, and the German Jew among the best Jews,—however you call him, he will rank among the best human beings. This is why we love the German fatherland and are grateful to it. We can by now be good Jews only by being good Germans, yet equally we can be good Germans only by being good Jews. We shall be both, or shall be neither, at the same time.

The term "the Chosen People" is, to us, an historical reminder of religious and ethical significance, a warning from our history to strive after the ideal, after self-examination and humility. It means to say that we are Germans of non-German ancestry, yet that, in the double and interlinked national feeling, we find a double reason for being humane, for every kind of moral activity.

"Be honest to goodness," Steinthal finally addressed his fellow-Jews, "and you will have fulfilled your mission for eternity."

This article represents the sincere conviction of the Jews of that time. There is still a feeling of the higher and lasting spiritual significance of nationhood in the reference to the "secrecy" of God's rule on earth, yet it is felt to belong in the past, whereas in the present only the moral significance of this religious tradition can be maintained. A psychological observation of C. G. Jung's on the life of individuals seems to apply here to groups as well. This observation says that achievements definitely attained at one time but afterward lost from consciousness or not further developed when life demanded it, tend to turn negative and, finally, destructive. To the extent to which the sense of the living spiritual significance of Judaism receded in Jews, anti-Semitism could become a danger beyond the level of ordinary social friction. The surrender of spiritual independence produced a germ of serious weakness in German Jews.

In 1899 Houston Stewart Chamberlain, a renegade Englishman who became the son-in-law of Richard Wagner, himself one of the first promoters of anti-Semitism among serious writers, combined the antithesis of the "Aryan" and the "Semitic race spirit" into a full-blown ideology of anti-Semitism. A generation later Adolf Hitler and the National Socialists merely translated this ideology into political practice. Extermination squads, death camps, and gas chambers were neither as inexplicable nor as incidental as is commonly believed. According to Darwin, "survival in the struggle for life" was the only admissible proof of "The favored Race" (or, identifying race and nation, of national superiority). If survival was taken to be the final proof of a claim to world domination, then it was blasphemous but logical to attempt to prove this by the physical extermination of Semitic "underlings"—by genocide. This survival was held to be the outcome of "natural selection" and of divine favor combined. The Nazis, in order to prove themselves "The Favored Ones," thus usurped both the power of Nature and the might of God, the roles of natural selection and of divine providence. They took it upon themselves to become the devil of the Gospel—the Antichrist.

Jews at the End of the Nineteenth Century

In the later nineteenth century, neither "national" nor "racial" anti-Semitism led to any such excesses in Germany, while in Russia, Poland, and Rumania pogroms were a direct outcome of the anti-Semitic drive. A liberal spirit of tolerance still permeated polite society and the larger towns. Isolated rowdyism against Jews in small towns and villages met with immediate and sharp police action. A recurrence of the medieval charges of ritual murder in the wake of the anti-Jewish wave, as at Xanten on the Lower Rhine in 1891 and at Konitz in West Prussia in 1900, and the excitement caused by the ensuing trials, could poison the atmosphere of the district concerned and cause Jews to move to larger towns. Yet even without the universal horror provoked by the anti-Jewish pogroms in Russia, which prompted the raising of generous relief funds, the German political parties were almost unanimously opposed to lawlessness. The Conservatives might condone propaganda against Jews, but not action. The Roman Catholics, themselves often included in the antagonism against anything "foreign," and the Social Democrats joined the Liberals in opposing anti-Semitism altogether; the latter had been readmitted to the German Diet since 1890 on a national and democratic party program, drawn up by Edward Bernstein, and their parliamentary leader, August Bebel, scathingly characterized Jew-baiting as "the socialism of fools."

Even so, the widespread attitude of constant and derogatory distinction had serious effects. The constitutional equality of rights was not abrogated but administratively sabotaged. In theory Jews were eligible for any career for which they qualified. In practice, unless converted, they were barred from appointment to the judiciary, civil service, and municipal employment, were entirely excluded from the corps of active officers, and only in exceptional cases promoted to reserve officers. The same invisible barriers prevented their access to academic posts. Paul Ehrlich never held an official appointment; Albert Einstein had to go abroad as a young physicist. On the other hand, Jews in previously established academic posts had no difficulties.

136

Moritz Abraham Stern, at Göttingen, was one of the outstanding mathematicians of his time. At Berlin, Moritz Lazarus and Heymann Steinthal continued their work on the psychology of nations, and Levin Goldschmidt, the foremost authority on commercial law, was the author of a code for international arbitration, generally adopted as the standard work on the subject. The neo-Kantian philosophy of Hermann Cohen, Professor at Marburg, also dominated its field beyond the borders of Germany.

Restrictions on employment went even further than the official boundaries. With the extension of state enterprise, such restrictions also came to apply to posts in higher education, the postal services, and railways and shipping, and some of the private key industries followed the administrative practice. In an age of rapid industrial expansion, Jews such as Paul Fürstenberg in Berlin and Moritz Warburg in Hamburg were leading figures among the private bankers. But the dominant importance of the national banks quietly ended a tradition of well over two hundred years, which since the time of the Court Jews had made Jewish bankers the financial representatives of governments.

Discrimination against Jews, unless they "proved their worth," was acutely felt in the field of personal social relationships. Students' associations would not accept any but members of "pure Aryan extraction," and a number of other organizations, not wishing to appear less nationally minded, followed their example. Such bias poisoned the spontaneity of personal intercourse between Gentiles and Jews, which had been quite natural during the preceding decades. It frequently made Jews feel socially insecure, awkward, or, in the opposite direction, pushing and reckless. This in its turn did nothing to ease the relationships. On the other hand, the hearty patronization of "philo-Semites" protesting their freedom from such base prejudice could be just as offensive. But even the most rabid anti-Semites would almost without exception boast of their personal friendship with Jews. Below the stratum of formal social life there remained a vast field of good sense, friendliness, and helpfulness on both sides.

Thus the social reception of Jews lagged in general far behind the degree to which they had been integrated into the national and economic life of Germany. In this social sense they were in fact in a worse position than they had been before their civic equality was solemnly enshrined in the German constitution. However, the new restrictions were child's play compared with the hardships most of the older Jews had had to overcome in their beginnings. However sorely their nerves were irritated by an incessant barrage of defamation that legal protection did little to alleviate, they stoically shrugged their shoulders and went on hoping that, in the end, liberty could only be followed by brotherhood. Although in an age of nationalism the humanistic ideals of the beginning of the century to which they adhered had increasingly lost currency, the Jews of the time were quite realistic in not overestimating the actual importance of discrimination. For they shared a lack of recognition with considerable elements in the German body politic, with Roman Catholics, with workers, and with the whole of industry. Jews were underrated but not isolated.

In a general sense groups such as the Jews are usually welcome in an expanding society, where their initiative, versatility, and adaptability to new tasks are needed and appreciated. In a contracting society they find all such places already taken. The Germany of the 1880s was vastly expanding but with the ideology of a contracting society. For Bismarck's alliance with the Liberals had given free play to economic development at the price of their subservience to a feudal order. This economic development now increased to the proportions of an imperialist capitalism extending far beyond the boundaries of any nation or even of any continent. The feudal structure, however, remained static in its composition and in its sense of values, dominated by landed property and military service. At the court of William II the youngest lieutenant took precedence over an industrialist who, in his own realm, might wield almost imperial power. To the landed gentry, the backbone of this feudal society, trade and industry were equally suspect as dangerous to their own predominance. Though many a Jewish heiress helped to regild a faded noble escutcheon, the ideology of "throne and altar" remained exclusive. And this exclusiveness was maintained by identifying the national cause with the conservative party, by denouncing Social Democrats as "subversive," by casting doubt on the loyalty of Roman Catholics and "cosmopolitan" Liberals, and by Jew-baiting. The ideological basis of German nationalism was simply too small and narrow to cover the actual reality of the significant components of a nation's might.

In fact, the rapid growth of industry, trade, and commerce, the spreading of the large towns almost overnight, and the emergence of Germany as a world power created opportunities far greater than any individual or even any group within society could exhaust. In this vastly expanding economy Jews took their full share and maintained their position in proportion to its growth and wealth. Albert Ballin, starting out from his father's small business as an emigration agent, became the director of the Hamburg-America Line (Hapag), and from modest beginnings had by the turn of the century built it up into the largest shipping company in the world, more than twice as large as the total capacity of the French mercantile fleet and famed for both the speed and comfort of its ships. In an age of merciless cutthroat competition between the international shipping lines, Ballin succeeded in replacing this competition by cooperation; he became chairman of a pool called the Atlantic Conference, which combined and regulated all Continental, English, and American shipping interests. With similar foresight and adroitness he tried to prevent the naval armament race between Germany and Great Britain, yet, though enjoying the friendship and confidence of William II, he could not prevail against the ambitious nationalism of German naval circles in an aim that could have prevented the 1914–18 war.

The career of Emil Rathenau shows the industrial development of Germany within a single lifetime. Born in 1838 and trained as an engineer, he founded a flourishing engineering works, building boilers, textile machines, and the like. Despite its success this business somehow did not satisfy him. He liquidated it and, still in his early forties, retired for seven years into private life, studying new scientific developments and traveling widely. He sensed the industrial possibilities of the new electrical inventions, then in their infancy and widely regarded as mere playthings, and took out licences on Edison's patents for electric lighting and for the telephone. His General Electric Company (AEG) made vast improvements to the manufacturing processes and introduced the first electric street lighting to Berlin in 1888. To overcome the teething troubles of the first telephone installations, Emil Rathenau worked in an honorary capacity at the national Post Office for three years. Yet even when technically satisfactory, the new service seemed to be a complete failure commercially; only twelve telephones were installed in the first year, and it required all his vision and tenacity to continue its propagation. The advantages of electric power had to be demonstrated to win it confidence: a cable transmitting sufficient electric energy over a distance of one hundred miles to feed one thousand electric bulbs, a waterfall, and a new alternating-current motor caused a sensation at the technical exhibition at Frankfurt in 1891. "If we consider," Emil Rathenau said on this occasion, "that the instinctive musing of mankind, the purposeful striving of research workers, inventors and the men of the future—as I would like to call engineers—aims at reserving to human endeavour, and ever more extending, the field of constructive thought and individual activity but, on the other hand, at leaving it to machines to perform all merely mechanical, robot work by subjugating natural forces, then I may boldly call this beginning a path on which centuries can advance with success, a new step on the road to beneficial civilisation."

As an industrialist and engineer, Emil Rathenau himself was such a "man of the future," a man of vision far beyond his own work. "It was moving to hear him talk in his simple language of what, to him, seemed self-evident. Yet what he described was the future, and this future he could visualise as clearly as we can see our own times and what we know of the past. Thus people came from afar to ask him what would become of this technical process, of that method of transportation, of this form of economy, of that development. He would answer them quietly and was only astonished that they did not decry his observations as glimpses of the obvious." This vision was, however, fully matched by a cool, critical, reasoning power. The General Electric Company attained worldwide dimensions not only because it took a leading role in large-scale manufacture of all manner of goods from small items such as electric bulbs to the construction of turbines and electric railways, as well as in the introduction of the chemico-electrical production of aluminum and many other fields, but also because Emil Rathenau was a master of financial policy. Personally, however, he did not hold one single share in his concern. The man who in his work did things in princely style, privately—and in this he was typical of a good many Jews of his time—retained his simple household and frugal way of living. "Money with him ends at three marks and begins again at three millions," said a witty friend.

This striking contrast between Rathenau's personality at work and in private life, and between the difference of achievement in the two periods of his industrial activity, was not due only to his being carried far beyond his immediate range on the crest of a wave of industrial expansion but also to his being strong enough to ride it. There was also the difference between an engineer's private enterprise and the industrialist's creation of a large-scale demand for electricity to satisfy it. In fact, it was the promotion of electricity that gave wings to Emil Rathenau's vision, to which he devoted himself with all his latent resources and with a sober passion. What electricity meant to him he hinted at when saying that Berlin, "the city of intelligence, must also become the city of light." He had grown up in the age of Enlightenment, a new stage in the age-old Jewish service of the spirit. Then it meant fighting the darkness of prejudice, promoting the light of knowledge, of culture, and of education. With a new turn of the screw of secularization, this aim came to mean to Emil Rathenau the promotion of electric light. In the age of positivism, a selfless servant of the spirit became an industrialist.

The bustling vigor of industrial expansion, fed by and maintaining a rapidly increasing population, swelled and transformed the cities. Palatial houses were built within large gardens; miles and miles of utilitarian, brick-built, treeless suburbs extended everywhere in equal and uniform ugliness. The tempo of life quickened. The emphasis on material goods led to unheard-of industrial productivity by organization, specialization, and the application of scientific methods. The increase of trade and material wealth loaded tables with the choicest products of remote continents. Material comfort came to be an expression of self-valuation. A broad, optimistic, self-assertive style of living seemed to imply that this enjoyable state of affairs would go on forever. Yet there was another side to this brilliant façade, both socially and spiritually. Socially, a capitalist economy created class distinctions much more marked than they had been before. In the small industrial undertakings of the mid-century, the workers had still been individually esteemed craftsmen. Now unskilled or semi-skilled workers sufficed in many industries. Being a mere cog in a huge machine, a number on a wage sheet, easily interchangeable, the worker appeared as impersonal as the limited company he served. No longer able to derive a sense of dignity from genuine satisfaction and pride in his work, he became a "proletarian," a member of a mass movement such as the Social Democrats. Yet among the middle classes of the cities, loss of the feeling of individuality was almost equally marked. They were embittered by the spirit of competition that permeated private as well as business life, giving people a sense of loneliness and isolation.

The contemporary disregard for the spiritual side of life blunted a sense of values, replacing it by rigid social conventions. The age did not achieve a style of its own but mixed historical motifs, luscious plush curtains, and artificial palms surrounding Renaissance furniture. There was an insatiable hunger for ever more facts, for sensations and scandals; but without visions, the "creators and feeders of life," the sense of reality itself grew doubtful and elusive. Schopenhauer's pessimism became the philosophy of the time, a philosophy that called reality as deceptive as Maya's veil and life the unfolding of a blind world will, tragically unraveling its own creations. Schopenhauer held that only art, and in particular music, could provide release from this senseless tragedy by transcending the egoistic will and transforming it into pure contemplation.

This pagan belief in a blind fate, in the senselessness of life, was indeed the corollary of positivistic materialism, as against the faith, both Jewish and Christian, in a seeing Creator, in the meaningfulness of world and life. Aestheticism, more and more desperately unfeeling and amoral, seemed to offer to the individual the only distinction from the crowd. On the other hand, art became the only access left to the

absolute, replacing religion. Yet an almost passionate interest in literature, art, and music also transcended the narrowness of nationalism
and could provide a feeling of belonging to the greater European community of the educated. In this idea of a cultural supernational community, and with its vivid sense of social responsibility, Liberalism,
although politically defeated, had indeed unified Europe on the cultural
plane.

The life of Jews in Germany towards the end of the century under-
went significant changes. The attraction of the cities became even
stronger. Now almost a third of all German Jews were concentrated in
Berlin and Frankfurt. Mass congregations tended to become composed
of impersonal subscribers rather than individuals who determined the
spirit of their community, as had been the case in smaller towns. At the
same time, social distinctions were sharpened, with the wealthy upper
middle class living in the villas of the fashionable outer districts, the
largest group occupying the spacious flats that were characteristic of
Continental towns, and last a small minority of hawkers and manual
workers, mostly immigrants from Eastern Europe, living in the poorer
districts. Jews in small towns and villages lived much as before. There
was comfortable wealth even below the level of bankers and industrialists, and far more ready charity than acute distress.

The outward picture of a flourishing community was, however,
somehow at variance with its spirit. High hopes had been placed on the
accession of the emperor Frederick William, the liberal son-in-law of
Queen Victoria, but on ascending to the throne he was already stricken
by the fatal illness to which he succumbed after less than three months.
His successor, the young Emperor William II, did not actively encourage anti-Semitism, but the Empress patronized Court preacher Stöcker
without checking his violent campaign against the Jews, and socially
her attitude set the tone. Jews were still expected, as Treitschke had
put it, to "prove their worth" individually—a flexible formula that,
while allowing the social acceptance of outstanding Jews, normally
meant their conversion. The preceding era of Liberalism had firmly and
unquestioningly envisaged that "progress" would go hand in hand with
toleration. Scientific, industrial, and economic progress was by now
abundantly in evidence, yet the feeling of human brotherhood seemed
to have receded almost beyond reach. Progress had failed to usher in
the Messianic Age. Thus to the Jews the social anti-Semitism of the
time meant more and seemed worse than constant, irritating antagonism—it meant a crisis of faith.

Gone were the days when religious reform, an adaptation of Judaism
to contemporary feeling and expression, had seemed the way toward

making the Messianic age a present reality. Weary indifference replaced former enthusiasm. The achievements of the past had hardened into a tradition that a new generation accepted and maintained without testing its basis anew, without any attempt at investigating whether there might be anything wrong with the whole structure of emancipation. The prevalent view of life in this outwardly thriving community is perhaps most strikingly illustrated by the fact that the upper stratum of Jewish society almost without exception adopted the current view on birth control, limiting the number of their children to two at the most, if not one. Six, eight, or even more children had been usual in the preceding generation, under far less auspicious external conditions. The climate of opinion appeared altogether less and less compatible with religious convictions, and the energy of Jews was directed outward even more than before. Being a Jew became a liability, an embarrassment, a fact not to be mentioned if it could be helped. The existence of anti-Semitism was just as unmentionable as an admission of Jewish descent. Educated Jews flocked to theaters, concert halls, art exhibitions, and lecture rooms, yet from the fair selection of world literature on their bookshelves the Bible might be ominously missing.

The combination of pressure and lure made religious apostasy once again, as it had been in the beginning of the century, a common event among the upper classes. The wealthy were lured by titles and social distinctions that, apart from conversion, had a fixed tariff by way of contribution to charitable causes. The professional classes were under pressure because, apart from the gamble of emigration, baptism was often the only path open to an appropriate career. Even so, the overwhelming majority of Jews set themselves with quiet, stoic pride and determination against yielding either to pressure or to temptation, deeming it beneath their dignity to buy the advantages of social recognition or advancement by renouncing their harassed community and uncertain faith. Baptized Jews found themselves isolated. The scions of well-to-do families, seemingly so assimilated as to be indistinguishable from their gentile neighbors, learned with astonishment that conversion or a mixed marriage would forever bar them from their parental home.

Although the conscious Jewish faith of the time lacked the living spark, it was by no means devoid of strong expression—though not immediately recognizable in its significance. For two generations Judaism had been increasingly concentrating on its moral and social implications. Thus a high-minded seriousness and impeccable conduct, active rather than ceremonial, contained the survival of religious conviction. Such exemplary conduct, far more extensive than is usually realized, made its appearance in strict commercial probity, in generous charity more often anonymous than flamboyant, in the humane treatment of servants and—perhaps its most subtle expression—in single-minded devotion to scientific work.

The crisis of faith in Jews that might well have led to a lessening of their sense of social responsibility actually had the opposite effect. The striving after moral perfection extended, at least in intention, to purity of inward thoughts and secret desires, to an ideal approaching that of saintliness, only just balanced by sound common sense. True enough, the high moral tone of their lives owed some of its fervor not merely to religious teaching but also to the will of individual Jews to "prove their worth" in their own way. They were unaware that, in doing so, they were strongly influenced by Christian teaching and by the Christian interpretation of godliness as moral perfection, as Christ-like purity rather than by the Jewish tradition that the world as God's creation of necessity includes both good and evil in its existence.

In a deep sense this conduct was also activated by the age-old belief that every Jew bears witness for the whole of Israel. The very insecurity of Jews as a community came to intensify this sense of coresponsibility in every individual Jew. In its positive expression of striving for exemplary conduct, this meant an outstanding realization of the true meaning of Jewish religion. In Jewish tradition, however, the collective responsibility of Jews as a community to God for their shortcomings had been expressed by the annual sacrifice of a "scapegoat" to be accepted as a symbol of redemption by God. Thus the individual acceptance of this collective responsibility on its negative side caused a readiness by Jews to identify themselves with their weaker brethren. For all their feeling of being individual citizens of their nation, such identification meant a somewhat guilty response to the negative generalization that any particular case of backsliding was characteristic of "The Jews"—a generalization on the part of the host nation that could only be effective because it touched a point of emotional response in the Jews themselves.

The exposed conditions of life under continuous stress drew Jews together. At the same time, high standards had to be maintained and if need be, enforced. These aims were answered by the extension to Germany in 1882 of the Order of B'nai B'rith. This was a fraternal and philanthropic association run on loosely masonic lines and founded in New York in 1843 by a Jewish immigrant from Germany, Henry Jones (Heinrich Jonas). Its German branch developed a structure and spirit of its own that became the model for new Continental, English, and Palestinian lodges. Strict in its demands on character and bearing in selecting its members, yet maintaining harmony above religious and political differences and placing increasing emphasis on religious education, the Order brought about a sense of distinction coupled with obligation, a firm emotional bond, a loyalty of almost religious intensity. Recruited from independent businessmen and members of the professional classes, it created centers of social and spiritual life and came to exert a strong influence on congregations beyond its immediate range. Internally, unobtrusive help was always available for members in difficulties. Externally, the Order came to build up an impressive social welfare structure, settlements providing relief and recreation for those in distress called "Toynbee Halls" after their English model, a chain of children's holiday homes, old-age homes, and maternity clinics.

In a broader field the Association for Jewish History and Literature, founded in Berlin in 1892 by Gustav Karpeles, the author of a *History of Jewish Literature,* met the desires of part of the Jewish population to draw closer together by arranging lectures and discussions, and by establishing libraries and reading rooms. Within twenty years two hundred branches sprang up throughout Germany. A Yearbook that maintained its appeal from 1898 till 1938 catered to a wider Jewish public by presenting historical essays in popular form, combined with autobiographies from the early days of emancipation that seemed idyllic in retrospect, and with heartwarming short stories.

In this circle the scholars of the Science of Judaism still found an echo. Otherwise their work, solid and careful but becoming more and more specialized despite its extension into ever-widening fields, lacked popular appeal. Exceptionally, a work such as Moritz Lazarus's *Ethics of Judaism* (1898), written with an insight sharpened by his work on the comparative psychology of civilizations yet based on neo-Kantian philosophy, could find widespread interest. But not even Moritz Güdemann's *History of Culture and Education of Western Jews* (1880), which combined pioneering research with attractive presentation, could break the emotional barrier in educated Jews who looked upon Judaism as a slightly obsolete second-best, suitable only for those who were not quite up to their time or could do no better. This rule found an exception, however, where scholarly treatment also served an apologetic purpose, such as David Hoffmann's *Shulkhan Arukh* (1885). Indeed, much of the work of the time had to enlist learning in the ranks of defense.

Since the anti-Semitic wave gave no appearance of abating, a new spirit of determination arose among Jews. Students were the first to react to insults based on their descent. In 1886 the student association

"Viadrina" was formed at Breslau, soon afterwards followed by similar student fraternities at other German universities. The colors worn according to the custom of German students' associations marked them out as Jews. Combining proud and conscious evaluation of their Jewish heritage with the aim of completing the struggle for full civic equality, they stood up for their convictions with a determination that did not fail to gain them the respect even of anti-Semitic students when they met them on their own ground—with sharp weapons. A more important aspect of this was, however, the greater self-reliance displayed by this younger generation.

A similar spirit was called for in the wide political field. In 1891 five hundred outstanding German Christians from all walks of life had combined to form an Association for Warding-off Anti-Semitism which, by publishing a periodical and a *Mirror of Anti-Semitism,* spread factual information and highlighted some of the disreputable characters among leading anti-Semites. A Jewish committee led by Paul Nathan, editor of the best political monthly periodical in Germany, had got together for the same purpose. Yet despite this counterpropaganda that did not reach the masses because of its limited means, sixteen anti-Semitic deputies were elected to the German Diet in 1893. Jews now felt that they had to take their defense into their own hands and themselves fight for their rights.

In the same year the *Centralverein deutscher Staatsbürger jüdischen Glaubens* (Central Association of German Citizens of Jewish Faith) was founded to this end, as the result of the wide appeal of a pamphlet *Protected Jews or Citizens* by Raphael Loewenfeld, director of the Schiller Theatre in Berlin. Under its respected and upright leaders, Maximilian Horwitz and Eugen Fuchs, the Association became a mass movement mobilizing virtually every Jew in defense of his honor and rights and those of his community. A nationwide organization and well-attended public meetings overcame the apparent lethargy with which Jews were watching the spread of the anti-Semitic movement. Such meetings demonstrated that Jews at large would no longer remain as a sitting target for unqualified abuse. Invoking the spirit of Gabriel Riesser, protagonist in the legal fight for emancipation, the *C.V.* likewise strove in the conviction that truth, if widely enough disseminated, must ultimately prevail. This was a faith that could rekindle the flickering flame of Jewish courage and hope, prevent their patriotism from becoming embittered, provide them with the factual information needed to refute anti-Semitic propaganda within their own environment, and that could give a feeling of effective protection to those most helpless and exposed, the small people of the remote countryside. The Association did not attempt to defend individuals, but it could and did provide skilled legal aid in cases that concerned Jews collectively, such as the charge of ritual murder at Konitz; or it could enlist competent scientific evidence against attacks on the Talmud or *Shehita,* the ritual method of slaughtering animals. The most loud-mouthed anti-Semites learned that slander could be called to account in the courts and they had to watch their step accordingly, though the German law of libel remained deficient on the question of collective charges. Above all, there was now an organized body representing German Jews in their legal status that could negotiate at the governmental level. No legal means could penetrate to the spiritual roots of anti-Semitism, yet the *Centralverein* effectively curbed its worst excesses. The wall of administrative discrimination against Jews only gave way in isolated cases, but unrelenting determination kept alive in Germany far beyond the Jewish sphere a feeling of the undeserved injustice of such discrimination, a sore on the German body politic.

Zionism

To understand the next step, a new phase in the development of Jewish life, we have to cast a glance beyond the German scene, to Austria, France, and the European East.

Toward the end of the nineteenth century the Dual Monarchy of Austria and Hungary was a mighty empire, still maintaining the prestige and supranational tradition of the medieval Roman Empire of the German Nation, so long established as to appear imperishable. But there were dangerous cracks in this impressive façade. Austria had suffered military defeat at the hands of Prussia in 1866—a blow to her self-respect that Bismarck's political genius alleviated by mild conditions and a close political alliance, quite apart from the bonds of common language. The dominant German majority found itself opposed by the violently nationalistic minorities of Czechs, Poles, Croats, Slovenes, and Serbs, all of them striving for independence and only kept together by close-knit common interests and loyalty to the old Emperor, Franz-Josef.

Jews were in an awkward position in this struggle, on the one hand hated by the Slav nationalists for remaining loyal to the German language and civilization, on the other hand, and at the same time, rejected by the German majority. The Germans answered the nationalist minorities with a national movement of their own, competing for power through the strongly anti-Semitic Christian Social Party, under the leadership of the Catholic clergy. With the virtual victory of this party, Vienna, hitherto one of the most liberal capital cities of Europe, became a hotbed of anti-Semitism. It was here that young Adolf Hitler learned the technique of swaying lower middle-class masses by means of anti-Semitic slogans, by evoking race hatred.

In the Austrian parliament a Jewish deputy, Joseph Samuel Bloch, unmasked the ignorance and hypocrisy of the anti-Semitic leaders. Discarding his parliamentary immunity, he successfully challenged them to legal action where their charges could be exposed in all their hollowness. The Austrian Israelitic Union, founded in 1885, which

148

accepted a membership on the basis of race and not of religion, combined a legal aid bureau with lectures on Judaism. But if even the censure of the Emperor, who labeled anti-Semitism "Vienna's disgrace," failed to carry force, Jewish countermeasures could hardly be expected to succeed.

There was another aspect to Vienna, the great city facing eastward down the Danube to the Balkans, where generous relief work was being carried out among the Jews of Galicia, who were sandwiched dangerously between the ruling Polish nobility and the Ruthenian peasantry. Baron Maurice de Hirsch, son of the Bavarian Court banker and himself a railway magnate who lived in Brussels, had in 1888 endowed a Foundation of twelve million francs to train in artisan employment and support young Jews from these overcrowded centers.

And above all, there was Vienna itself, long resigned to noisy parliamentary scenes, to the insoluble clashes of minorities, to "catastrophic but not serious" political prospects, determined to survive by "muddling through." Here was the glittering elegance of the most refined culture, the colorful pageant of military parades and church processions, the wealth of an old civilization, the incomparable richness of artistic tradition. This graceful, leisurely, hospitable city of waltz rhythms and wine had one concern of passionate seriousness, shared alike by porter and industrialist, by Christian and Jew: perfection in art. The death of an actor at the *Burgtheater* seemed like a national tragedy, leading musicians were heroes, outstanding writers the demi-gods of Vienna.

This softly padded, happily excitable, severely critical world of literature, stage, and art was to a disproportionate extent sponsored, run, and represented by Jews. Apart from economic and industrial pursuits it was chiefly in this realm that they found real equality as well as a chance to distinguish themselves, though Jews of wide renown were working at the university too, especially in medicine; and in the army, unlike Germany, the Emperor promoted officers with liberal impartiality. At the *"Burg,"* Adolf Sonnenthal was the outstanding actor of his time, as Bogumil Dawison had been before him. At the opera, Pauline Lucca still enraptured the crowded house with her voice, her acting, and her charm. Gustav Mahler as conductor—as a composer he was as yet hardly known—revolutionized operatic performances by opposing the "slovenliness" of a great tradition, insisting on the integration of singing and acting and the setting of the whole in a concept of artistic perfection. In the lighter side of music, Oscar Strauss, Leo Fall, and Emeric Kalman competed with glittering operettas and brilliant waltzes. A whole galaxy of young Jewish talent strove for recognition in literature, among them Hugo von Hofmannsthal, who wrote beautiful and mature poetry at the age of sixteen; the great-grandson of an ennobled Jewish banker, he had grown up among the Austrian and Italian aristocracy. Arthur Schnitzler, Stefan Zweig, Richard Beer-Hofmann, and Peter Altenberg were all to attain international recognition, apart from scores of other Jewish writers and journalists.

Among the journalists Theodor Herzl had established a reputation as a dramatic critic and playwright and was admired as a master of the subtle, cultivated, witty essay. The *Neue Freie Presse,* a daily paper of international renown, made him their Paris correspondent—one of the most sought-after and envied positions in European journalism. He became a well-known figure in the salons of this, the most brilliant of European capitals. His dazzling reports concerning the stage, literature, and art also came to include political and social questions. Indeed, social unrest and political tensions were all too apparent in the young Third Republic, still in danger of being overthrown by aristocratic, military, and clerical adherents of the royalist regime that had fallen victim to the Prussian victory of 1870. These tensions exploded in the Dreyfus case. From 1894 to 1906 this famous "affair" came to divide France into two fanatically opposed camps. It brought the country to the verge of civil war and, finally, led to the restitution of the moral credit of the Republic and to the severance of State and Church.

Theodor Herzl was present when on 5 January 1895 Captain Alfred Dreyfus, the first Jewish officer to have been assigned to the French general staff, was degraded from his rank at a solemn public military ceremony, prior to being deported to Devil's Island. He had been found guilty of high treason by handing over secret documents to the Prussian general staff. Although the incriminating documents had been cloaked in the veil of military secrecy, almost everybody believed the prisoner to be guilty. It took years until concerted effort established the truth that there had been treason indeed, but that the culprit was a high-ranking officer of the old aristocracy, Esterhazy, whose friend Lietenant-Colonel Henri had directed suspicion to Dreyfus and had caused his conviction by forged documents. The ceremony took its course. An officer broke the captain's sword; one after another a sergeant, a corporal, and a private tore his insignia from his uniform and threw them at his feet. Nobody heeded his outcry: "I am innocent!" Herzl also believed him to be guilty, yet he could not understand the exultation glowing on the faces of the spectators standing by. "Why are these people so delighted?" he asked time and again after the prisoner had been led away. "Granted he is a traitor, how can they find such intense joy in the suffering of a human being?" "You forget," he was told, "that this crowd is elated over the degradation of a Jew."

Herzl's pride revolted. But this revolt released a depth of feeling, a stream of creativeness hidden even from his own ironical, ambitious self. He felt transformed. For months he was in a fever, toiling by day and night in shaping his reply to that experience, sensing inspiration "like an eagle's wings above his head," feeling as if in a "gigantic dream." A small book emerged from all these labors: *The Jews' State*. Here was the age-old Messianic longing for Zion, transformed into the European conception of a modern national and political movement— Zionism. Herzl's vision saw the Jews, scattered for centuries among the nations, emancipated as individuals of varying nationality, as a people—One People. He raised anti-Semitism to the apocalyptic stature of common and unavoidable destiny. Neither struggles nor alleviation through the channels of philanthropy could bring a solution, only the establishment of a Jewish State by open negotiations with the nations to win their consent and help for planned emigration and colonization. The breathtaking boldness of this conception lay in daring to hope, in stating with confidence, that a dream of two millennia could become actual reality in the immediate future, if only the Jewish people wished it to come true.

This was what Herzl actually believed and meant; undeterred by the seeming impossibility of achieving a goal that, externally, meant entering international power politics without any power and, internally, uniting a community divided by allegiance to a dozen different nations, separated by language and by a wide variety of religious views ranging from medieval orthodoxy to socialist atheism. A friend to whom he showed the manuscript read it and, halfway through, broke down in tears—not, as it transpired, because he was so moved by the content but because he seriously feared that Herzl's mind had lost its balance. The thirty-five-year-old Herzl did indeed consult a psychiatrist, Max Nordau, who, like himself, had come from Hungary to Vienna and thence to Paris to win international fame as the author of *The Conventional Lies of Civilisation*. In Nordau, who was as completely assimilated as Herzl but the grandson of a famous rabbi, the spark struck fire: "You may be mad," he said, "but then I am as mad as you."

Herzl believed that both political influence and funds would be readily available if only he could win over to his cause some of the leading Jewish financiers. The first was Baron Maurice de Hirsch, who had followed up his Vienna Foundation for the training of Galician Jews with a much larger project still, the Jewish Colonization Association (ICA), which aimed at ending the unspeakable suffering of Russian

Jews by transferring them to a new, productive existence in the Argentine. Here was a man who, having lost his only son in early manhood, put all his energy as well as his financial resources into constructive work: "My son I have lost, but not my heir; humanity is my heir." Yet Baron de Hirsch did not believe in a national Jewish ideology. Herzl saw Baron Edmond de Rothschild in Paris who also would not support a political movement, although he had helped untiringly and despite all misgivings to establish the first small Jewish colonies in Palestine on a secure and modern foundation—"the father of Jewish colonization in Palestine." Under the difficulties of Turkish rule, Rothschild could see progress only in slow and steady infiltration, in strictly nonpolitical work. In London, Herzl found a handful of steadfast individual supporters, yet a spontaneous, enthusiastic mass response only came forth when he addressed the poor Jewish workers at Whitechapel in the East End of London, the refugees from Polish and Russian pogroms.

In September 1895 he returned to Vienna, promoted to the post of dramatic critic and *feuilleton* editor of the *Neue Freie Presse*. It was one of the most important positions in the literary and artistic life of the city. The paper's reviews determined the success or failure of a play, the renown of an artist. A young writer could become famous overnight by having one single essay published "under the line" on the title page that separated the cultural part, the center of attention, from the "mere" political news above it. Literary fame, adulation, envied social position, and financial independence were the very real perquisites of this post. Yet they appeared to be utterly incompatible with Herzl's vision. The very word *Zionism* could not be mentioned in his paper. The whole Jewish bourgeoisie was solidly entrenched against a conception that seemed to undermine the whole basis of emancipation and to furnish a deadly argument in favor of anti-Semitism. Eastern orthodox rabbis feared in a Messianic movement turned political an attempt to force the hand of Providence. Socialists, seeing in the class struggle the means of creating a classless supranational society, the brotherhood of men, could but regard a national movement as reactionary. The merciless wit of Karl Krauss, one of the outstanding Viennese journalists of Jewish descent, lampooned Herzl as "The King of Zion," an arrow charged with poison.

Herzl, having finished his book, believed that this was all he had to do, that others, better fitted than himself to carry out his vision, would take over its realization. Yet none of the leading Jewish personalities whom he had approached responded, and the sharply divided reception accorded to Herzl the artistic writer and Herzl the prophet of Jewish renaissance could only encourage him along the one track, deter him from the other. Fame had never been so serious an obstacle to a deeply spiritual urge, to a mission in which Herzl saw "the Sabbath of his life."

He was not, however, so isolated as it appeared; it was just that he knew nothing of the love of Zion surviving among Jews everywhere, of his precursors, and of the European East and its fervent Jewish life. In small villages throughout Europe there had always been men who would let their own families starve rather than withhold financial support from those who prayed for them before the Wailing Wall in Jerusalem, the last remnant of Solomon's Temple. Pious Jews were still buried with a little bag of earth from the Holy Land under their head, so that they might be reunited with their forefathers. This longing for Zion, spiritualized and secularized during the age of emancipation, had yet been kept alive both in Jewish hearts and in the synagogal service. Symbolizing the spiritual unity of Jews in the Diaspora and the hope of Messianic redemption, this longing was revitalized by any fear for their temporal position. As in Herzl, this feeling was the first glow of Jewish solidarity in those who returned to Judaism after having strayed afar.

Thus Moses Hess, one of the early pioneers of socialism, had advocated Jewish nationalism in his book *Rome and Jerusalem* (1862) as the solution of "the last nationality question." It had been sympathetically reviewed by Heinrich Graetz, the historian, but otherwise regarded as a paradoxical phantasy of the "communist rabbi" who did nothing to implement it. But in the same year Zebi Hirsch Kalischer (1795–1874), an orthodox rabbi at Thorn in East Prussia, had emphasized in his Hebrew work, *Derishat Zion (Care for Zion),* the need for colonizing Palestine, proving from traditional sources that it was the right and duty of Jews to do so without awaiting the arrival of the Messiah. This led to the foundation at Frankfurt of an Israelite Association for Colonization in Palestine, which found strong and lasting support from orthodox rabbis such as Esriel Hildesheimer, the leader of the Berlin rabbinical training school, and Isaac Ruelf, who had himself seen the plight of Russian Jews.

The chief motive force of this colonization had, however, come from among the Russian Jews. The *Hoveve Zion (Lovers of Zion)* had aroused a widespread movement that found pioneers in particular from among students who were willing to undergo any measure of hardship for the sacred task of reviving the ancient land and, as it was felt, the glory of ancient Judaism by reverting to the holy soil from which it had sprung. With almost superhuman efforts they had indeed succeeded in establishing the first small settlements, yet despite Rothschild's help and sympathy, and support from Jewries everywhere, everything seemed to combine against them. In 1884 a conference was held at Kattowitz where the frontiers of Germany, Austria, and Russia met, attended by delegates from all European countries. In the chair was Dr. Leo Pinsker, a physician from Odessa who had published in 1882 in Berlin a pamphlet entitled *Auto-Emancipation,* which combined a gloomy view of the chances of emancipation with a plea for a Jewish State. The conference did not adopt this national view, yet the Turkish government forbade further immigration or settlement of Jews in Palestine. Jewish national feeling, however, had spread fast. Even in Vienna itself there was a students' association, Kadimah, of nationalist conviction.

When Herzl realized to what extent his ideas had been expressed before him, he declared that had he been aware of this he would have written nothing. Still, there was a great difference. Nobody before him had held out the hope that the "Jewish Question" could be settled with the help of the nations—the hope of redemption from without as in the early days of emancipation, now transferred by him to a collective level. Only such a thoroughly assimilated Jew could carry the idea of "progress" this far, could trust modern civilization to redeem age-old suffering with the certainty with which medical science had come to treat epidemics hitherto regarded as transcending human power. A Western Jew had formulated the inarticulate feeling of hundreds of thousands of Eastern Jews, and their admiration for the emancipation that had been achieved in the West gave him authority. The followers he won in the West were individuals. From the East he received a wave of enthusiasm, the trust and confidence of the masses. He had brought the breath of a wider world into their narrow lives, great though they were in inner values.

This confidence, while investing Herzl with almost undisputed leadership, implied two tasks, both enormous, yet at the same time interdependent and almost mutually exclusive. The first of these was to organize his following, potentially large yet dispersed over many lands, composed of mystics and rationalists, of orthodox Jews and atheists, of humanist idealists and racialist free-thinkers. The second task was to feed this faith in a national solution of the Jewish question by visible success in diplomatic and political negotiations with sovereigns and ministers. Herzl put all his strength into these two tasks. In addition to them, however, he had to attend and face a different one that made his life a kind of gymnastic exercise on a tightrope. He had to keep his post at the *Neue Freie Presse.* For, apart from its attractions, it yielded him the income he needed to support his own family and to meet both much of the cost of the Zionist organization that he had set up, and his own traveling expenses.

In the service of his mission Herzl grew into a diplomat, statesman, inspiring orator, and first-rate organizer, besides remaining a writer of distinction. And his vision fused all these facets of his personality into a "curiously magic effect," a magnetic power. He had at his side a small band of devoted and capable enthusiasts, yet none of them, except Max Nordau, could offer the common cause any direct contact with royalty or the diplomatic sphere. Still, almost providential good luck was on Herzl's side; where the support of the Jewish world failed him, Christian love of Zion came to his aid. William H. Hechler, chaplain to the British Embassy in Vienna, was fervently interested in the millennium, as were a good many English parsons of the time. From a prophecy of the seventh century he had two years previously calculated the date of the millennium as the year 1897–98. In Herzl's movement he saw a "prophetic turning-point." During the time of the first Russian pogroms he had collected money to help the Palestinian settlements and had distributed it there himself. Now he offered Herzl direct access to the German Emperor, through the mediation of the latter's uncle, the Grand Duke of Baden, one of the most distinguished liberal princes in Germany.

Thus, only a few months after the publication of *The Jews' State,* Herzl seemed indeed on the way to spectacular success. The tall figure, elegantly groomed, strikingly handsome, with fiery dark brown eyes in a pale face and an almost blue-black Assyrian beard, somehow recalled bygone ages of feudal splendor in his poise, ease, and charm. He won over the Grand Duke to sponsoring his cause with the Emperor. And William II, cherishing romantic dreams of reviving the German Emperors' protection of the Holy Land in the Middle Ages and at the same time of extending German influence to the Near East, seemed willing to intervene with his friend the Sultan of Turkey on behalf of Zionist aims. Moreover, by the happy mediation of a gentile journalist colleague, von Newlinsky, the editor of the *Correspondence de l'Est* in Vienna, Herzl obtained within the same year an audience with the Sultan Abdul Hamid II himself, the results of which were "at any rate not discouraging." The Sultan was opposed to granting Palestine to the Jews as an independent State. But the idea of an autonomous country under Turkish suzerainty was discussed, with the prospect of a loan by Jewish financiers to Turkey in the background; her financial difficulties were only too well known, not least to the financiers whom Herzl still hoped to win over should the project mature.

Founding a weekly periodical *Die Welt (The World)* as a party organ,

Herzl lost no time in utilizing the visible, though not yet tangible, progress he had made. Despite determined resistance from within the movement against appearing too early in public, Herzl convoked a World Congress of Zionists for August 1897. The internal resistance was, however, negligible compared with the barrage of antagonism he encountered from official Jewish quarters. The Congress was to be held at Munich; the Jewish community, terrified, protested against the honor, so that it had to be transferred to Basle. The Rabbinical Association of Germany issued a solemn declaration in the general press, stating that the endeavor to establish a Jewish national state in Palestine was "in contradiction to the Messianic promises of Judaism." The declaration, while carefully guarding "the worthy efforts which aim at the colonization of Palestine by Jewish agriculturists" against any suspicion of nationalistic aims, protested in the name of "religion and patriotism alike" against the forthcoming Congress. One of the two dissenters from the declaration was Leo Baeck, then twenty-four years old and rabbi at Oppeln in Silesia. German Jews were, however, not alone in condemning Jewish nationalism. Dr. Nathan Marcus Adler, Chief Rabbi of England, was similarly opposed to it. The Central Conference of American Rabbis expected that the establishment of a Jewish State would bring "not benefit but infinite harm." The theological point was as controversial as the differences between predominant political interest in the West and the East. Eastern rabbis such as Samuel Mohilever of Radom expressly based their support for Zionism on the traditional Messianic promises.

In the face of this almost solid body of resistance by Western Jews, Herzl succeeded in making the first Zionist Congress a memorable event. The 204 delegates, representing Zionist groups in most European countries, in the United States, Palestine, and Algiers, felt themselves to be the first Jewish national assembly since Roman times. Although expressing widely differing ideas in diverse languages, they were united under the blue and white flag with the Star of David, and more so still by the feeling of a common purpose.

Max Nordau's eloquent analysis of the position of Jews throughout the world impressively contrasted the material needs of Eastern Jews with the moral conflict of those in the West. Because of the political danger he had to omit any mention of Russia, which contained half the then existing Jewish population of the world. Nordau's romantic eulogy of the ghetto sounded strange as voiced by a Western Jew so far removed from it. He set a fashion for Zionist writers and speakers by fighting Jewish "assimilationists," disregarding the strong religious forces of Messianic hope inherent in and kept alive by German Jews throughout the vagaries of the age of emancipation. These were the very same forces that Zionism, at a further stage of development, now sought to transfer from Jews as individuals to the Jewish people. Despite all this, however, Nordau's address conveyed a sense of community between Jews bridging all existing diversities of outlook and development—a feeling not expressed with such power since Leopold Zunz and Heinrich Graetz.

The chief unifying force of the Congress, however, was Theodor Herzl's own personality. He was not unaware of this. "In Basle I created the Jewish State," he noted in his diary, adding "though with opportunist modifications and with weak performance." In fact, the "Basle Program" had to tone down the aim of a Jewish State to that of "a publicly recognized, legally secured home in Palestine." Max Nordau had invented the expression *Heimstätte,* "home," to give less ostensible offense, counting on its politically innocent interpretation as a shelter for all persecuted Jews, especially those from Russia. However willing to further this latter, philanthropic aim, Jewish bankers refused support for the establishment of a Jewish Bank, which the Congress had voted.

The following year, 1898, promised the fulfillment of Herzl's highest hopes, the justification for his manner of storming the heavens. The German Emperor, William II, journeyed to Palestine and was prepared to receive there, in the Holy Land itself, the Zionist deputation with Herzl at its head. Herzl, himself enthusiastically welcomed by the Jewish colonies, greeted the imperial suite on its way from Jaffa with a choir from one of the colonies, Mikweh Israel. The Emperor recognized him and treated him with friendly courtesy. A formal audience followed in Jerusalem. Herzl petitioned the Emperor to intervene with the Sultan for the grant of a Jewish Chartered Company in Palestine and Syria under German protection. This was received in a gracious mood, though without a definite promise. The fact of the audience itself was an unprecedented success, firing the imagination and hopes of the multitude of Jews in distress. Yet it was followed by an anticlimax. There was no reply; there was only silence. Herzl, wondering what might have gone wrong, tormented himself over any mistake he might have made. Only much later did he learn that the Emperor had in fact sounded the Sultan on the project but had met with blunt rejection.

It took nearly three years of difficult negotiations with the corrupt Turkish court before Herzl himself was again granted an audience by the Sultan, followed by further negotiations. The final outcome was an offer for Jewish colonization—throughout the whole Turkish realm, with the sole exception of Palestine. After years of exertion Herzl had come up against a blank wall.

Though deeply disappointed, he was far from giving in; he was the leader of the Zionist movement, he said, because he "could not be made to yield." He suspected Russian influence behind the Turkish refusal and was determined to break it down. Indeed, against all expectations, he secured from the most violently anti-Jewish power of the time an official pledge to support the establishment of a Jewish commonwealth in Palestine at the "Sublime Porte"; the Russian ministers wished to soothe world opinion after the terrible Kishinev pogrom.

While trying to strengthen his hand still further for a renewal of negotiations at Constantinople by gaining the support of other European powers, Herzl was stimulated by a surprising invitation. The British government indicated its willingness to support Jews in distress. A first project, that of opening up Wadi El Arish in the Sinai peninsula, foundered over the objection of the Egyptian government to the drawing of water from the Nile for irrigation of the settlement. The Brisith Colonial Secretary, Joseph Chamberlain, followed it up with the formal offer of an autonomous Jewish settlement in Uganda, on some of the most suitable land in East Africa.

In view of the plight of the Jews in Russia, this offer was most tempting, only—it was not Palestine. Max Nordau called it an "Overnight Shelter." Yet when the project was submitted to the Sixth Zionist Congress in 1903, the delegates were first electrified by the fact that a Great Power recognized Zionism as representing the Jewish People, but then were utterly dejected by its content. The Russian delegates viewed Herzl's guarded recommendation as treason to the Zionist ideal; two delegates from Kishinev itself voted against the project. A turmoil of conflicting emotions all but split the movement; the Russian Zionists threatened to establish a Zionist organization of their own. Herzl, with his heart siding with the Zionist aim, his head with that of the African project, was deeply hurt at being called a traitor to his movement. He still endeavored to use the Russian promise of support for renewed negotiations in Constantinople but his heart, ailing for years, could no longer stand the strain. He died in 1904, only forty-four years old. In a span of but nine years he had indeed not conquered the world for his mission, but he had wrested glory from defeat. And his vision persisted and retained the power of transforming reality.

On Herzl's death Vienna was startled to realize that he had not merely been the adored *feuilleton* editor of the *Neue Freie Presse* but the leader of a great movement. "Suddenly, to all the railway stations of the city, by day and by night, from all realms and lands, every train brought new arrivals. Western, Eastern, Russian, Turkish Jews; from all the provinces and all the little towns they hurried excitedly, the shock of the news still written on their faces. . . . The funeral procession was endless. A tumult ensued at the cemetery; too many had suddenly stormed to his coffin, crying, sobbing, screaming in a wild explosion of despair. It was almost a riot, a fury. All order was upset through a sort of elementary and ecstatic mourning. . . . It was this gigantic outpouring of grief from the depths of millions of souls that made me realise for the first time how much passion and hope this lone and lonesome man had borne into the world through the power of a single thought." This was the experience of Stefan Zweig, a young Jewish writer who had been as skeptical of Herzl's Zionist "hobby" as had the whole of literary Vienna.

Into the Twentieth Century

A contemporary of Herzl in Vienna, of much the same age, had only just advanced into his work when Herzl's path came to an end. Sigmund Freud's way led in the opposite direction. Not the "breath of eternity" of Herzl's fiery vision marked his approach, but slow, systematic, painstaking, scientific study; not Jewish revitalization but a further stage of secularization of spiritual values. Yet, while Herzl failed to reach his goal in outward reality, Freud came to discover a new dimension of the human mind—the unconscious. Utilizing his discovery for the treatment of hitherto inaccessible disorders by his method of psychoanalysis, Freud laid the foundations of modern psychology.

Born in Moravia in 1856, Sigmund Freud was made professor extraordinary of neurology at the University of Vienna in 1902. Fascinated by the Bible as soon as he learned to read, he had originally meant to study law as a means of social activity. But then Darwin's doctrine of evolution attracted him "because it promised an extraordinary advance in understanding the world." In his scientific approach Freud was, after Darwin, the outstanding exponent of the endeavor to encompass the phenomena of life in rational terms, to reduce imponderable qualities to measurable quantities. As a late disciple of the age of enlightenment, Freud sought to shed the light of the conscious mind on the darkness of the unconscious, to bring order into it, and to fight disease. At the same time, the explorer in him searched for the deep-lying roots of psychic energy—as he conceived it, the instinctual drives. The unconscious thus to him had the double aspect of a repository of consciously unacceptable matter, of forgotten facts and repressed wishes, but at the same time a subsoil of basic energies.

These basic psychic energies, however, Freud viewed with the positivistic approach of his time as being merely biological and physical phenomena. His findings incomparably enlarged and deepened man's potential capacity for knowing himself. His demonstration in infantile sexuality and of its influence throughout life as a source of unresolved conflicts opened a way to the treatment of neurotic disorders. Freud's insistence on the importance of sexual life met with a storm of indignant and prolonged rejection. But it mirrored with scientific integrity and candid realism the actual situation at the time, not confined to Vienna—a situation that had to be hushed up because of rigid social conventions.

While thus courageously holding up a mirror to his time and being foremost in overcoming its limitations, Freud in other respects was himself bound by these limitations, by the positivistic tendency to reduce theology to biological anthropology, of which he became the chief representative. His rationalistic and materialistic interpretation of his findings mean a devaluation of values, a reduction of both spirit and soul to the primitive level of early childhood sexuality. In his understanding, human action was explainable by one single principle, the "pleasure principle." Love of God and service to God were in Freud replaced by or transformed into unqualified, dedicated devotion to European science and its temporal points of view. In the service of science he became a devotee of materialistic "theology."

What one might call the "theological" motive of Freud's psychology may be seen in the pattern of the Oedipus complex, which he regarded as the primary cause of all neurotic disturbances. It is the pattern of the male child, unknowingly wishing to kill his father in order to marry his mother. It was not incidental that this pattern was found in Greek mythology, related to a cult of the Great Mother, which had been as materialistic, mother- and nature-bound as was the age of positivism in Europe. The overcoming of matriarchal religion had indeed been the beginning of Jewish monotheism. This Oedipus pattern in no way reflects a quarrel between Freud and his own father. But what he did do unknowingly was to fight the Father of fathers. In his book *Totem and Taboo* he investigated the primitive roots of religion and morality and stated: "The hero is he who kills the father." Finally Freud seemed to take on this heroic part himself: in an essay on religion, entitled "The Future of an Illusion," he denied any reality to God by making him a mere "father image."

It is remarkable that with such convictions Freud could remain a Jew. He was in no doubt about his Jewish allegiance as an inner necessity, although he could not really understand it. What he could see was that his Jewish background, apart from imparting to him a characteristic psychological structure, had provided him with two gifts essential for his work—a comparative freedom from prejudice and a readiness to stick to his convictions in opposition to the views of a compact majority.

Freud's description of his emotional position, however, characterizes not only himself but also a large group of educated Jews since
the beginning of the twentieth century. He was a Jew, he said, "who
does not understand the sacred language, who is completely alienated
from his ancestral religion, as from any other, who cannot share
nationalist ideals and yet never denies his allegiance to his people, who
feels his individuality to be Jewish and does not wish it otherwise. If
someone were to ask him: 'What is there still Jewish about you if you
have given up all those things that you have in common with your
fellow-Jews?', then he would answer: 'Still a great deal, probably the
main thing.' But he could not at the moment put this essential factor
into clear words." Freud explained that what in him exerted an "irresistible attraction" to Judaism and to Jews were "many dark forces and
emotions, all the stronger the less they could be formulated."

These "dark forces" retained their attraction throughout his life.
When he had connected all his findings in a closed and almost rigid
system, he had to undergo a dangerous operation for cancer. This was
followed by the experience, to quote his own words, of "a transformation, a piece of regressive development if one may call it so" that
took him back to the cultural and religious problems of his youth. In his
last years he came to amend his view of religion as an "illusion" by "a
formula which does do it better justice: that the power of religion rests
indeed on its content of truth, but that this truth is not material but
historical." This confession of the existence of a nonmaterial truth, still
shyly circumventing the nonscientific expression of "spiritual" by calling it "historical," marks perhaps the personal completion of a lifetime
full of discoveries.

From a proper perspective it may even be possible to name those
"dark forces and emotions" which did not release Sigmund Freud until
he had done them "better justice." In the oldest of Jewish rituals, that
of circumcision, the natural force of sex is fully preserved but inextricably linked with the spiritual significance of human creativeness as the
most intimate bond with the divine power of creation. Freud attempted
to secularize sex, to acknowledge only its natural side. Yet his unbelief, even to the extent of trying to kill the image of the Father God,
could not prevent the higher, "nonmaterial" truth from making itself
felt in his own life.

To return from Freud's later years that brought him worldwide recognition to his prime in the early years of the century, he provides an
outstanding example of an attitude of apparent and conscious unbelief
covering deep loyalties and partly unconscious beliefs—an attitude
widespread among educated Jews of the time.

Europe before 1914

The first decade of the century was a golden age of wealth and security. For more than a generation no major war had disturbed the conviction that, in Europe anyway, armed conflict was a terror of the past. However strong the dividing forces of nationalism remained, the cultural unity of Western life was not only an emotional reality; it found a tangible expression in that one could travel the length and width of the European Continent without a passport. Industry and trade were still fast expanding, though with increasingly savage competition. The standard of living rose. Tastefully decorated department stores, almost without exception built by Jewish owners from small beginnings, became centers of town life, in vain opposed by the smaller shopkeepers and their organizations. Pleasures and holiday traveling, a privilege of the few a generation before, became customary for many, while sport was still reserved to those who could afford more leisure. Insurance could shield against the risks of life and even the economic consequences of death to families bereaved of their breadwinner. The advances of medicine greatly reduced the fear of illness and early death.

The part of Jews in fighting diseases may be instanced by Paul Ehrlich's synthesis of antidotes for syphilis and lethargic encephalitis. Studying the cells of living tissue with an intensity as single-minded as had been Ferdinand Cohn's, Ehrlich discovered that by microscopic staining it was possible to study and test the influence of chemical agents on the anatomical structure of tissues. Thus, never tiring in his search for chemical agents that would attack cells infected by a specific disease without harming the healthy tissue, he founded the modern discipline of chemotherapy. Ehrlich's fight against syphilis, the scourge of mankind, was complemented by August von Wassermann's diagnostic reaction for this disease that bears his name, and paralleled in importance by Wassermann's serum therapy of typhoid fever.

The most important contribution made by a German Jew to Western science, Albert Einstein's "special principle of relativity" of 1905, revolutionized physics but at the time did not attract wide attention. In German cultural life, however, Jews continued to hold distinguished positions. Max Liebermann became a leading painter of the Impressionist school. Otto Brahm, theater director and stage manager at the same time, helped the new social realism of Ibsen and Hauptmann to win recognition. S. Fischer became the publisher and friend of most of the leading writers of this modern literature. Of the great Liberal newspapers, Sonnemann's *Frankfurter Zeitung* and Rudolf Mosse's *Ber-*

liner Tageblatt and the Ullstein papers and press were influential far beyond Germany. The political and literary criticism of Maximilian Harden's *Zukunft* made him a power in his own right.

The Jewish communities participated in the increasing wealth of Jews by receiving a special income tax, levied on their behalf by the State at the same time as the general tax collection. In Berlin, the largest community with over 100,000 Jewish members in 1900, this fixed income amounted to several million gold marks, apart from comparable sums collected in voluntary contributions for charitable and educational purposes. Administered by capable honorary officials, this wealth maintained a vast structure of religious services, schools, libraries, hospitals, and the like, the whole of which constituted an autonomous cultural sector of Jewish life, though closely interrelated with its environment. Its social services, extending and merging into the interdenominational field, were especially varied and noteworthy. In Frankfurt, the second-largest of the Jewish communities in Germany, only about one-third the size of Berlin but inspired by an old and proud tradition, this social work was, with the aid of a voluntary organization of Jewish women, extended to cover personal care for the prevention of prostitution, in particular among poor immigrant girls. The fierce determination of Bertha Pappenheim, in charge of this work, to wipe out "this stain on Jewish womanhood," in particular in the East of Europe, led her to new methods of preventive care and to founding an international organization for the fight against the white slave trade.

Not only adequate means but also skilled scholars of international repute were now at the disposal of learned projects. The Society for the Advancement of the Science of Judaism, founded in Berlin in 1902, was led by the historian Martin Philippson, who had been rector of the University of Brussels, and by rabbi Jacob Guttmann, an authority on medieval philosophy. It set up an ambitious program that enlisted the cooperation of experts throughout the world. The Society took over the *Monatsschrift,* still the leading periodical devoted to the Science of Judaism, and published or subsidized a large number of individual works. Furthermore, the Society undertook the collection of all historical documents relating to the history of Jews in Germany in a series *Germania Judaica,* a similarly comprehensive collection of the works of the early Talmudic period in a *Corpus Tannaiticum,* and a third comprising a *Grundriss der Gesamtwissenschaft des Judentums (Outlines of the Total Science of Judaism).* A program of this size, requiring for its completion the work of several generations of Jewish scholars, reflected the unbounded optimism and confidence of Jews at the beginning of the century that progress, wealth, and scholarship would continue indefinitely. All three of these series were destined to remain incompleted by 1930; work on the first would be resumed on a more modest scale in 1956.

Relief work took on similarly impressive proportions. When the first Russian pogroms alarmed the civilized world, a Russian Relief Committee was set up in Frankfurt. In 1901 the *Hilfsverein der deutschen Juden* (Relief Organization of German Jews) was founded in Berlin, directed by James Simon, a wealthy merchant and a collector and patron of art, to whose generosity the public galleries of Berlin owed much of their international standing, and by Paul Nathan, a politician and writer who had been foremost in organizing resistance to the anti-Semitic wave in Germany. Cooperating with the Frankfurt Committee, the *Hilfsverein* became the leading agency for relief work, famous for the scope, precision, and speed of its assistance in the case of catastrophes such as the pogrom of Kishinev. Apart from this side of its activities, the *Hilfsverein* established a central office that attended to the needs of immigrants to Germany from the east, amounting to 200,000 Jews between 1904 and 1914.

Extending its assistance beyond mere alleviation of distress, the *Hilfsverein* established and maintained a chain of fifty educational institutions in Palestine and the Balkans, ranging from kindergartens to teachers' seminars. This side of its work was, in view of German interests in Turkey, encouraged by the German government. For this reason, however, it led to a conflict with the old-established Alliance Israélite in Paris which sought, with similar activities, to further the influence of the French language and civilization. The political background of this competition defied all efforts at harmonizing the activities of these two large organizations.

The picture of a flourishing community, bustling with activities of all kinds, also showed deep shadows. A greatly reduced birthrate and a marked increase in mixed marriages, the children of which were almost without exception brought up as Christians, threatened group extinction within a few generations. The increasing concentration of Jews in a few large cities and in comparatively few vocations spelled danger for many of the smaller communities with their far more intimate and personal Jewish life, quite apart from the even greater danger of loss of roots in an often lonely existence in a capital town. A banker and a small shopkeeper, an orthodox cattle dealer in Hesse, and a sophisticated journalist in Berlin, Vienna, or Prague no longer shared the same social background, the same outlook on life.

Even within the same family circle, a Jewish tradition that, however, diluted, still held living values for the older generation, no longer appealed to the young. Franz Kafka was not the only son who felt that getting rid of his father's Jewishness seemed to him "the most effective act of piety one could perform." Hence this younger generation went out in search of whatever was new in literature, art, the theater, and philosophy. Nietzsche's philosophy came to exercise a strong influence on many of the younger Jews—not only the pagan Nietzsche who followed Darwin, but also the "good European," the poet, the writer of penetrating insight. Western thought and art, however, was in itself contradictory and diffuse and could no longer give the guidance that former generations had absorbed from the principles of Liberalism, from the humanistic conception of goodness, truth, and beauty. Schopenhauer's trust in art as the sole access to the absolute became somehow equivocal, considering that four representative European artists of the same generation had lost their mental balance: the painter van Gogh, the composer Hugo Wolf, the novelist Guy de Maupassant, and Nietzsche himself.

Thus a good many Jews, the sons of "good families" as well as Jewish workers, were attracted to socialism, not for its heavy trappings of Hegelian dialectics and Comte's positivism, less still for any class dictatorship of the proletariat, but for the ultimate hope of social justice in a "classless society" of a united mankind, the Messianic hope secularized in Karl Marx's doctrine and propounded with an almost apocalyptic certainty as infallible science.

There were others, however, who were disgusted by socialist materialism, despaired of any positive values, and sought a precarious superiority in criticism, in exposing and debunking the values of the past. Many journalists were of this type as well as, among philosophers, Fritz Mauthner, with his skeptical analysis of language. The decaying sense of spiritual values, despair at finding a meaning in life, caused a number of suicides among young and promising Jewish intellectuals who felt divided and torn within themselves. Jewish self-hate became a recognizable feature of the time. It was most strikingly epitomized in a Jewish student of philosophy, Otto Weininger who, at the age of twenty-three, shot himself in the room in which Beethoven had died, after publishing a book *Sex and Character*. This book was stimulating, yet dangerously confusing. Weininger contrasted the male and female characteristics, spirit and nature, as exclusive opposites. In an outpouring of hate, he identified Jews and Judaism with nature, with the female sex characteristics he despised and feared in his young and uncertain masculinity. In the beginning of the twentieth century Weininger reexperienced the conflict of early Christians in whom the spirit, harmoniously and closely combined with nature in Jewish tradition, had turned independent and inimical to life.

A long process of secularization, the ever-closer identification of the features of the environmental civilization with the components of Jewish tradition, had come to blur the sense of inner identity in Jews. This process continued. Positivism had reigned supreme for too long. Too long religion had been looked upon as obsolete, as incompatible with the results of science. Without a conscious appreciation of religion, however, the guiding force of Jewish tradition was lost, the sense of being connected with, of being one link in the chain of generations that extended backward to the beginnings of civilized life on earth, of being part of a people of timeless significance—the People of God. This loss of continuity meant inner uncertainty and still greater dependence on external recognition, individually and collectively. The emotional condition to which it could lead was tersely described by Franz Kafka, with a somewhat sweeping generalization, as that of a "typical Western Jew": "This means, expressed with exaggeration, that not one calm second is granted me, everything has to be earned, not only the present and the future, but the past too—something after all which perhaps every human being has inherited, this too must be earned, it is perhaps the hardest work. . . ."

This loss of continuity, though characteristic of a fairly large educated group, did not, however, become typical among German Jews. They may be contrasted with Eastern European Jews who, on leaving the protective shelter of compact Jewish settlements with their unbroken medieval tradition, still had to undergo the experience of absorbing Western ideas and to suffer their disturbing and disintegrating effect. There was no shortcut from the Middle Ages to the present; it remained a transition requiring several generations. In the West, however, the evolution turned full circle.

As long as emancipation had still to be fought for, Jews, while adapting their tradition to environmental conditions, had valiantly maintained it. The success of emancipation followed by racial antagonism had, however, led to a crisis of faith. Now an unprecedented revival of religion took place, unparalleled in other Jewries. Emancipated Jews, fully at home in the Western world, speaking its languages and trained in its thought, came to look at Judaism afresh, to rediscover its significance as a new force in their lives, sparkling with promise, instead of the deadweight of the past it had seemed for so long. This new link with the past had indeed, as Kafka felt, to be reearned the hard way, to be reconquered rather than just taken up. For precisely this reason it produced a fusion, a synthesis of Western Judaism, which had not been reached in the nineteenth century. This hard-won synthesis of Western Judaism, the third to be achieved after Maimonides' fusion of Greek and Jewish thought and the integration of Judaism with medieval civilization by the Jews of Spain, survives German Jewry as its most precious legacy to Jews all over the world, to the Jewries of the future.

The Synthesis of Western Judaism

The new appraisal of Judaism was above all due to the work of four outstanding men: Hermann Cohen, Leo Baeck, Martin Buber, and Franz Rosenzweig. Although it was only gradually evolved over a period of years and gave rise to controversy as well as common endeavor, the attainments of these four men appear in retrospect as aspects of one concerted whole. While its components inspired varying groups of German and foreign Jews at different times and did not penetrate to an equal depth, its total effect amounted to a reinvigoration of Judaism, to a new consciousness of its meaning that permeated and transformed the outlook of a large proportion of German Jews. This effect was chiefly due to the personalities of these men both as individuals and as exponents of widespread movements, such as Leo Baeck in Reform, and Martin Buber in the Zionist movement.

Leo Baeck

Leo Baeck was an unknown young rabbi at Oppeln in Silesia when in 1905, thirty-two years old, he published his book, *Das Wesen des Judentums (The Essence of Judaism)*. This book provided a philosophy and a theology of Judaism as a way of life, presented in a series of historical quotations so as to make the subject describe itself. A century of Jewish scholarship was distilled in these quotations. Their presentation recalled the conception of Heinrich Graetz that the idea, the totality of Judaism, had found its complete expression in the history of the Jewish people. The scientific approach inherent in this book, however, was that of Wilhelm Dilthey, professor of philosophy in Berlin, from whom Leo Baeck had learned to study ideas as patterns of thought determining the shape of historical events and institutions. His book combined the influence of Graetz and Dilthey in a unified manner. There was far more to it, however, than that. This slim volume contained the most determined fight waged for the cause of Judaism since Mendelssohn's *Jerusalem,* though indicated only by its title and without any polemics, let alone apologetics. This title, *Das Wesen des*

Judentums, challenged Adolf von Harnack's, the leading Protestant historian's, chief work *Das Wesen des Christentums,* that had scornfully denied to Judaism the very claim to be a religion. No rational proof would have sufficed to establish this claim. But Leo Baeck spoke from a background of profound religious experience. He emphasized the paradox implied by this experience between God's remoteness and nearness, between the mystery of divine existence and the concrete commandment, between *this* world and *that* world, and yet stressed the unity of experience contained and held in this inherent polarity. The irrational background of Judaism was not merely demonstrated, as Steinheim had done; it was conveyed with calmly expressed yet passionate feeling. Likewise, the oscillation between polar opposites, the paradox of religious experience, was firmly balanced by a rational clarity of purpose. The revelation of God and the revelation of man's ethical task are but one, Baeck stated, and thus ethics constitutes the very essence of Judaism.

What made this book a synthesis, a homogeneous blend of diverse and even heterogeneous forces, not otherwise achieved throughout the nineteenth century, may be found in the balance of profound thought and lucid exposition, in deep piety expressed through wide and precise learning, in the combination of an uncommon sense of structure with a detached and analytical approach. Here was a historian presenting Judaism as if it had never been viewed before, a theologian reformulating ancient tradition while preserving it, a philologist with an unfailing flair for selecting the significant detail, and a philosopher viewing the evolution of ideas as parts of a living, unified whole—all these qualities combined in one man.

But these gifts, great and rare as they were, would not have enabled Leo Baeck to write this book. It required something more, a decisive quality of independence, of inner security and freedom, that was lacking in preceding generations. Their knowledge of Jewish tradition had been as wide as his own, though less methodical, yet they were too much contained in this tradition to express it with anything like the same measure of identification and detachment. On the other hand, the generations since Moses Mendelssohn had been so fully occupied in acquiring and mastering European methods of thought, so anxious to fit their own understanding of Judaism into the scope of these methods, that they were unable to view and present their religion in its own right, on terms of equality with Western civilization. It is this new maturity of self-expression that Judaism attained in Leo Baeck, a firm yet modest awareness of its own lasting values, an open-eyed appraisal of its place in the strategy of religious ideas, a poise and a dignity that could make it as tolerant as it was worthy of toleration.

The distinctive qualities of Leo Baeck that eventually made him not only the representative of German Jews but also the representative German Jew, were creative piety, outstanding scholarship, inner independence, and a sense of the unity of Judaism and of Jewish life in all its aspects and facets. The call "to live in scientific pursuits, to be devout as a scholar for the sake of life, to be a free man for the sake of life and of science, no man's serf and serf to no endeavour," which he ascribed to Maimonides, was also his own. In the final analysis no individual can be understood in terms of external influences, yet the forces that shaped him in his formative years allow us to see more clearly how he became himself.

Leo Baeck's Career

The small town where Leo Baeck grew up, Lissa in the then German province of Posen (Poznan), was near the compact Jewish settlements of Poland and retained something of their warm human atmosphere and intimacy, of close personal interest in people and their lives. The little town was also a frontier post of marked national tension between Germans and Poles, accentuated by the religious differences between Reformed Protestants and Roman Catholics. Its Jews had marked German patriotic feelings without, however, alienating the Poles. Thus the boy grew up in a small, self-contained political unit enlivened by strong and visible contrasts, the outcome of history and politics, both religious and secular. These captured his interest and must have made him more acutely aware of the conditions of Jewish life in this three-cornered setting.

Notwithstanding these stresses, however, and in contrast to the militantly national and anti-Jewish attitude of Protestantism prevailing in Germany at the time, local religious contacts between Germans and Jews were of the friendliest. A pocket of the Calvinism that had prevailed in Poland before the Jesuits rewon the country for Roman Catholicism, survived in Lissa. A lively humanistic tradition dating back to the Reformation was maintained in the grammar school at which Leo Baeck was educated; it had been founded by Amos Comenius, one of the great educationists of that age, and preserved the intimate link between religion, scientific endeavor, and education that came to be Baeck's particular concern. Thus he grew up in a spirit of religious toleration that did not gloss over the existing differences but included them in a feeling of community. His father, Samuel Baeck, the rabbi of the Jewish congregation, lived in a house leased from the Calvinist minister, who stubbornly refused to adjust the nominal rent to the normal level. The boy learned early that religious toleration could and did work, if only the groups concerned were secure in their own faith and setting, and not merely indifferent.

Samuel Baeck was his son's first teacher and certainly one of the great formative influences of his life, not only by introducing him to the traditional ways of Jewish learning at a tender age but, more important still, by the atmosphere of piety permeating his own house and work. Leo Baeck's piety was an intensely personal feeling of being "rooted in the Kingdom of God," the ultimate source of his individuality as a created human being: "All creation is revelation, namely the entry of the One Eternal into an individual, and each such entry, every revelation simply means creation. Whatever is, whatever is to be, emanates from the One, the Eternal and bears witness to Him. It is infinite because it emanates from Him." This proud and humble awareness of being a transmitter of divine creativeness, as distinct from a sense of creativeness as a personal quality or property, was the core of Leo Baeck's piety, even and above all in his scientific work. He once quoted the words of one of the Fathers, R. Halafta, a scholar of the second century, that if ten men sit together and occupy themselves with the study of the Law, the Divine Presence, the *Shekhinah,* rests among them, and this also holds true when there are only five, three, or two—nay, even if one man undertakes his studies with all the devotion of his heart and mind, the Divine Presence is with him (*Mishnah Aboth* 3:6). That is how Leo Baeck felt it and how it could be felt through him. His piety, his sense of being rooted in, linked up with, and committed in service to this Presence gave him inner freedom, yet kept him divorced from ever completely identifying himself with the world in which he lived and for which he cared, or with any of the many causes of his concern. For this freedom and independence were matched by a strong sense of social obligation and service.

Leo Baeck's piety bore a basic similarity, whatever the differences of approach, to that of the *Haside Ashkenaz,* the Devout of Germany of the Middle Ages, in their particular combination of passionate love of God, devotion to learning, and strong sense of social service. His was a free, unobtrusive, sober type of piety delighting in the simple gifts and pleasures of life, capable of wide and warm human sympathies, extending a never-ending interest in other cultures, civilizations, and religions without losing its own firm ground.

At the age of eighteen, Leo Baeck completed his rabbinical and scientific training at the Jewish Theological Seminary, which was still the center of the conservative Jewish outlook. He met Heinrich Graetz, the master of Jewish historiography, for just one term before his death. Leaving the Breslau Seminary after three years instead of the usual six, he continued his studies at the *Lehranstalt für die Wissenschaft des Judentums* in Berlin, still dominated by Abraham Geiger's spirit of Jewish Reform, with its combination of enthusiasm for the timeless message of Judaism and critical scientific investigation of its changing historical forms. Yet to Leo Baeck the transition from Breslau to Berlin meant neither a demonstrative step nor a change of direction. Baeck, who was to become the leader of the Jewish reform movement not only in Germany but throughout the world, forever retained Zacharias Frankel's conviction that liturgical and similar reforms should not be imposed but should develop slowly from a general need. Thus reform to him meant traditional Judaism in modern form, reinterpreted rather than drastically altered. Under his influence *conservative* and *Reform* lost their distinctive differences and tended to merge into a plain but more comprehensive Jewish feeling.

If, therefore, Baeck's studies in Breslau and Berlin did little to alter his independent mind in regard to indoctrination, they provided him with the training, the tools he needed to become a modern rabbi, not only a preacher and teacher but a scholar as well. Both these institutions were leading exponents of the Science of Judaism. Leo Baeck became the living standard-bearer of this nearly century-old scientific tradition, its leading representative, and a pioneer in extending it into new fields. He was, however, able to develop this tradition further, as opposed to merely maintaining it, because in addition to mastering its methods and craft, he found a fresh approach to its problems. By the end of the nineteenth century the historical treatment of the past, so new and fruitful in its beginnings, had become somewhat stale. Volume after volume of research had elucidated the facts, the problems, and the solutions of past periods. Yet in this sea of precise detail and learned comment, the feeling of unity and continuity of Judaism was in danger of being lost; an understanding of past periods only in terms of this or that particular age and its conditions led to the spiritual aridity of historicism.

It was on this particular point that Leo Baeck revealed a new approach in his *Essence of Judaism,* not as a result of his Jewish training but owing to Wilhelm Dilthey, professor at the University of Berlin, whose favorite pupil he became. Indeed, he had left Breslau to go to Berlin because of the attraction of its university. Dilthey retained or regained the independence of the historical sciences by assigning to them the function of comprehending meaning, as distinct from the natural sciences, which provided causal explanation. Instead of trying to fit the evolution of ideas into a preconceived scheme and to sit in judgment on past periods, as Hegel had done for instance, Dilthey revived the concept, discovered by the romantic age, and discussed by Hegel, of organic growth, of ideas evolving according to their own inner laws and momentum. Leo Baeck learned from him to "reexperience" the problems and struggles of men of the past so as to understand them in terms of their own times and, above all, in reference to the ideas for which they stood, and thus to view them both in their own right and as exponents of a phase of development. In such a way a set of ideas could be understood as a whole, as a structure and pattern capable of taking on varying forms and expressions, but also determining the shape of events and institutions. As a further step, by way of the philosophical rather than of the psychological and historical approach of this method, patterns could then be grouped and compared according to typological characteristics, which Leo Baeck later on came to apply, for instance, in distinguishing between "classical" Judaism and "romantic" Christianity. In his *Essence of Judaism,* however, Dilthey's method of "understanding" a complex system such as Judaism provided Baeck with the necessary distance to view it as a whole, to allow it to describe itself, as it were, true to life, as if looked upon by an outside observer. This detachment, attained by the German philosophy of the time, was the necessary counterpart to Leo Baeck's own inner independence that his own piety gave. The problems of self-understanding are complicated when Judaism cannot naively be taken for granted, because it needs to be experienced in each civilization and generation.

And yet, a further prerequisite was needed to bring about a synthesis of Western Judaism: the maintenance of continuity with the Jewish tradition of the nineteenth century and avoidance of a break. However, great the advantages of Dilthey's approach, it had one serious defect if applied to the description of a religion, namely, that in viewing sets of ideas as patterns, as parts of a structure, it denied them normative validity. Both this link and this normative quality Leo Baeck obtained from Hermann Cohen's philosophy, which viewed religion as an unending ethical task.

Although the *Essence of Judaism* attained its final shape only when it was virtually rewritten in 1922, the achievement of its first version of 1905 must be viewed against the contemporary background to be fully appreciated. It was a time when religion as a whole might well be deemed to be on the point of eclipse under the massive weight of positivism and Marxist socialism, when it was threatened with dissolution by historicism, and when it was abstracted into mere ethics by the prevalent idealistic humanism. Beyond its immediate aim of replying to Harnack, by pointing to the irrational side of religious experience,

Baeck's work strengthened and deepened religious feeling in Jews and gained the attention of Gentiles.

By way of comparison we may here cast a glance at the position of the preceding generation, represented at its best by Hermann Cohen, in both his person and his work.

Hermann Cohen

Hermann Cohen was renowned throughout Europe as the founder and head of the Marburg School of philosophy. This school was called neo-Kantian, for when in the eighteen sixties the great metaphysical system of Hegel and Schelling appeared no longer tenable, only two ways seemed to remain open to encompass the whole of civilization in a unified view: to return to Kant, who had marked the limits of human reason but had also shown the power of the human mind to create its own cosmos, or to gather the bricks of a new building from a revaluation of the history of philosophy. This is precisely what Hermann Cohen did. He reinterpreted Kant's theory of experience as covering the whole of scientifically ordered knowledge, and he interpreted the history of philosophy as the way by which human reason could combine this knowledge and lead to considered action. On this basis, by reevaluating the guiding thoughts of the history of mankind, he built his own system. This "critical idealism," opposing both positivism and pantheism, combined Kant's critiques with Plato's view of ideas as the underlying laws of reality, hence its name that was far remote from what is usually termed idealism. The huge task of combining in one system disciplines such as the natural sciences and ethics, which in their own work drew further and further apart, did require radical abstractions. To keep them as close as possible to the original sources was Cohen's never-ending effort: "he passed through the history of philosophy as if walking through a pillared hall full of sacred statues," as a friend of his put it. At the same time, these abstractions made his work difficult to grasp, stimulating, and controversial.

His *Logic* had included a philosophical foundation of the natural sciences, based on the mathematics of motions in space. In 1904 his *Ethics of Pure Will* was published. Cohen introduced the concept of God into the very center of ethics as the guarantor of truth, as the ultimate basis for the realization of right in law, and of morality in life, in the State, and in a commonwealth of nations. He viewed both the State and humanity as the eternal tasks of man, and eternity as the proper ethical perspective of an infinite future that, however, is to begin here and now, everywhere and at any time. This was, indeed, the core of Cohen's innermost conviction of monotheistic Judaism and its Messianic message. It was here that Cohen and Baeck came closest to one another. Yet at the same time Cohen reduced the function of religion to ethics—and in this the difference between the two generations in Baeck and Cohen becomes evident. Although his view of ethics as an absolute, clear-cut, and unvarying command became difficult for later generations to accept, it perhaps needed their experience of the opposite idea of the State as a mere instrument of naked power and amoral expediency to rediscover the intrinsic truth of his vision.

The Cohen who felt that he had to be sternly rational to cope with his sytematic work was, however, not all of the man. After the *Ethics* had just been published, he wrote to a friend: "My destiny is of quite a special kind. If there are men who bring the *sacrificio dell'intelletto,* I am bringing that *del sentimento.* You know how I am linked to the inner life of our religion with the deepest strivings of my heart and with the most intimate feelings of my spirit; yet here too, my fate is abstraction, and only those who are genuine in themselves can understand and suffer me."

Hermann Cohen was a born philosopher, not merely a professor of philosophy. In order to contain and balance his "volcanic" temperament and his unusual sensitivity to the finest nuances or implications of persons or books, he was forced to develop a heightened consciousness, a rapid reference to a stable medium of comparison. Ideas, more real to him than persons or events, became this medium. He would even see persons as basically expressing an idea. Thus to him abstraction was a natural way of orientation, of understanding and relating essential features, and his education in the sphere of German philosophical idealism had helped him to develop this major philosophic tool into a fine art, a kind of filigree of thought yet nevertheless a sturdy method for maintaining a high and unified view of reality.

At a time when the scope of philosophy narrowed and split into its component parts, Cohen maintained the solemn conviction of the dignity of his discipline, inherent in Plato's view of a philosopher king. At German universities it was still regarded as a professor's task not only to combine original research and teaching but also to represent, as it were, the nation's spirit as her spokesman, and the meaning of scientific endeavor to the people. Hermann Cohen could do this with complete sincerity and conviction, with the full approval of his university, unwavering even throughout the anti-Semitic flood of the eighteen-eighties. On his first visit to Friedrich Albert Lange, the historian of materialism, whose attention had been caught by Cohen's interpretation of Kant, he had been asked: "On the understanding of Christianity we differ, I suppose?" Cohen replied: "Not in the least—what Christianity is to you, prophetic Judaism is to me." Lange, who was a devout Christian and a religious socialist, could see the point, and the common ground of social feeling based on religion led to their lifelong friendship.

The two roots of Western civilization, to Cohen's mind, were Greek philosophy and the Messianic social ethics of the prophets. German idealism as one of the representative philosophical expressions of Western civilization owed to Greek philosophy, in particular to Plato, the methods of this discipline. The prophets, although lacking this method of thought, were in his view superior to the Greeks because of their belief in God, the ruler of the universe, implying a creative view of the future (whereas even Plato's Utopia could not visualize anything beyond the stabilization of idealized conditions). In Cohen's view this conception expressed indeed, in its barest outline, the synthesis of Western Judaism. It was this view that enabled him to teach philosophy at a German university with complete confidence, the conviction that Western civilization owed as much to its Jewish heritage as the emancipation of the Jews owed to the beneficial influence of Western civilization. Cohen went even further by defending a "sound cosmopolitanism" in addition to natural patriotic feeling, by referring to the German classical period: "German classicism had this sense of world citizenship in common with Prophetic Judaism; its historical root lies in the Messianic idea of God."

Such views may show the strength of Liberal convictions and their religious undertone in Jews of the older generation, even at the beginning of the twentieth century, as opposed to any positivistic, economic, or biological determinism. Hermann Cohen was born in 1842 in Coswig in the small North German principality of Anhalt, where his father was *hazzan* (reader) and teacher to the Jewish community; he also became his son's first teacher. It must have taxed his parents' slender means to the utmost to send this brilliant and gifted adolescent to the Breslau Jewish Theological Seminary at the age of sixteen. While studying there, he decided to take up philosophy instead of becoming a rabbi, hardly realizing how much his synthesis of Greek philosophy and Judaism owed to Jacob Bernays, one of his teachers at the Seminary, and notwithstanding the fact that his emphasis on the prophets and his ethical interpretation of their Messianic message was chiefly due to the influence of Abraham Geiger. For from Breslau Cohen went to Berlin, where he found friendly support and scientific guidance in Heymann Steinthal's circle—a kind of apprenticeship that led to his academic appointment at Marburg at the age of thirty-one, and only three years later to the chair of philosophy. It was an amazingly swift career and an equally successful one—the renown of the Marburg School attracted students from all over Europe, not least from Russia.

With all the high earnestness of his bearing, Hermann Cohen was simple in himself and always ready to help others. He remained a Liberal in the sense of the idealism of 1848, with its vision of a strong and unified German State that could implement a high degree of personal liberty and humanitarian care. After Bismarck's unification of Germany, the feudal framework of which he but grudgingly respected, he did not give up his democratic views. He was not unduly impressed by capitalist expansion: "Kant," he said, "had no inkling of capitalism, otherwise he would have decreed a worldwide stocktaking prior to peace among the nations." Socialism and idealism, to Cohen, meant the same thing, a very practical attitude of personal responsibility; socialism of the Marxist type he opposed as forcing the millennium, as inverted romanticism. His deep spiritual and historical consciousness and philosophical approach, however, prevented him from ever feeling or being in outright opposition to his time and prompted him, and many men like him at European universities, to maintain a sane balance between the demands of the moment with a steady gaze at the permanent conditions of civilization—at ethical "eternity."

From his *Ethics*, published in 1904, Cohen went on for the next eight years to work on the third part of his system, *Aesthetics*, with which we are not here concerned. Before we consider the last years of his life, which were highly significant for the development of Jewish thought in Germany, we must, however, cast a glance at the wider Jewish scene.

The Jewish Scene from 1904 to 1914

The decade from 1904 to the outbreak of the First World War in 1914 was characterized by increasing ideological differences between the main Jewish groups, combined with the barely relenting external pressure of anti-Semitism. For the preceding twenty years or more the system of unified congregations, comprising both reform and orthodox synagogues in larger communities and leaving them free to arrange their services according to their conviction, had worked well and without friction, although no administrative system could prevent the slow, corroding influence of religious indifference. The large majority of

Jews had come to regard their religion as one of the spheres of life that they could take for granted. They took part in it and were prepared to support readily and liberally any deserving cause, ranging from social aid or learned projects to the exciting rediscovery of a small group of Jews, the Falashas, who from times of antiquity had survived in Abyssinia.

This leisurely peace had been disturbed since 1905 by the Free Association of Orthodox Judaism, which sought recognition of orthodox Jews as a separate group, representing reform and orthodoxy as Jewish "denominations" comparable to Protestants and Catholics. The large majority of German Jews, now adhering in a conservative mood to the mild reforms of the mid-nineteenth century, resented both such a break of internal unity and any interference with their own way of life. A spearhead of the reform movement founded a Union for Liberal Judaism, emphasizing the spiritual meaning of Judaism while removing contradictions between doctrine and liturgy by a fairly extreme pruning of the latter. *Principles of a Program for Liberal Judaism,* published in 1912 by Caesar Seligmann, rabbi in Frankfurt, on behalf of the Union of Liberal Rabbis, became a bone of contention both for those to whom this comparatively moderate program went too far and for those to whom it did not go far enough. The struggle over the *Principles* split the Frankfurt congregation but took on even wider proportions. In 1912 a world organization of orthodox Jews, Agudat Yisrael, was founded at Kattowitz in Silesia. It was directed by Jacob Rosenheim of Frankfurt and endeavored to mobilize the large orthodox groups of the European East so as to reinforce the small orthodox minority in Germany itself. In declarations and counter-declarations that did not help to clarify the position, let alone to map out the large area of common ground between the two groups, the orthodox side went as far as to assert that the spirit of the *Principles* was incompatible with the traditions of Judaism. This fruitless controversy subsided only with the outbreak of war in 1914.

The ideological struggle had been both intensified and confused by the Zionist movement, at any rate in its short-term effects. Theodor Herzl's death in 1904 left the Zionist Organization in a highly critical situation, with the hope of an immediate establishment of a Jewish State shattered by the refusal of Turkey to allow large-scale colonization in Palestine and with the diversion to an intermediate goal, the Uganda project, objectionable on principle to those most immediately concerned, the Russian Jews. David Wolffsohn of Cologne, elected president of the Organization, saved its unity and, with it, its existence. He was one of Herzl's closest friends and helpers; born in Lithuania, he had been imbued with a love of Zion and had from his youth been familiar with problems of Jewish colonization as a pupil of R. Isaac Ruelf, one of the promoters of the pro-Zionist Association to this effect. The Uganda project was liquidated and a compromise was reached between the two warring groups within the organization, the "political," which wished to stop small-scale colonization in Palestine till a "Charter" could be obtained, and the "practical," which wished to continue limited infiltration there without waiting for a diplomatic miracle. The compromise meant that both diplomatic efforts to obtain a charter and colonization should continue. In fact, a Palestine Office was opened in Jaffa; Arthur Ruppin, its director, was as tireless as cautious in overcoming the tremendous difficulties of early settlement, which included the founding of Tel-Aviv.

The tension between "political" and "practical" Zionists extended far beyond problems of immediate approach. The first group was largely composed of emancipated Western Jews, first and foremost Herzl's closest collaborators such as Max Nordau, David Wolffsohn, and Max Bodenheimer, a lawyer, also of Cologne, where the headquarters of the Zionist Organization were established from 1904 to 1911. The belief in a political solution of the "Jewish Question" implied, for all their conviction about the positive values of Judaism, a withdrawal, a way of escape from the pogroms and economic distress of the European East, as well as from the moral distress of anti-Semitism in the West. The "practical" group, however, predominantly composed of Russian Jews, could be so labeled only because of their insistence on continuing colonization in Palestine and nowhere else. They looked upon the task of tilling the soil of the Holy Land with religious devotion, as the source of ancient creativeness. To Ahad Ha'am, their spiritual leader, the Jewish People was the source of creativity. In his view the "biologic law of the nation" demanded the reawakening of the spiritual identity of Jews by restoring the national, ethical, and spiritual ideals of prophecy to their central position in life. Palestine should thus become a national center, a "powerhouse of Judaism, generating spiritual electricity", so as to overcome the "taint of galuth," of the spiritual as well as geographical dispersion of Jews, by a "revitalization of the heart," by education for national responsibility as against individual goals.

Hence the Zionist element of Western Jewry expected the fulfillment of Zionist aims by liberation from without, notwithstanding the faith and will required of Jews themselves. Eastern Jews understood it as redemption from within, not by mystical self-purification as in the Middle Ages but with an equally mystical belief in the creative effect of a reunion of a people with its ancient soil. The West contributed Herzl's vision, diplomatic activities, organization, and economic schemes; the East, a national renaissance of the Hebrew language and small-scale colonization in Palestine.

In retrospect, the immense changes since the beginnings of the century may be gauged by the fact that the aims of Zionism could actually be implemented in the State of Israel only after the upheaval of two world wars. In its early stages, "political" Zionism appeared to be a predominantly secular movement. In the West it attracted mostly young educated people to whom traditional religion had become meaningless and who could find in Zionism a modern, quasi-religious creed, a distant, ideal aim kindling their enthusiasm, invoking a selfless spirit of sacrifice. With the rejection by 'political' Zionism of gradual infiltration in Palestine, even problems of colonization there were met with indifference. The national view of Zionists, being equally compatible with every possible religious or anti-religious attitude, had little bearing on any of the internal Jewish questions of the time. A purely national view would have involved advocating a modification of the status of full political equality of Jews, for example, minority status that did not then exist. Such a suggestion would, however, have been tantamount to political suicide. Thus Zionist supporters carefully emphasized that every Jew has two countries, that of his birth, which controls his political, economic, and spiritual relationships, and Palestine, which governs his soul. Consequently, only propaganda remained as an internal Jewish activity.

Without having to refer to any problems of reality, this propaganda could depict in glowing terms the glory of a Jewish State once it was attained. It stressed the necessity of Jewish solidarity, at any rate with remote Jewries. Nearer home the tone changed into sharp and bitter criticism, casting doubt on the value of a nationality to which no alternative could yet be offered, mocking the patriotism of Jews and castigating "assimilationists" without opposing assimilation. Such criticism, leveled by Zionists who were themselves thoroughly assimilated Western Jews, had a confusing and irritating effect. Yet this Zionist criticism rightfully drew attention to the fictitious element in the structure of the emancipation of Jews, the mistaken conception that a brotherhood of mankind could be attained by individuals who disregarded their human bonds of nationality and faith instead of accepting and then transcending them. This had indeed tended to sever Jews from their essential roots in their own community and in many Jews had brought about a weakening of inner independence and inner security. Thus the profound religious significance of Jews as a Chosen

People had throughout this period of emancipation clashed with the ideology that regarded Jews as individual citizens of Western nationality. The ensuing uncertainty of this basic concept was indeed the most dangerous outcome of the inadequate ideology of emancipation, while a merely secular national conception of Judaism would have tended to be almost as dangerous a substitute.

One of the most serious and lasting aspects of this Zionist propaganda was, however, that it failed to honor, and thus to maintain consciousness of, the very great and real achievements of this age of emancipation in the Jewish sphere. A new and stronger feeling of community in Jews could only be evoked because it had never really been lost. Even the fact that Jews had come to value themselves as individuals, in the end strengthened their need to relate themselves anew to a community, no matter what its form was. The Zionist ideology, by failing to acknowledge the Jewish values of the age of emancipation and to link them up with the inner loyalty that this age had striven to achieve, disrupted that sense of continuity in the development of Jewish life which was a vital asset for the future.

With the hopes of an early fulfillment of Zionist aims receding more and more, the idea of gradual education came into the foreground. Wolffsohn's and Nordau's defeats at the tenth Zionist Congress of 1911 were significant in this respect. The former was succeeded as president by Otto Warburg, professor of botany at the University of Berlin. In line with the "practical" group, he stressed the importance of the actual work in Palestine as an end in itself, irrespective of a charter, and contributed thereto his own research on land development and on the plants and trees most suitable for the climate of the country, in particular the citrus species. The headquarters of the Zionist Organization moved to Berlin. The following congress went even further by accepting the continuation of Jewish life in the Dispersion as an unalterable fact, but called upon every Zionist to make *Eretz Yisrael,* the land of Israel, the center of his existence and to order his life accordingly. The effect of this hidden religious meaning of Zionism, the waiting to enter the Promised Land and to build it up, came close to the expectation of previous generations for the coming of the Messiah as a guiding and activating force, an indefinite but ever-present possibility. This vitalization transformed the outlook of Zionists by making them proud of their Jewish descent and detaching them from dependence on the surrounding nation and civilization. It gave them boundless enthusiasm, a sense of responsibility, and some of that inner unity which piety could bestow on the deeply religious. The mighty past of Jewish history had a bearing on their own lives, although its traditional evaluations were impatiently discarded. A national program that rejected the incorporation of Jews into European Liberal society and suspected their middle-class outlook had to evolve its own valuation. Germany became the ideological laboratory of Zionism, where its theory and philosophy were elaborated. The Jewish Publishing House of Berlin was for a long time the most important center for Zionist publications.

Some of the basic features of the State-to-be were agreed upon early, such as Hebrew as its national language and common bond, and the evident necessity for a more normal distribution of professions, a drastic changeover from business or the liberal professions to agriculture and artisanship. A marked social feeling among young Zionists also insisted that not only the national status but also the social conditions of the Jewish masses would have to be improved. In fact, Socialist convictions even more than Jewish tenets came to dominate Zionist discussions, all the more so because they determined the shape of the cooperative settlements. Yet even with fairly unanimous agreement on such basic features, the ideological trends of the future State still left a wide field to individual imagination, and in this respect the Zionist movement of the time was a loosely knit web of many different strands. Only one of these, not even the strongest within the movement itself but one that transcended its then limited range, was "cultural Zionism," an attempt to make the national society of the future a true community, and to give it a basis of Jewish values.

Martin Buber

This was what Martin Buber's work within the Zionist movement stood for. Born in Vienna in 1878 he had, as a result of his parents' separation, been educated from his second to his fourteenth year in the house of his parental grandparents at Lemberg, in Galicia. His grandfather, Salomon Buber, was one of the outstanding representatives of the *Haskalah,* the Eastern Jewish movement of enlightenment. A wealthy merchant who took a leading part in communal affairs, he yet found time to edit volume after volume of old collections of *Midrashim,* homiletic interpretations of Scripture interwoven with legend, poetry, and wisdom. His editions were models of competent and devoted scholarship; the great European libraries entrusted their manuscripts to him for textual comparison. Such a grandfather could not fail to impress this young boy. However, Buber also received a deep impression from his first contacts with communities of the *Hasidim,* those devout mystics who opposed, and were opposed by, his grandfather's world. Their rabbi lived in a pompous palace that disgusted him; their enraptured and entranced way of praying, the boy found odd. Yet when he saw the rabbi walk through the rows of his reverent followers and observed the men dancing joyfully with the Scroll of the Law in their arms, he obtained an intuitive understanding of leadership and community, of "common reverence and common joy as the basis of true human community."

For years this seemed to have been no more than a passing impression. The student in Vienna, Berlin, Leipzig, and Zurich was seized by the "fermenting intellectualism" of literary interests that carried him far away from the East into Western literature, art, and philosophy. Buber, like many young men of his generation, was strongly influenced by Nietzsche's Dionysian philosophy of life—of a heroic and dangerous life as against one of saturated comfort; of a spirit responding to instinctive urges and accepting their demonic side as against abstract rationalism; of passionate revolution rather than reason and order. Indeed, it was common to much of the philosophy of the early twentieth century to emphasize values as against circumstances, psyche against logos. George Simmel, under whom Buber studied in Berlin, taught a philosophy based on this "transcendence of life." Edmund Husserl's "phenomenology" in Germany, Bergson's ideas of the *élan vital* in France—all these of Jewish descent—had some similarity to those views which Buber came to hold. He differed from them decisively, however, in applying this approach to a people, the Jewish People, rather than to the individual.

While still a young student Martin Buber became a passionate devotee of the Zionist movement. It gave him new roots in a community, it liberated him from the spiritual isolation threatening the uncommitted intellectual. As editor of the party paper he early gained some influence with the movement. His view at that time was to oppose the "inner ghetto" of Jewish life by the "conquest" of a Jewish renaissance, to "enthrone again the unified, unbroken vitality of the Jew" in contrast to "pure spirituality," and to prefer "a beautiful death while straining every nerve of life" to smug self-satisfaction. He assumed that a people was "held together by primary elements: blood, destiny, civilizing power as far as this is conditioned by its specific character as evolved from the blood, but not by secondary elements such as utilitarian purposes or creed, by economic or religious groups." Opinions such as these, if unqualified and not counterbalanced, were not only Western but in a sense pagan and dangerous to the survival of Jews. Buber himself, but a few years afterwards, called them "lyrical doctrinarianism."

For even in these early years of the Zionist movement he also held that the whole task of a young Jew was to "become human, and to become so in a Jewish way." He had indeed clashed with Herzl himself over this question of the Jewish content of the Zionist movement. Yet on this point Buber was a pupil of Ahad Ha'am, a spokesman of that Eastern group of Zionists by whom Herzl felt constantly opposed and to whom he would not give way. The "Jewish way" that Buber had in mind was, however, far from adopting a traditional religious content or form. He felt, as he was to put it later, that "Jews in whom Judaism came alive without a sense of community, are sterile, while those in whom a sense of community came alive without Judaism go astray." He set out to discover Judaism under the aspect of a national community. At first he had expected a new Jewish art to arise that would convey such inspiration, but no Jewish art of such quality was forthcoming. After his clash with Herzl he withdrew for years from active participation in the movement in order to study mystical movements of all lands and ages, as the meeting ground where humanity experiences the divine. During these studies, which led to a number of publications, and in a roundabout way as it were, Martin Buber rediscovered the *Hasidic* movement that had so deeply impressed him in his boyhood, and it became the center of his life and his teaching.

The Hasidic mystical movement originated in Eastern Europe in the mid-eighteenth century, and it still lives on there, although in a state of decay. Its historical significance lies in the fact that it was able to overcome the nihilistic danger of Sabbatianism. Buber was not, however, concerned with a historical approach in the first instance. He found in this movement what he had been looking for—religion not merely as propounded in sermons and practiced in synagogues but as a force within everyday life, as a social feature influencing and ordering human relationships. The core of Hasidic piety meant a hallowing of ordinary life even, and particularly, in its seemingly profane, routine, and humdrum aspects. For it taught that "sparks" of the divine glory are scattered throughout the world even among apparently vulgar, empty, improper things or beings, only waiting to be redeemed and reunited with the Holy One. To him who translates the sense of being created in the image of God into the task of looking for the divine "spark," the holy essence in whatever people, things, or situations he meets, life indeed becomes transformed. The *Zaddik,* the spiritual leader, can be a true helper and guide because, in giving advice on simple practical problems, he lifts them out of their ordinary context and shows their inner meaning, their deeper significance, the point where the religious and the social planes converge.

To Martin Buber, concerned as he was for the religious core of Zionism, this discovery or rediscovery of Hasidism fulfilled the demands for a new religious feeling that could give meaning to a national aim. Hasidic piety conveyed an acceptance of life as being meaningful; it helped to discover sparks of the spirit in all human activities and occurrences; it led to zest, joy, and a feeling of community, to action rather than meditation, to individual responsibility. It was a religious attitude that could be conveyed without requiring specialized scholarship, that could with comparative ease be transferred from its original background of orthodox Jewish life and would carry on its vitalizing message to the different settings of secularized Western Jews. Even more, here was an attitude to life of general human significance.

The *Hasidic Tales,* which were selected from a vast mass of material and published at intervals after 1906 within the wider framework of German literature, illustrated this way of life by numerous small anecdotes while also outlining the history of the Hasidic movement. These with his other publications established Buber's reputation as a distinguished European writer who was at the same time an Eastern sage. These tales were widely appreciated, indeed far beyond the Jewish sphere, as a new aspect of Judaism, as an expression of piety that could foster a much-needed approach to religious values.

To Martin Buber himself the *Hasidic Tales* represented a personal synthesis of a Western philosophy and Jewish religious feeling, in which the different facets of his personality—the research worker, the creative writer, the teacher, and the leader—all found adequate expression. In working through the raw material of popular pamphlets, which more often than not gave garbled versions of the Hasidic rabbis' sayings, he realized that no literal rendering, nothing short of recreation would do justice to what they had had in mind. He had to mediate their sayings through his own person, and had, in his own words, to "become as it were their pupil across the ages so as to be loyal to their intentions."

To German Jews, however, these *Hasidic Tales* brought from Eastern Europe a type of piety that, in essence, was very similar to that of their own forefathers, long forgotten by then and received as something new—which, as presented by Buber, went far beyond the actual elucidation of a historical movement.

Buber's strong social sense, increasingly tending toward religious socialism, made him counterbalance his work on mystical movements by editing a series of sociological monographs that, written by leading German sociologists, dealt with actual questions of social psychology and their ideological background. His interest in both socialism and mystical movements he shared with his friend Gustav Landauer.

Within the Zionist movement, too, Buber reemerged from his semi-retirement after a few years. His *Discourses on Judaism,* of which the first three were published in 1911, were given at the invitation of a Zionist students' association in Prague, among whose members the philosopher Hugo Bergmann, the writer and journalist Robert Weltsch and, in its wider circle, Max Brod and Franz Kafka came to be widely known. Beyond their immediate effect, which gave Martin Buber a loyal following within the younger generation of Zionist writers and politicians, these addresses exerted a stirring and inspiring force that made Buber "the spokesman of his and the following generation" (Rosenzweig). The cause of this deep impact may be seen in the fact that his interpretation gave many young Jews who despaired of finding their own way a secure sense of self, while at the same time lifting nationalism out of narrow self-glorification into a generally human, ethical task.

The *Discourses* raised the question of the actual meaning of Judaism and defined it, in national terms, as an "inherited particularity" of character and spirit conditioned by blood, as a sequence of generations that makes the living, the dead, and the unborn a unified community. The experience of such a community, so Buber held, implies the destiny of the individual; its future is his task and responsibility as the preparation for the Messianic Age, in the spirit of a "servant of God." In this task nation and religion come together. Trusting the creative stream of national life to bring about the social forms it would need in a future State, and holding that the inner unity of the individual could be achieved by the creative forces of the blood, Buber did not underestimate the difficulties and hazards of reaching such inner unity. On the contrary, he emphasized polarity, the dynamic tension between world and God, as a principal trait of Jewish life. This is why defection from God is a recurrent motive of Jewish history. Striving after unity, however—the unity of God and world in a unified human soul—makes Jews creative and renders Judaism of supranational significance. Such striving after unity, leading to decision and realization in actual life, is a personal as well as a general human task. Insofar as the achieving of such unity means a "return" to God and implies an experience of rebirth, it is a religious development that presupposes a state of crisis as its starting point. On a personal level such a crisis may be the state of being torn between opposites; on the collective level it means the disorientation and despair of Dispersion. Viewing the national renaissance of Zionism against the highest achievements of individual integration, Buber held the seemingly negative sides of Jewish life in the Dispersion to be as much a part of the total picture and as important as its bright side; thus he came to reevaluate the peddler and the moneylender of Jewish history as well as the saint, scholar, and philosopher, to emphasize the trials and humiliations experienced by individual Jews as well as their achievements. He believed that the evolution of Judaism had come to a standstill in the nineteenth century and stressed Jewish nationality as against liberal reform, the incomprehensible vitality of religious experience as against rabbinism, the superiority of inwardness as against official Zionism. He even extended such criticism to past Jewish history, holding that the true life of Judaism had rested more in its subterranean currents than in its overt representatives, more in the prophets, the Essenes, the early Christians, the Aggadah, and in the mystics and in Hasidism—a view that, while significantly extending the range of historical awareness, tended to replace an incomplete picture by a one-sided one. There was, however, a strong emphasis on the ever-recurring possibilities of synthesis, religious in the times of the prophets and early Christianity, philosophical in Spinoza, social in religious socialism, national in the rebuilding of Palestine.

Buber's sharply critical attitude toward the Jewish life of the time, and his tendency to deny it the character of genuine Judaism reflected the militant, revolutionary aspect of the Zionism of those days. On the other hand, the Zionists' own national conception was more than a little colored by racial views unacceptable to the vast majority of German Jews, who regarded themselves as Germans of Jewish origin and persuasion and, what was more important, were so regarded by Gentiles at large, with the exception of the most rabid anti-Semites. In fact, the Liberal convictions adhered to by most Jews veiled even to themselves the strong Jewish emotional bonds they retained in this secularized form while, on the other hand, the Zionists, with their glowing enthusiasm fixed on a still largely utopian ideal, tended to underrate their own Western roots. In this way, however, divergences between the two camps that were largely a matter of emphasis, assumed the character of mutually exclusive, incompatible standpoints. This caused much friction, especially since in internal Jewish politics the Zionists usually sided for tactical reasons with the orthodox group against the majority, who leaned towards mild reform or held conservative views, even though the national view of Judaism commended itself in particular to younger Jews of very free, if any, conscious religious convictions. Indeed, the divergence of attitude went far deeper than that between reform and orthodoxy, with the exception perhaps of the latter's secessionist wing, which had left the otherwise unified congregations. In the crude oversimplification of political propaganda, the understanding of Judaism as "nation" or "religion" assumed the character of mutually exclusive alternatives.

The tension came to a head in the so-called Palestinian language war. The *Hilfsverein* as has been mentioned above, maintained a chain of schools in Palestine, ranging from kindergartens to a technical college at Haifa known as the Technion. The latter was administered by a Board of Governors on which for a long time non-Zionists and Zionists had peacefully worked together. While the *Hilfsverein* had introduced the Hebrew language as the language of instruction in its general schools, agreement had been reached that, since modern Hebrew was not fully enough developed for tuition in complicated technical subjects, a transitionary period was required before extending it to the *Technion*. When, however, the 11th Zionist Congress of 1913 had enjoined the development of a Hebrew school system, to be crowned by the project of a Hebrew University in Jerusalem, the Zionist members of the Board presented an ultimatum demanding that Hebrew be used as the sole language of instruction at the Technion. This was followed by a strike by many students and teachers in the *Hilfsverein* schools and by a blaze of propaganda of international dimensions. A matter of expediency had suddenly become a question of principle. A spirit of national independence showed its determination in a demonstration against philanthropic patronage, however skilled its work, however well-meaning its intentions—although a sinister influence of German diplomacy in the *Hilfsverein* was also suspected.

The Gentile world in Germany paid scant attention to these tensions within the Jewish body politic. Roman Catholics, in the minority in Germany, advocated strict toleration, whereas in Austria and Hungary, with the Church in a position of power, they adopted a conversionist policy toward the Jews. The tone was set, however, by the Protestant Church, still as strongly identified with German nationalism as thirty years before. In the same spirit, the State continued to regard loyalty by Jews to the Jewish faith and community as lack of complete conformity with the idolized national ideal. Although from time to time distinctions or promotions were conferred upon individual Jews to emphasize their civic equality and the absence of prejudice on the part of the authorities, it remained the rule that only baptism completely removed the invisible barriers to the career and social acceptability of Jews.

Walther Rathenau, the son of Emil Rathenau and his successor on the board of the General Electric Company, outlined the defiant attitude of a significant group of leading Jews when he pointed out in a pamphlet *The State and the Jews* (1911) that the very fact that social advantages were implied in religious conversion prevented them from taking this step despite the looseness of their own links with the faith of their forefathers. Religious conversion, he went on to say, also meant silent acceptance of the grievous wrong done by this government policy to a sector of the population that was responsible for a considerable proportion of German economic life, and that provided a disproportionately large share of the voluntary contributions to public welfare and charitable causes, to the furtherance of scientific research, to literature, and to art.

This was indeed the naked truth, but to give it free and adequate recognition would have required a spiritual security that the empire of William II lacked; it would have needed a broadening of its outlook to which the Prussian nobility, predominantly confining its activities to agriculture and to military and administrative service, suspicious of large-scale industry and with only limited cultural interests, could not agree. Yet this attitude was not confined to the landed gentry which, on the other hand, did not object to a substantial number of mixed marriages within its own ranks. Liberals too—such was the lingering relic of the anti-Semitic wave of the 1880s—would eagerly read the books and articles of Jewish writers, could enthusiastically admire Jewish artists on the stage or in the concert hall, yet would have earnest doubts on the so-called Jewish Question—doubts that gave way to relieved certainty in the case of baptized Jews. The economist Werner Sombart, who ascribed to Jews a decisive part in the development of capitalism, expressed this embarrassed wavering with characteristic advice: "The European States grant to their Jewish citizens full equality of rights, but tact and intelligence will prevent the Jews from making full use of this equality."

In a world of fierce competition in which Jewish contributions, if not entirely debarred, had to be outstanding to command attention, such advice was easier to give than to follow. At the same time, it was a world in which Jews, with family and communal roots reaching back for centuries, felt completely at home, more often than not preserving even the regional characteristics of their native town or district when moving to the larger cities. Spiritually, too, if it may be so called, Western humanism as represented in Germany from Lessing and Kant to Goethe and onward had become the dominant creed of German Jews, well compatible with, nay, seeming to reflect and include their Jewish convictions. It was a three-generation-old tradition, capable of intensification by deeper awareness of Jewish values, with a consequent differentiation from its Western components. Short of a catastrophe, however, it could not be twisted or broken, for the religious forces that had been transferred and transformed to Western culture from their erstwhile focus on sacred lore were too strong. Thus, when in the course of an investigation of the "Jewish Question" by the *Kunst-*

wart magazine, a Jewish writer, Moritz Goldstein, in an article entitled *"Deutsch-Jüdischer Parnass"* complained that Jews representing German culture were resented rather than appreciated and pleaded for voluntary restraint and a measure of cultural separation, the ensuing discussion showed a wide divergence and confusion of views among Jews and Germans alike. The writer did not, however, make any attempt to create such an independent autonomous sphere, which could only have led to a kind of cultural ghetto unless it were directed toward the creation of a new national community such as that for which the Zionists strove.

On the Gentile side, the "Jewish Question" was the problem of recognizing the creative contribution of Jews to German life—a problem largely determined by the terms of reference used in assessing so complex a feature as a modern national culture. On the Jewish side, it was a matter of awareness, of an inner attitude rather than of any external activity. As Moritz Heimann put it: "What a Jew on the loneliest, most inaccessible island still recognizes as the 'Jewish Question,' that alone is it." He was one of the finest Jewish spirits of the time who, as reader to the publisher S. Fischer, gave up much of his own writing to literary midwifery for others. He added: "It is quite possible to live in relation to two centres, the two focal points of an ellipse—some comets do so and all the planets."

In the last analysis, however, the attitude of the surrounding world to Jews depended on their attitude to Judaism, as Leopold Zunz, the founder of the Science of Judaism, had rightly foreseen. And in this respect, hopeful signs were not altogether absent. Hermann Cohen's address at the World Congress for Religious Progress of 1910 on "The Significance of Judaism for the Religious Progress of Mankind" made a deep impression on the large inter-denominational audience. Early in 1914, sixty leading German theologians and philologians petitioned the Ministry of Education to make good an old injustice by establishing a chair for Jewish scholarship at a German university. The project was shelved, owing to the outbreak of war.

The First World War, 1914–18

The 1914–18 war, terminating fifty years of peace among the leading nations of Europe united by the bonds of a common civilization, came as a shock, all the greater for having been thought well-nigh impossible despite the many preceding politiical crises. The lights were going out all over Europe, as Sir Edward Grey put it. Liberal convictions of peaceful competition within an overriding cultural community, the belief of Socialists that an international solidarity of workers would prevent all future wars, the hopes of pacifists—all these were swamped by national enthusiasm and righteous indignation. A high spirit of sacrifice and a stern determination to stand by their country in its supreme need animated and united each of the Western nations in their suicidal fight against each other, none of them doubting the justice of their cause.

German Jews were no exception to this national fervor. At the beginning of the war many joined the colors as volunteers; those overseas hurried back, trying to break the allied blockade; Zionists returned from Palestine, giving the lie to doubts about their loyalty to their country of birth. Jewish soldiers could not help hoping that their sacrifice would after all ensure the equality of opportunity so long denied to their folk, and that their blood would help to remove the existing disabilities. A domestic truce had been declared, the ban on promoting Jews to commissioned rank being waived at the beginning of the war. They shared in distinctions and in losses; over 12,000 out of 120,000 gave their lives for their Fatherland in those four years.

Not only the front line required devoted service. The German army, with its distrust of industry, had neglected to mobilize industrial resources and the distribution of raw materials. Walther Rathenau, as chief of the War Materials Office, overcame this oversight in time. Albert Ballin, defeated in his efforts to prevent the war altogether by a naval agreement between Great Britain and Germany, put his ships to the task of securing foodstuffs, many of which ran dangerously short during the later years of the war. Among raw materials nitrogen was equally essential for agricultural fertilizers and the manufacture of munitions, and lack of it would have defeated the German war effort but for Ernst Haber's fixation process, based on previous work by Adolf Frank and Nikodem Caro. August von Wassermann, the discoverer of the test for syphilis that bears his name, organized the vaccine service of the German armies and contributed to the prevention of tetanus in wounded soldiers.

Initial enthusiasm waned as the hopes of a quick and decisive campaign, of "a war to end all wars," dwindled before the reality of huge armies interlocked in the muddy trenches of the Western front and before the hardships of life at home. The chauvinism of armchair patriots waxed, trying to vitalize sagging morale. Once more, scapegoats were looked for. Once more "the Jews" were blamed for whatever went wrong—the scarcity of food, the lack of consumer goods, racketeering, the very war itself. Anti-Semitic deputies in the German Diet slandered the Jews, alleging they were falling short in their duty to their country. The Prussian Minister of War gave way to this agitation by ordering in November 1916 a census of Jewish soldiers at the front, in reserve formations or armies of occupation, in army bureaus, and those unfit for service. This insult, though such an intention was denied, could but embitter those wounded in action or facing death by day and night. The results of the inquiry, made public with lame apologies, showed how groundless it had been.

On the other hand, the German High Command did not hesitate to make use of the prestige of German Jews where this suited its purposes. On advancing into Russian Poland in 1915, Major-General Ludendorff issued a Yiddish proclamation "To my dear Jews in Poland," promising them protection by his army, and freedom and political equality for the future. Severe fighting and the destruction inflicted by the retreating Russian army had wrought havoc in the occupied countries, Lithuania, Poland, and Western Galicia; over 100,000 refugees had fled to Austria and were accommodated in temporary camps. Feeding and clothing the nearly two million Jews in Poland and Lithuania, threatened with starvation and epidemic, were a terrible problem for the German army of occupation. Two years' crops had been all but destroyed in Poland by the fighting. The Poles themselves, flattered by both groups of belligerent powers, were unwilling to share their own inadequate resources with the Jews, and the Central Powers were short of food owing to the allied blockade. In cooperation with the *Hilfsverein* in Berlin and local organizations, the generosity of American Jews prevented a catastrope. The Joint Distribution Committee for the Relief of Jewish War Sufferers—"the Joint" as it came to be called—headed by the banker Felix M. Warburg in New York, a most respected immigrant from Germany, rose to the measure of need. The occupying authorities welcomed the help that they themselves were unable to provide.

This spirit of goodwill on the part of the German military authorities was largely due to the mediation of a Jewish Committee for the East that, formed in Berlin at the beginning of the war and representing all Jewish groups, furnished the authorities with the information they required in regard to the cultural and religious necessities of Eastern Jews, and smoothed out differences of approach. Jewish Departments were set up in Poland that helped to restore communal life and to further education within the possibilities of wartime conditions, complicated in Poland by the strongly anti-Jewish nationalism of the Poles and by the antagonism of orthodox and socialist Jewish groups, as well as by a nationally organized dispute regarding Hebrew or Yiddish as the language of tuition.

The closer contact with Eastern Jews formed by many German Jews within the army of occupation did much to revise a long-ingrained prejudice against them. Behind the unfamiliar medieval garb of long black caftans, behind long beards and sidelocks, soldiers and officers found Jewish learning, warmth, piety, and humor. They were met with moving hospitality in destitute and underfed families, they were touched by the enraptured devotion of synagogue services, they were impressed by the cozy atmosphere of close Jewish settlements. Here was an aspect of Jewish folk life, of an intensity, long unknown in the Western world, that came as a romantic discovery to many young Jews in Germany. The writer Arnold Zweig and the etcher Hermann Struck, both assigned to the Higher Eastern Command at Wilna, combined in presenting this aspect in a book *The Eastern Jewish Countenance*. Yiddish folksongs, theater, and novels became popular toward the end of and after the war.

The Cohen-Buber Ideological Conflict

In Germany the tension between the Jewish Liberal majority and the Zionists led to a new ideological conflict. Among the latter, the patriotic enthusiasm of the early stages of the war had caused a crisis, but the reappearance of anti-Semitic trends was answered by a strengthening of Jewish feeling. Thus, when in 1916 the Committee for the East published a periodical, *Neue Jüdische Monatshefte (New Jewish Monthly)*, to represent German Jewry under wartime conditions, Martin Buber countered with a Zionist monthly. He revived the title *Der Jude (The Jew)* of the periodical published in 1832 by Gabriel Riesser, the celebrated protagonist of the Jewish cause in the fight for emancipation, for "religion and freedom of conscience" of the individual Jew. Buber now turned this fight into a national cause: "We do not demand freedom of conscience for the adherents of a faith, but we demand freedom to live and to work for a national community so that, at present kept down and largely treated as an impotent object, it should become the free subject of its destiny and its work, so that it should grow to fulfill its task for mankind." The very claim of Zionism to the spiritual legacy of the age of emancipation, signified by the adoption of this title, meant a direct challenge to Gabriel Riesser's spiritual descendants.

Hermann Cohen had left his chair of philosophy at Marburg in 1918, disappointed over an important academic issue. Without giving up hope of completing his system with the fourth part, which was to be a psychology of cultural consciousness, he went from the small town he had made famous to Berlin, the capital city, to serve "his Jews" at the point of greatest concentration, distraction, and danger. He centred his activities there by lecturing at the *Lehranstalt für die Wissenschaft des Judentums* on Greek, medieval, and his own Jewish philosophy. There appeared to be nothing sensational about it at the time nor did he immediately cause a stir among cultured Jews but, in retrospect and in a far wider sense, this "return" takes on the deep significance it had to Cohen himself. Personally, it meant closing the arc of his life span by returning to his beginnings with the wealth of wisdom and experience he had gathered on his way, retreating to some extent from a world increasingly dominated by power politics and economic competition. To the philosopher, however, this retreat was an advance. His passionate feeling did not accept as final or even satisfactory the place accorded in his *Ethics* to religion as subservient to ethics. An honest and fearless thinker, he paused to reconsider the problem.

Thus, instead of the many strands of human development combined in cultural consciousness that he had visualized as the crown of his system, the unifying force of religion claimed the center of his attention. Judaism, thought to be safely tucked away, incorporated in thought and life, once more became his urgent concern. In this urgency Cohen's sensitivity to contemporary trends realized a necessity far greater than that of tidying up a philosophical system. Western life had become more ambiguous, and it contained fewer and fewer of those nutritive elements, those guiding ideals with an immediate emotional impact, that had made its appeal irresistible to the Jews of the preceding generations. Hence a deepened consciousness of Jewish values, a strengthening of the Jewish side in the bipolar life of Jews, was indeed essential. Cohen's shift of emphasis came to reflect a turning point in the standing of Judaism in the eyes of educated Jews.

Hermann Cohen himself became the spokesman of his generation, a representative of what was best in German Jews. This was perhaps even more evident where his concern included Eastern Jews beyond the frontiers of Germany. In the beginning of 1914 he had traveled through Russia, giving lectures on his philosophy; this tour became a triumphal procession. At the same time, he was hoping to help Russian Jews to institute higher schools of their own in protest against the introduction of a numerus clausus limiting the admission of Jews to Russian higher education. Beyond this immediate goal he believed that the evolution of a Liberal Jewish movement in Russia might provide a creative alternative to the sudden change-over from traditional orthodoxy to nihilistic radicalism, which he had observed in several of his many Russian pupils at Marburg. The war and the subsequent Russian Revolution prevented him from following up these aims.

The ideological development of wartime Germany, with its increasing appeal to a sense of national power and pride, seemed to be in utter contradiction to Cohen's Liberal humanism that regarded the State as an instrument of education, a link in the development of mankind to the Messianic goal of eternal peace among all the nations. Within this conception, the Jews, as bearers of Messianic ethics, of "the spirit of mankind," were deemed worthy of preservation as a separate group within the nation, with a "nationality" of their own, as it were.

Cohen's attack on Zionism, made in 1916 in response to an invitation from the anti-Zionist Jewish students' associations, was prompted by his feeling that his hard-won ideological synthesis was being blurred and endangered by an exclusively national conception of Judaism. His original view was a clear-cut distinction between Judaism as religion versus the Zionist view of Jews as a nation—as he saw it, nothing but a nation. Martin Buber, replying in an Open Letter in his own periodical, roundly denied the existence of any such ideology. Thus the controversy led to immediate agreement on the basic point that Judaism could not be interpreted in merely national terms. Within this agreement, however, two strongly contrasting attitudes emerged. Buber counterattacked Cohen's view of Jews living as a "nationality"— understood as a mere natural fact—within Western host nations, with the conception of Jewish folkhood as a factor of religious significance. "The world of ethics in its historical development," Cohen maintained, "is our true Promised Land." He identified prophetic Messianism, as the religion of mankind, with modern Judaism, "and this centre of gravity removes any anomaly between our being Jews and Germans" while, on the other hand, realization of the Jewish message is linked up with dispersion among the nations and requires loyalty to a strong state as the bearer of ethical principles. Buber considered this view of the State as a "fiction" of "the untrue or high-flown 'humanity' of yesterday," as a wrong idealization, and Cohen's glorification of the Diaspora as "a misrepresentation and distortion of the basic fact of exile." Cohen defended the Jewish feeling of being "at home" in the Western world; Buber countered with being "on the way" to a new understanding of Judaism as the creative spirit of a people and its future realization as settlement in the Land of Promise.

Not only two generations and two ideologies but two conflicting attitudes confronted each other in this discussion. Cohen's earnest ethical rationalism used ideas to provide both a model of reality and its guiding principles, whereas Buber's dynamic and emotional bent looked upon thought as inspiring action. Their respective emphasis on State versus People revived, with a new turn of the spiral, the similar antagonism between Hegel's and Schelling's philosophy, reflected in Geiger's reform and Bernays's neoorthodoxy almost a century before or, farther back in Jewish history, the two main lines of this antagonism in *Halakha,* the religious law, and *Aggadah,* the living commentary on the Law by imaginative and poetic folklore. From the point of view of inner consistency and harmony with ancient Jewish tradition, Martin Buber held much the stronger position. While Hermann Cohen tried in abstract theory to justify a synthesis that really came true only in living experience, he scored by his sense of reality. Buber's vision, on the other hand, was focused on an eternal Zion of human perfection and social justice, on a Palestine where "no power politics would be at stake, a settlement that, independent of the bustle of the nations and removed from external politics, can gather all its forces for internal development and, therefore, for the realization of Judaism."

This controversy highlighted a divergence that, in internal organization and socially, remained the watershed of Jewish life. Unlike the earlier phase of emancipation, however, a feeling of unity was maintained overriding the divergences. This was to a large extent due to Leo Baeck who, at the end of 1912, had been called as minister to one of the largest reform synagogues of Berlin, lecturing at the same time at the *Lehranstalt* as a colleague of Hermann Cohen. From his youthful days he had refused to associate himself with the anti-Zionist bias of many Jewish Liberals. As an army chaplain he was away from Berlin during the war. Yet he reacted immediately to the controversy between Cohen and Buber by a paper of gentle superiority, published in Buber's own periodical, which increasingly came to represent more than the Zionist sphere.

Judaism, so Leo Baeck pointed out, is a feature of unique and indivisible individuality, the "unity of a people living in its religion and through it, from which, for this reason, everyone eradicates himself when this religion loses its force for him, and everyone excludes himself when surrendering this religion; a religion, moreover, speaking to all human beings, desirous of existing as a general truth for all human beings, yet existing only through this people so that, when this people no longer lives, it must be lost from the earth." This manifestation has remained unique in the history of mankind, "a word of the Creator of the world that has not been repeated." It would therefore be futile to split this indivisible unity into its component parts, however useful it might be for purposes of presentation now to stress the national basis and then the ideological content, or however much authors might differ in type or temperament and therefore in either "seeing" or "hearing." Provided only that there are great thoughts, their divergence is one of creative tension, not of mutually exclusive contradiction: "there is no contradiction, for instance, between the idea of Hermann Cohen that reinserts Judaism into the world history of the spirit and gives it once more the place of a world religion, and the [Zionist] conception that sometimes opposes [Cohen's conception] by pointing to the basis of our individuality, to the particular depth of our life, to our religious feeling. In such tensions grows the life. . . . Within and without, the idea of the Jewish mission has sometimes been ridiculed, but at least it contains the touch of greatness, and it would be a great day when once more the first emissaries would go forth to proclaim the truth of our God. Within and without, the idea of a free Jewish home in the land of the fathers has sometimes been ridiculed, but at least it also contains the touch of greatness, and it would be a great day when the homeland that will receive bodies and souls in search would come into being."

The idea of a mission of Judaism remained an inspiration, instead of entering the realm of tangible reality. Yet the great day that heralded "the establishment of a national home for the Jewish people" was nearer than could then be divined. During the war, in 1915, the seat of the Zionist Executive had been transferred from Berlin to the United States of America, then still a neutral country. The entry of the United States into the war shifted the center of gravity of the Zionist Organization to the Allied camp. The outcome of a diplomatic tussle for Jewish sympathies, together with Dr. Chaim Weizmann's efforts, was the Balfour Declaration of 2 November 1917. Allied sympathy for the Zionist cause meant acute danger to the Jewish settlers in Palestine, which was under the authority of Turkey, which was allied to Germany and threatened by an impending British attack. In the spring of 1917, Kemal Pasha, the Turkish military governor, suspecting the Jews of treason, had ordered their evacuation to Syria. It required a concerted effort by German Zionists, through German representations with the Turkish government and the intervention of the Queen of the Netherlands and the King of Spain, to secure their protection.

From the closing stages of the First World War, characterized in the West by the decisive support of American troops and in the East by the downfall of the Tsarist regime in the Russian Revolution of 1917, we return to the closing years of Hermann Cohen's life and his final development. In 1915 he had published the first result of his new appraisal of religion, *The Concept of Religion in the System of Philosophy,* dedicated to the Marburg School. He no longer subordinated religion to ethics nor did he ascribe to it independence, which would have meant giving it a separate part in the system, alongside logic, ethics, and aesthetics. The new significance of religion is seen in its "peculiar character" or "specificness"—which, by remaining outside the accepted fields of philosophy, can permeate all of them. The God of ethics—so Cohen realized by this differentiation—is the God of humanity. The Lord of religion is the God of the individual. Religion, without jeopardizing the aims and tenets of ethics, transcends its impersonal confines in God's love for man, man's love of God, in the individual's feeling of sin and guilt and the experience of a Redeemer forgiving it, and finally in the discovery of man as "fellowman," in compassion and sympathy.

This new view of religion as a relationship or, as Cohen called it, "correlation," takes a central place in his great *Religion of Reason from the Sources of Judaism,* which, dedicated to the memory of his father, appeared posthumously in 1919. As a philosophy of religion, this work might be regarded as the customary fourth part of a philosophical system; but without ever losing sight of the connecting links, Cohen did not incorporate it into his system, nor had he given up his plan for completing the latter by a psychology of cultural consciousness. Although still using a philosophical approach, this work extends beyong the limitations of an academic discipline. Its idea was to demonstrate the prophetic monotheism that he held to be "the central problem of the evolution of the spirit of civilization," the Jewish belief in the One God in which he saw "the immovable bulwark for all the future of ethical culture" as a consistent structure, a general form of an individual religion. Cohen did not claim that Judaism was the only religion of reason, but he held its sources to be the oldest, purest, and therefore the most suitable for attempting such a general representation. His "Religion of Reason" is a monument of that synthesis of Western Judaism which Hermann Cohen himself and the Liberal idealism he stood for had achieved.

This momentous work had, as it were, two faces, one looking back to the past of Jewish tradition, the other forward into the future. By presenting Judaism as a "religion of reason," Cohen restated the theme of Moses Mendelssohn's *Jerusalem,* namely, that such a religion was common to the educated sector of mankind. Contrary to Mendelssohn's view, however, that the age of enlightenment had already arrived at such a basic faith, within which Jews had only to retain their religious laws, Cohen held that prophetic Judaism itself was this religion of mankind, both as basic reality and as an eternal task. This difference of confidence marks the distance traveled and the achievements in the thought of German Jews during this phase of emancipation.

The very notion of *reason* contains a similar transformation. To Cohen reason is the source of all cognition, knowledge, and insight, the "rock" from which all concepts spring, like the water of life under Moses' touch, their "organ" and criterion of truth. In this sense religion too has a share in reason, which allows religious concepts to be included in the unity of human consciousness without blurring the boundaries between religion and philosophy. Cohen refers to his predecessors, the Jewish philosophers of the Middle Ages, as "our legitimate theologians," above all to Maimonides, who like him used the Greek methods of thinking to combine revealed truth and scientific knowledge, faith and reason into one homogeneous whole. Yet this Greek view of reason as a capacity of the human mind, however dear to him, is only one side of his approach. The other side is a religious appraisal of human reason as God's creation, as man's portion of the divine spirit—as a wonder. Hermann Cohen's is not a rationalism bought at the price of emotional shallowness.

Indeed, the emphasis imperceptibly shifts from a philosophy of religion to religion itself, presented by a philosopher. The God of humanity, as shown in the *Ethics,* is now not only felt in His uniqueness and otherness, "incomparable to any creature," "opposed to the world" by this incomparability, but the origin of nature and reason alike, also as the God of love, of mercy, and of peace. In a memorable chapter of his work Cohen outlines the discovery of the individual by the prophet Ezekiel, the namesake with his own Hebrew name, from the consciousness of personal, individual sin and from the experience of forgiveness by attaining "a new heart." In this individual aspect, religion is distinguished from mere ethics. Although even spirit as ascribed to God is "no less a metaphor than "voice," "hand," or "mouth"—we know only human spirit—, the human experience of a "spirit of holiness" does form a true bond between man and God, who reveals Himself in continuing creation. And God remains the refuge, the hope of all human suffering and distress, the God of the poor, the Lord near to those who are forsaken.

Thus, notwithstanding its rational presentation, this work is aglow with passionate religious feeling. Here Hermann Cohen no longer restrained his heart, no longer sacrificed his fervor to the cooling process of thought. Indeed it had been his heart, the pathos of Messianic expectation, that permeated even his understanding of political events, that had preserved the inner unity of his personality, and made him the outstanding individual he was. And as the confession of faith of an individual, representative of an epoch, his work faces the future, kept alive by its own inner fire even for generations that may no longer accept its philosophical framework, contested even while it was written. Franz Rosenzweig, predominant among Cohen's pupils during his last period and deeply moved by his Jewish spirit without sharing his philosophical premises, expressed this aspect of the future hyperbolically by "foreseeing in spirit the Hebrew folio editions of five thousand years hence, printed by Siberian and Patagonian presses in New Guinea and the Cameroons," in which—as in Talmud editions—"Cohen's text is drowned in a flood of three or four commentaries."

Franz Rosenzweig

Franz Rosenzweig came to be the most powerful spiritual force in the Jewish life of the postwar period, carrying on and promoting a revival of Judaism that completed what I have called the synthesis of Western Judaism. His brief life of meteoric luminosity showed that heroic quality of Jewish existence which, difficult to notice under normal circumstances, came to startle the world, for instance, in Leo Baeck's bearing in a Nazi concentration camp. Franz Rosenzweig became a legend in his own lifetime and may yet, as he himself foresaw, become a guiding star for future generations. Yet "life must have been wholly lived in the here and now of time before it can be eternal life"; this saying of his also holds true of him.

In retrospect, it appears to be of more than accidental significance that the dates of Rosenzweig's life mirror those of Moses Mendelssohn in reverse: he was born in 1886, a hundred years after Mendelssohn's death, and he died two hundred years after the initiator of the age of emancipation was born, in 1929. Rosenzweig did indeed reverse the somewhat centrifugal trend of this phase of emancipation, the expectation of redemption from without, from contact with Western civilization, by an unprecedented intensity, depth, and width of Jewish feeling. He rediscovered Judaism as a faith of fascinating novelty notwithstanding its timelessness, as a way of life of unsuspected totality, to be won as much as rediscovered. Yet this deeper experience of Judaism completed and fulfilled Mendelssohn's vision of Jews as able to live within the sphere of Western civilization and to contribute to it from their own inner resources—as Jews. Franz Rosenzweig closed the circle of this phase of emancipation, of this period of Jewish history.

He was intimately related to the history of emancipation within his own family. His great-grandfather, S. R. Ehrenberg, superintendent of the Jewish Free School at Wolfenbüttel, had had among his pupils Leopold Zunz, the founder of the Science of Judaism, and the historian I. M. Jost. The aim of the school was "to transform ignorant, ill-bred *bahurim,* crude in speech and ideas, into well-bred, polished young men." One result arising out of these beginnings was represented by Franz Rosenzweig's cousins and friends, who became fervent Christians. A still more characteristic outcome of the evolution of emancipation were Franz Rosenzweig's own parents: his father, a successful manufacturer of dyestuffs at Kassel, of tireless energy and devotion as a town councillor; and his mother, charming, idealistic, and full of enthusiasm for art, music, and poetry. Their Jewish convictions were stronger than met the eye but, superficially, their interest in Judaism was no more than formal. A "thin thread" of Jewish tradition was handed on to the boy through a great-uncle who lived with the family, rather than through his parents. Adam Rosenzweig, a xylographer, combined a passionate Jewish feeling with a deep love for the German romantic painters and draughtsmen of the mid-nineteenth century, for Dürer's and Rembrandt's graphic art, for Goethe's poetry, and through him the boy became familiar with both these worlds.

Rosenzweig's education seemed to follow the conventional pattern of the only son of a well-to-do family. He studied medicine but found that it was not to be his métier, although he passed his examination to prove to his father that he could do so. Then he changed over to history and philosophy. As a pupil of the Liberal historian Meinecke, he combined both disciplines in a brilliant study *Hegel and the State.* His chance find, among Hegel's papers and in his handwriting, of the draft of what he discovered to be the earliest system of German idealist philosophy, led him to an almost sensational piece of academic detective work, the proving from internal evidence that the important sketch was Schelling's work, which had been preserved in a manuscript copy written by Hegel. A distinguished academic career lay before the young historian who, strikingly handsome and as swift of foot as in his intellectual penetration, had only to grasp his opportunity.

Rosenzweig's study of Hegel, however, had convinced him that German Idealism, in the atmosphere of which he had grown up, was an end and not a beginning. Hegel, crowning the endeavors of all previous philosophy to express total reality by a coherent understanding of the ideas underlying and determining it, had seen God as immanent in history, and His expression as accessible to human reason, comprehending itself by reflecting on its own history. There was no way beyond this. It could only be bypassed, as Cohen's neo-Kantianism had tried to do by a comprehensive "cultural consciousness," reversed as in Karl Marx's dialectical materialism by making ideas a by-product of economic systems, or as in the subjective philosophies of Schopenhauer and Nietzsche, or else transcended as in Schelling's late philosophy of revelation. Indeed, religion, to Rosenzweig and a circle of his friends, came to promise the only way out of the "curse of historicity," of the misleading notion of "progress" to which Hegel's philosophy had led by the end of the nineteenth century. Yet to Rosenzweig it seemed inconceivable that a modern scholar, a man of scientific training, used to logical analysis and to the historian's discipline of viewing ideas in the context of their time, could take religion really seriously. In long discussions with a friend, Eugen Rosenstock, a Christian of Jewish descent and a first-rate legal historian, Rosenzweig experienced that neither his scientific relativism nor his rudimentary Jewish convictions could be maintained against a living faith. Zionism or baptism seemed to be the only choice. He decided to become a Christian, with the one reservation that he would do so as a Jew.

In preparation for this step he attended the synagogue service on New Year's Day. When his mother heard of his intention and that he wanted to go there again on the Day of Atonement, she told him: "I shall ask them to turn you away—in our synagogue there is no room for an apostate." He went to Berlin and spent the Day of Atonement in a small orthodox synagogue. He never mentioned to anyone what he experienced on that October day of 1913. Yet it was the decisive event of his life, a religious conversion bringing about a radical change both of his outlook and of his career. He remained—in fact, became—a Jew.

From later references by Franz Rosenzweig to the Day of Atonement in his letters and works, we may gain a glimpse of his experience. When, shortly afterward, telling his cousin that he had "reversed his decision" to become a Christian, Rosenzweig added that, though he still agreed with the Church that no one can reach the Father save through Jesus, "the situation is quite different for one who does not have to *reach* the Father because *he is already with him*." He later described the Jew who, in a tension that seems irreconcilable on this Day of Atonement, "confronts the eyes of his judge in utter loneliness as if he were dead in the midst of life." The liturgy recollects the ancient Temple service during which—on but this one day of the whole year—the high priest pronounced the ineffable Name of God—"the Word and Fire of Revelation." The divine truth was beheld in the sanctuary, in the mystery of resemblance, as the Countenance "which looks upon me and out of which I look." And on the last, most solemn profession of the day, "man himself, in the sight of God, gives the answer which grants him the fulfilment of his prayer of return. . . . In this moment he is as close to God . . . as is ever accorded to man." This moment comes to determine his life: "By the one shining moment of grace, of choice, man turns to a 'must' that is beyond all freedom."

Franz Rosenzweig gave up his plan of an academic career and turned to the study of Jewish classical literature and theology, with the same, almost violent, determination with which he had previously put away his violin forever when music threatened to overwhelm him. At the *Lehranstalt* in Berlin he came across Hermann Cohen. He was fascinated by him as a philosopher and as a true and constructive thinker, and was deeply impressed by his passionate religious feeling. Not even Cohen could soften Rosenzweig's radical break with that humanistic idealism from which he had turned to religion, from the view of man's moral autonomy to that of man before God. Yet Rosenzweig felt that Cohen in his final development had, unknowingly and even against his own intention, broken through the crust of his idealism into a direct confrontation with the reality of life "in the sight of God," had maintained the "undeniable right of the soul against all demands of civilization." On this ground they met. Rosenzweig's loyalty made up for many disappointments of Cohen's last years, and the old man's clear-sighted love recognized the heroic quality in the younger. It was Cohen who gave Rosenzweig, like an accolade, the "lordly word to the hero" on his way that became the motto of his central work: "[In your splendor,] hail thee, ride for the cause of faith" (Ps. 45:5)—except that Rosenzweig wished the first three words to be added only after his own death.

Cohen, who devoted the last months of his life to furthering a project of Rosenzweig's to which I shall presently refer, did not live to see the completion of his pupil's chief work, *Der Stern der Erlösung* (*The Star of Redemption,* 1921). It was written in the midst of the war on army postcards, sent home one by one from an aircraft observer's post on the Macedonian front, from hospitals, and from the halts of an army in retreat. Yet its unhurried, inspired style and the accomplished architecture of its nine parts in three volumes does not betray its origin. In this work Rosenzweig produced "a theory that grew out of an ardent longing," the philosophical foundation of his theological position. His religious conversion, of lightninglike suddenness after months of "torture," had been the answer to his vital necessity to gain a foothold beyond the relativism of historicity. In its general significance this answer meant the rediscovery of "metahistoric Judaism," of timeless, unchanging reality, of the anticipation of eternity within life. This had been the view common to past Jewish tradition and still shared by Mendelssohn, the view of revelation as imposing its truth on reason that Steinheim had propounded in the middle of the nineteenth century. Rosenzweig found this timeless existence in the "eternal life" of the Jewish People, whose awareness of being allied to God had ever remained the "fiery core" of its faith. Forgoing growth and not subject to decline, this people had already reached the goal toward which the nations of the world were still moving. He saw eternity foreshadowed and mirrored in the liturgical rhythm of the sacred year with its Sabbaths and festivals. Corresponding to the "eternal life" of this People is the "eternal way" of Christianity, both being mutually related and interdependent for the whole of human history, till the Messianic Age.

In thus establishing Judaism as one of the suprahuman powers on earth, Franz Rosenzweig regained its essential freedom from Western civilization, an independence beyond his own time and circumstances—a freedom that had virtually been lost by an undue inner identification of Jews with the movement of enlightenment, with political and religious Liberalism, and with humanistic idealism. Rosenzweig did not thereby advocate a withdrawal of Jews from contemporary Western life, as did the Zionists. On the contrary, as well as being aware of the religious forces inherent in socialism, even in its atheist form, he realized the necessity for Judaism to become secularized so as to play its part as one of the sustaining forces in the crisis of Western civilization: "The ability to secularize itself again and again proves its eternity."

His own work in its philosophical aspect was party to such secularization. There were two reasons for this. Rosenzweig's findings, relevant far beyond the extent of the Jewish sphere, had to be presented in the forms of Western thinking so that they could be checked. The second of these reasons, one of at least equal importance, was a personal one. Rosenzweig's religious experience, the answer to a radical challenge by "the poisonous juices of a philosophy of doubt and blasphemy" such as Nietzsche's that had also largely been his own, required to be linked up with, and incorporated into, the systematic context of his modern, secular views, lest he be split into two incompatible halves. This experience, matching in depth the challenge of his position, carried him far beyond the position of previous Jewish tradition, to theological concepts paralleled only in the esoteric doctrine of dialectical Cabbalah, as G. G. Scholem observed. Rosenzweig needed a new philosophical approach for his task of integrating his religious experience within his total personality.

He claimed his work to be a system of philosohy containing—

although distributed within its text rather than separately presented—logic, ethics, and aesthetics. These parts and the inclusion of the Eastern religions, Islam, Indian and Chinese creeds, and pagan mythology circumscribe it. Its architecture reflects the influence of Rosenzweig's studies of Hegel. For part of his outline, however, he found common ground with the latter's great antagonist, the *Philosophy of Revelation* of Schelling's last period, and with Nietzsche's criticism of idealistic philosophy and of historicism. The methodical nature of his approach, however, was largely that of a "New Thinking," just then being evolved among his own friends and also in European philosophy—existentialism. Not that Rosenzweig ever was or became an existentialist in a specific sense, in the attitude conveyed by that philosophy of spiritual isolation and despair of the human individual. His own was almost diametrically opposed to this attitude. Yet there was a community of approach that belonged to the period. Rosenzweig attacked idealism on the grounds that its construction of the world foundered on the impossibility of taking into account the suffering and death of the human individual, which never mattered in its abstractions. His own point of departure was precisely the concrete situation of the individual who had to face death physically on the battlefield or spiritually in isolation, suffering, loneliness, and despair. In this approach Rosenzweig paralleled, for instance, that of Martin Heidegger, Cohen's successor at Marburg, who in these years also spoke of "being toward death," and there were further similarities in their emphasis on the intimate connection between thought and language.

From the view of a philosophy that accepts the concrete reality of the philosopher as its point of departure, time takes on a new significance. It is not, as in idealistic philosophy, dissolved in the timeless world of ideas, but past, present, and future become irreversible. The subjects of this philosophy are man—the particular individual with his own name—the world, and God. Rosenzweig demonstrates that all three are irreducible. The first part of his work shows these three constituents of the human universe as unrelated, closed and mute in the paganism of Greek antiquity, of mythical gods, of the tragic hero, of a "plastic cosmos"—aspects of an understanding of life that only belongs to the past in a historical sense but remains characteristic of ages unrelieved and unrelated by revelation. For it is revelation, seen as a consequence of creation and in turn leading to redemption, whereby the isolation of God, man, and world turns into mutual relationship, leading to a meaning of life—because the reality of common sense is, after all, divine reality—and leading to human fellowship and community. The theological concepts of creation, revelation, and redemption are taken by Rosenzweig not as theological terms but as objects of thought, as happenings unfolding their own inherent dynamic power. God, man, and world, related by creation, revelation, and redemption, together form the luminous Star of David—the "Star of Redemption" whence this work takes its title. Divine truth does not deny itself if invoked "with both hands, with the double prayer of the believer and the unbeliever."

The gates of the sanctuary, where this truth can be found after a transition from the danger of death to anticipation of eternity, open "into life." But although "only the transports of holiness also hallow the profane aspects of everyday," this truth required verification by daily conduct and personal responsibility, in matters great no more than in small ones. By writing his book Franz Rosenzweig attained a full and coherent justification for his position in both the philosophical and the spiritual realms. It was "his armor" against attacks from each of these two standpoints. In his breakthrough to a faith both old and new, to inner freedom both from dependence on contemporary European development and on the burdensome aspect of a Jewish tradition adopted without reexperiencing its meaning, he felt that he had written a book of "timeless" merit, that he had drawn a "beeline" on any subsequent development of Jewish life, apart from such guidance as it might come to provide to Western civilization. Indeed, he felt that by writing this book he had "cut himself off" from any further literary effort, except perhaps that he might have to add to it at the end of a long life. Insofar as the writing of the book merely meant the beginning of the verification of this faith within the harsh realities of the everyday, Rosenzweig could at the same time call it just "an episode" in his life.

The active task he saw in front of him was a reform of Jewish education—a concrete task of seemingly modest dimensions. Yet the idea behind this was far bolder and more thoroughgoing than met the eye. It was no less than to render the classical sources of Judaism, taught in their original language, once more the center of the culture of Jews—to recreate a "Jewish world." With this aim in view Franz Rosenzweig countered the resolutions on Jewish education of a Rabbinical Assembly of 1916, which visualized a predominantly historical program, with a bold proposal of his own, addressed as an Open Letter to Hermann Cohen entitled "It is Time," which was published in 1917, still in the middle of the war. His proposal was the creation of a Jewish Academy as the center of Jewish education. It should become such a center by training scholars who would at the same time be teachers. As Rosenzweig had brought together philosophy and theology in his *Star of Re-*

demption, so he envisaged a rejuvenating effect on the Science of Judaism by direct contact between the scholars and "the people" rather than that the former should remain in the ivory tower of pure research. On the other hand, he held that the standing of religious tuition would be enhanced and enlivened by teachers who were scholars in their own right. This synthesis of scholarship and education had been achieved in the Jewish "learning" of old, and it was the same combination that had given German universities their reputation. Hermann Cohen supported this project with all his fiery enthusiasm even during the last weeks of his life.

The Academy for the Science of Judaism was in fact founded in 1919, with a participation by educated Jews that differed markedly from the aloofness of former generations. A "new Jewish purpose that strives everywhere for a new understanding of Judaism" was the mark of the post-war era, and the Academy was fully alive to its demands—a scholar's responsibility to render the documents of the past not merely in their own historical context but, without detriment to scientific standards of research, to penetrate to those underlying ideological and emotional motives that determine their lasting significance. In the short span of its fifteen years of existence the Academy did indeed set and represent the standard of modern Jewish scholarship throughout the world. The standing of its leading members may be gauged by Leo Baeck's *Pharisees,* Ismar Elbogen's history of the Jewish liturgy, Isaac Heinemann's work on Philo, and Julius Guttmann' *Philosophy of Judaism.* The program of the Academy, under the guidance of the historian Eugen Täubler, enabled young scholars to start out on original large-scale work, such as Fritz Yitzhak Baer's history of the Jews in Spain, based on the original documentary sources, or Chanoch Albeck's studies on the Mishnah. To Hermann Cohen's Jewish writings, published by the Academy in three volumes, Rosenzweig himself wrote a brilliant introduction, a model of tender affection combined with critical detachment.

In one respect, however, the Academy fell short of Franz Rosenzweig's hopes. However open it was to the wider concerns of the time, it remained strictly within the field of academic scholarship, without attempting that combination of research and teaching which he considered to be essential for a revival of Jewish learning on a broader scale. In fact, he himself had probably underestimated the extent to which scientific work had been split up by specialization, in consequence of which inspiring teachers who were at the same time first-rate research workers had become rarer and rarer—that is, those who were able to concentrate on detailed problems while retaining or attaining a comprehensive view. Yet Franz Rosenzweig had seen in Warsaw during the war that intimate connection between Jewish life and thought which he wanted to impart to Western Jews, and he was convinced that this could be done even under the greatly differing conditions of the West. He could not, however, rely on any institution to give expression to his own vision. He had to do it himself. The Academy had been in existence for only a few months when, early in 1920, he outlined his new plan in a pamphlet, *Bildung und Kein Ende* (an allusion to Ecclesiastes: "Of the making of many books there is no end").

"It is new Jews that are needed, not new books," was Rosenzweig's main thesis which revolutionized the outlook of a generation. Only a revival of Jewish life, he held, could restore the foundation of Jewish letters—Jewishness should not be an exclusive nationality but a central and determining, humanizing yet not limiting force in the individual. He was under no illusions about the actual state of affairs. A century of passionate concern for Western culture had, he held, only produced a new cultural ghetto. Religious law was chiefly directed against the large majority of those who no longer kept it. The Jewish home had lost its former central position; the synagogue had become a "place of religious edification". Only emancipation itself, the struggle for equal rights, still held Jews together and provided the sole external stimulant for Jewish scholarship—a "frightening" view. Rosenzweig agreed with Zionist critics that only the Jewish individual himself was still healthy and whole, but he differed in his conclusions. If Jews were to be brought anew into contact with a great tradition, however blurred it might appear to modern eyes, if they once again were to "feel the sap of the old, inexhaustible stream running through their veins," the individual Jew must be taken seriously as he is, here and now, in his wholeness. Rosenzweig held that no set plan could outline a program of such return. The demand was only for readiness: "No other assumption is made than the simple resolve to say once: 'Nothing Jewish is alien to me'"—and confidence. For "confidence walks straight ahead. And yet the street that loses itself in infinity for the fearful, bends itself imperceptibly into a measurable yet infinite circle for those who have confidence."

The deceptively simple words "Nothing Jewish is alien to me" circumscribed the new attitude that Franz Rosenzweig brought to Jewish life in Germany—a comprehensiveness of feeling before which the very real barriers separating Zionists and "assimilationists," orthodoxy and reform lost their significance. And to those who were prepared to

come, Rosenzweig suggested to begin with, that the new post-war
Institutes of Jewish Adult Education could offer time and place for
their desires or questions, whatever they might be.

This program, for all its imaginativeness, remained silent on two
important points: who was to answer and guide such questions, and
how to attract those who would not come by themselves. Rosenzweig's idea of a possible solution of the first problem was only hinted at
by the dedication of his pamphlet to his friend Dr. Eduard Strauss at
Frankfurt, a research chemist by profession who, while studying the
history of religions, had come to rediscover the Hebrew Bible for
himself. The answer, therefore, that Rosenzweig could not reveal without frightening away those he wished to attract, was that laymen who
were themselves searching for the sources of Judaism could and should
guide those embarking on this course. The problem of attracting, and
the still larger one of retaining, large audiences to a serious study of the
old sources of Judaism required Franz Rosenzweig's own outstanding
organizing ability as well as his deep conviction.

In August 1920 he took charge of the Institute of Jewish Adult Education at Frankfurt. He re-named it *Freies Jüdisches Lehrhaus* (Free
House of Jewish Studies), recalling in the name the ancient *Beth ha-
Midrash*, the "House of Studies" of Talmudic times; by adding the
word *Free* he conveyed a notion of unfettered modern approach, of
admission without entrance examination. In his welcoming address
Rosenzweig expressed his confidence that the center of Judaism could
still be reached from any point on the circumference, and outline the
program of this novel venture "without a set curriculum, without
priestcraft, free from polemics and apologetics, universalistic in subject and in spirit." Outwardly the *Lehrhaus* hardly differed from any
imaginatively directed Institute of Adult Education. Franz Rosenzweig
arranged lectures by well-known speakers on popular subjects, Jewish
and general alike, to attract large audiences and to get the publicity he
needed. The real work, however, was concentrated in smaller study
and discussion groups, with the emphasis both on active and intensive
participation by the pupils themselves and on a return to the living
world of the classical sources of Judaism in their original language.

It was difficult, slow, uphill work, but Franz Rosenzweig's casual-
seeming yet stubborn energy succeeded in breaking down the resistance of Jewish youth organizations against the participation of their
members in ventures other than their own, so that the *Lehrhaus* became a unifying force in this social sense as well. Rosenzweig himself
was by no means the most successful of the teachers; he had moved
too far ahead of his time to be easily understood, however urgently he

so desired. But apart from his good fortune in enlisting the cooperation of fascinating local personalities such as the leading conservative rabbi, Nehemiah Nobel, in whom traditional learning, a deep love of Goethe, mystical leanings, Zionist convictions, and an elementary religious passion were strangely blended and in whose daily Talmudic study group Rosenzweig himself took part, and apart from winning the support of Martin Buber, who found at the *Lehrhaus* a new center for his activity as well as a galaxy of distinguished guest lecturers, Franz Rosenzweig exerted a magnetic attraction on young scholars from many walks of life in search of Jewish values. Some of them had traveled a parallel course, from indifference to Jewish life, often through Zionism, to the old traditional forms; Ernst Simon, for instance, came to play a major part in the renaissance of Judaism in the postwar years. Others, like Dr. Richard Koch, a lecturer on the history of medicine, or Rudolf Hallo, an art historian and archeologist, were "discoveries" who, reluctant at first to teach at the *Lehrhaus,* did so impressively by being just the kind of student teacher that Rosenzweig was looking for. Through his formative and catalytic influence on this group, Franz Rosenzweig widened the immediate effect of his teaching, which in this way came to permeate substantial sections of the Jewish youth movement, far beyond the direct reach of the *Lehrhaus*. His message was, despite the long and hard road it had taken him to reach it, in its essence exceedingly simple—the age-old one that God can be reached from any situation whatsoever, but it was also new in that this return could be spontaneous, almost experimental, without having to accept an old and weighty tradition in its totality, once and for all. In short, this message viewed Judaism as a helpful way of life, not ready-made but to be discovered in its significance for the individual.

Franz Rosenzweig extended this pragmatic, experimental approach even to religious law. Just as the individual Jew, he stated in his pamphlet *The Builders,* has to gain a firsthand, adequate knowledge of Jewish tradition to find out which parts of it are relevant to him, so religious practice can only be understood by practicing it. Thus, far from sponsoring a rigid orthopraxy, he stressed the dangers inherent in a sudden changeover to those who had not grown up in it, and outlined a deliberately unorthodox "hygiene of return" to traditional ways of life. He even contrasted "the Law of Western orthodoxy of the past century" with the far more comprehensive totality to be faced anew in "Jewish law, the law of millennia, shredded by thought and glorified by song, the law of everyday and the law of death, petty and yet sublime, sober and woven in legend, the law radiant with the homely candle and with the flames of the martyr's stake, a plantation surrounded by Akiba with a fence that Aher tried to break down, the cradle from which Spinoza sprang, the ladder on which the Baal Shem ascended—the Law, ever extended, never reached, yet always capable of becoming Jewish life, of being transformed into Jewish faces. . . ."

While Rosenzweig's example of a measured return to the traditional forms of Jewish life met with only a small response, his feeling for the unity and meaning of Jewishness inspired large groups, especially among the younger generation, and enabled them to bear the brunt of the years to come. His educational work could counteract within its reach the dissociating influences of the postwar era, because he had experienced and overcome the spiritual crisis that after the war became a national and a European problem. The contemporary significance of his work will become clearer when we cast a glance at the wider post-war scene in Germany.

The Aftermath of the First World War

Seen in retrospect, the 1914–18 war destroyed the balance of power in Europe that had enabled a sense of supranational community to exist despite national tensions. This war both highlighted and, in its conse-quences, deepened the crisis of Western civilization that characterizes the following decades. With the Russian revolution this civilization began to split into two seemingly incompatible halves. The center of power slowly shifted away even from the victorious nations, them-selves dangerously weakened, and the feeling of vengeance and moral discrimination took years to die down. It was, however, in the defeated nations, above all Germany, that the symptoms of a far more wide-spread and deep-seated disintegration appeared in their full destructive force. Within Germany once again the Jews were exposed to the full blast of this disintegration and, as a community, came to be destroyed by it. In both cases it was in the last analysis a moral problem, that of collective responsibility to a supranational community, which, vaguely felt and uneasily acknowledged by the respective nations or national groups but betrayed by their actual conduct, caused guilt feelings that were fastened on Germany and in turn, projected onto the Jews.

The harsh and humiliating peace treaty of Versailles belied the hopes that this had been a war to end all wars. With a territory shrunk by the cession of Alsace-Lorraine to France and of the Eastern provinces of Prussia to Poland, the democratic German Republic was compelled to accept an indictment of imperial Germany as the basis for paying huge war reparations. Austria was reduced to but a shadow of its former glory.

The Weimar Republic bravely and by no means unsuccessfully strove to form a unified nation out of the former federal states and to overcome the strong particularist trends still remaining. Its internal difficulties in addition to external handicaps, however, finally exceeded the constructive forces. These difficulties may in a wider sense be understood as a crisis of Liberalism.

In the nineteenth century, Liberalism had freed Western nations from patriarchal tutelage and despotic oppression, from political and religious parochialism. It had created a European community of culture and social feeling that was only broken up by the war. Yet in the postwar era the limitations of Liberalism became as fully apparent as its strength had been before. These limitations were equally grave in the political and the economic sphere. The second German empire had collapsed under military defeat; an almost bloodless "revolution" indicated the fact that the regime could no longer find its defenders— although a man like Albert Ballin did not wish to survive it, foreseeing that the mighty Hamburg-American shipping line he had created, a link in international communications, would be doomed. The young successor State could not command the unquestioning loyalty granted to a monarchy that had been heir to an old tradition and ultimately deemed to exist "by the grace of God." Without this unifying framework of a monarchy, the Liberal doctrine of social justice and of the freedom of the individual led to a multiple society. Full freedom of self-expression for each section of the community did not, however, result as expected, in fresh and spontaneous communal life; the outcome was rather a multiplication of parliamentary parties representing sectional interests without a strong sense of national responsibility. The landed gentry, stripped of its former power and dominant position, was not in the least inclined to yield with good grace. The ranks of those groups which opposed the Republic on principle were reinforced by soldiers who, returning from the war with all its horrors but also with its experience of group solidarity and fellowship, could not find their way back into the often inglorious humdrum of peacetime work and life. Because defeated Germany was not allowed a proper army, there was no disciplined body to give these men constructive work and self-esteem. Groups of them stuck together in so-called "Free Corps," united by hate against the bolshevist revolution, by spite against any established order.

Their chief grudge against the Weimar Republic, apart from a military dislike of civilian life, was the blow to their soldierly pride. Germany had not been invaded, and they would not accept the fact of military defeat nor forgive the German Republic for putting its signature to the declaration of war guilt even though under duress. The notorious forgery of the Protocols of the Elders of Zion, widely publicised by White Russian refugees from bolshevism to explain the Russian revolution as a Jewish conspiracy rather than as the breakdown of a barbarous autocracy, seemed all too plausible. Major-General Ludendorff who, wielding a military as well as political dictatorship during the war, had been chiefly responsible for sabotaging a viable termination of hostilities and had then precipitously demanded an armistice, gave the lead in evolving the legend of a "stab-in-the-back" by Jews, socialists, freemasons, and Roman Catholics as the cause of German defeat—the clearest personal instance of a projection of one's own guilt onto others on a large scale.

To these merciless foes the German Republic became a "Jews' Republic" and its black, red, and golden flag of the revolution of 1848, signifying the greater unity of Germany and Austria, was despised as "the Jews' banner." But the Republic, afraid of communist efforts to spread the Russian revolution to Germany, felt dependent on those very forces for its internal security and did not seriously punish their excesses. In the turbulent days of the breakdown of the old order in 1918 a handful of socialists, mostly writers and artists, tried to establish a socialist state in Bavaria under the leadership of the pacifist Kurt Eisner, who was fiercely attacked because of his Jewish birth. He was shot by the Nationalist Count Arco, himself of half-Jewish extraction. After his death the idealists, especially Gustav Landauer, who by popular education and genuine community sought to implement the spiritual revolution of his "Proclamation of the Spirit," were soon outdone by communist extremists, and the socialist experiment was quashed by military force in the service of the Republic. Landauer was beaten to death, while the writer Erich Mühsam and the young poet Ernst Toller were sentenced to long terms of imprisonment. Munich, one of the most liberal and easygoing of German towns, became the hotbed of anti-Semitism. It was in Munich that Ludendorff and the "unknown soldier" Adolf Hitler staged their ludicrous beer-hall "Putsch" in 1923, the last of several similar attempts to overthrow the Republic by paramilitary force, yet too pompously ridiculous to be taken seriously even within Germany. Hitler got away with a mild sentence of political detention in a fortress.

The aggressiveness of frustrated nationalists also led to a number of individual murders. Resistance to the war-guilt clause of the Peace Treaty brought about the assassination of Erzberger, one of its chief

German signatories. When Walther Rathenau, his father's successor in the General Electric Company, became Minister of Economic Reconstruction and then, reluctantly, Minister of Foreign Affairs, to put his own international contacts to use in overcoming the political and moral isolation of the young Republic, the fact that he was a Jew led to his murder in 1922 regardless of his political aims and achievements. Although a solemn state funeral strengthened the internal prestige of the Republic, the stern foreboding of this event resounded for long in Jewish hearts, as if the ground were quaking under their feet. But as yet this remained an isolated occurrence.

The crisis of Liberalism demonstrated itself most clearly perhaps in the economic sphere. The Liberal principle of free competition had been wholesome in the early stages of the industrial revolution, when in the long run every increase in production had served both the national interest and the manufacturer's own. Yet this was no longer true after an imperialist expansion of capitalism had led to such predominance of the strongest producers that, by combining in trusts or cartels, they could not only eliminate smaller independent competitors but actually impose their will on the State itself by identifying the national interest with their own. The crucial test of this bid for power came with the disaster of monetary inflation in 1923–24. In the economic depression of the postwar years, its small-scale beginnings had actually provided a stimulus to the economy by reducing the pressure of debts on farmers and industrialists. But once underway, the devaluation of currency went on for more than a year at breathtaking speed, by leaps and bounds, not by days but within a matter of hours, until a mere tramway ticket cost a matter of 2,000 million marks. Over wide sectors of economic life the currency ceased to function altogether as a medium of exchange, and farmers, for instance, reverted to barter; nevertheless the German legislative stubbornly maintained the fiction of valueless notes being equivalent to gold marks. Though wage-earners were protected by a sliding scale, fixed incomes were adjusted only after long delays. The value of savings, mortgages, gilt-edged securities, and endowment policies disappeared as into thin air. When the ghastly episode was over in 1924, its effect amounted to that of a revolution far more thorough than that of 1918. Its victims were the professional middle class, small-scale traders and manufacturers; its beneficiaries, the tycoons of mining and heavy industries, who amassed huge industrial empires by merely taking out credits and repaying their debts with devalued currency, besides a number of speculators who had swiftly learned the ropes and whose fortunes dwindled as quickly as they were made. These industrialists had coolly prevented a stabilization of the currency before it got completely out of hand. When after the world economic crisis of 1929 unemployment figures rose into the millions, they went on to hire those young men of the middle class whose future they had ruined, as a praetorian guard for their own protection, in the belief that they could control them. This was the social origin of the National Socialist rebellion.

Within this political and economic setting of the postwar era, Jews had to find their place. The Weimar Republic had removed the discriminations imposed by the empire, and emancipation was therefore complete. At the same time, however, antagonism against the Jews, now mainly based on "racial" grounds, spread at an alarming rate. Fanned by the general feeling of insecurity and disorientation, it sought its justification in the widely publicized cases of Jewish war profiteers or inflation speculators—a publicity that left the chief gentile culprits safely in anonymity.

Actually the Jewish population of Germany had diminished. Nonetheless, the large communities, above all Berlin, continued to increase, because practically all Jews from the provinces ceded to Poland opted for Germany and moved inland; in 1925 over 170,000 Jews, nearly one-third of the total Jewish population, lived in Berlin. Moreover, the plight of Eastern Jewry in the postwar era drove thousands of them to Germany, a few wealthy, but most of them utterly destitute. Their accommodation and incorporation presented a very real problem, all the more so since anti-Semitic propaganda added to the burden they represented in view of widespread unemployment and since, naturally enough, some of them were not overscrupulous in their ways of earning a livelihood.

The new freedom that made Jewish descent no longer a barrier to promotion led to a slightly wider distribution in the professional field. There had always been a sprinkling of Jews in the democratic parties. Now Jewish politicians could attain ministerial office, as, for instance, did Hugo Preuss, who drafted the Weimar Constitution. A number of Jews entered the civil service and some of them rose to the highest posts, especially when undertaking new or unusual tasks, inconspicuous but yet of considerable importance. For instance, Otto Hirsch, a civil servant from Württemberg, was put in charge of the Neckar Canal Company which, by linking the Rhine with the Danube across a mountain range, created a navigable waterway from the North Sea to the Black Sea. Men in such positions also felt that they were no longer prevented from taking part in internal Jewish affairs, and Otto Hirsch combined his official duties with a leading role in the regional association of Jews.

In the economic life of postwar Germany, Jews still played a respected but somewhat more restricted part. They had their share of
private banking. For instance, Max M. Warburg and Karl Melchior of
Hamburg were among the economic advisers at the Peace Treaty
negotiations, the latter becoming the German representative at the
World Bank. There were a large number of old, established firms that
maintained or extended their positions, and Jews took a prominent part
in new lines of activity, such as chain stores or film and aircraft production. With the emphasis of economic power shifting from medium-
sized to very large units of production, such as the chemical, mining,
and steel industries, in which comparatively few Jews were active and
then rarely in positions of consequence, the economic importance and
influence of Jews within the total German economy decreased. Many
Jewish firms, disinclined to gamble in the currency market, were unable to replace raw materials from the receipts for finished goods; they
were hard hit by the inflation, while nearly all the speculators who had
amassed fortunes from it, lost them again almost as quickly as they had
been won. Jewish firms participated again in the seemingly miraculous
recovery of Germany's economy after 1924 resulting from the stabilization of the currency, the settlement of reparations, and the influx of
foreign, above all American, investment capital. Yet the prewar position of Jews within the German economy was never regained. This at
least is the opinion of skilled observers, although the difficulty of arriv-
ing at this conclusion may perhaps be even more significant than the
fact itself, since the economic activity of Jews was so completely integrated within the German economy that it no longer represented a
sector with fairly clear outlines; thus only comparative statistics that
do not exist could give a complete and reliable picture.

The incorporation of Jews into the cultural life of Germany was if
anything even more complete than at any time before. At the same
time, however, Judaism attained a force and depth that it had lacked
for generations. A centrifugal, outward-flowing movement continued,
while at the same time a centripetal, inward-directed movement gained
momentum. The reason for this twin development lay in the twofold
effect of the crisis of Liberalism in its cultural aspect. Liberal belief in
progress had taken no account of the possibility of a breakdown such
as the visible disintegration of the Western world, and its conception of
the rights of man and of tolerance came in for bitter mockery under the
harsh realities of post-war existence—one look at the success of the
bolshevist terror sufficed. On the other hand, the Liberal conviction of
the civilizing and democratic effects of culture and education was still
as valid as ever. However, in this respect too, Liberalism had, as

Nietzsche remarked, striven for a formal "freedom *from*. . . ." rather than "freedom *to*. . . ." Hence this freedom that had now been attained was practically limitless but also lacked direction and guidance. The apocalyptic atmosphere of a "weariness of Europe" was indicated by the sensational success of Oswald Spengler's forecast of a *Decline of the West*. Even Albert Einstein's theory of relativity owed the popular aspect of its world fame to a misunderstanding of "relativity" in the sense of nothing absolute, as if no firm and secure values remained, as if everything was "just relative," subjective, and provisional. On the other hand, this freedom, being genuine, produced a keen and daring spirit of experiment, a lack of prejudice and openness to new ventures such as no set traditional society could have encouraged. This is why, though politically insecure and economically struggling, Germany—and in particular, Berlin—became the hub of the cultural life of Europe in the postwar era.

In this Indian summer of German culture Jews played a prominent part as patrons, both actively and receptively. Even mere participation in this cultural life fascinated and held a large group of German Jews with sufficient power to make them feel their Jewish background to be an incidental factor and no more. The postwar atmosphere of full political equality added momentum to the centrifugal tendency that had been part of the period of emancipation almost throughout its course. In addition, doubts in the Liberal beliefs so long associated with the Jewish reform movement also tended to weaken the latter. Believing themselves to be indifferent to any religion, retaining a far stronger background of religious convictions than they were aware of, these Jews believed in Humanism, in humanitarian ideals, in Western civilization, and in a vague cosmopolitanism—a small fraction even sought refuge in German nationalism. By 1927 mixed marriages amounted to 27% of the total—a figure that tends to show to what degree the "racial" dogma of National Socialists was irrational propaganda and nothing more.

The reasons for the opposite, inward-directed, centripetal movement toward a deep-reaching revival of Judaism were equally strong. This movement owed its existence to the vision and energy, to the inner forces of Judaism itself, while its urge came from the crisis of Liberalism and its bearing on the direction of Jewish education. Since the early days of emancipation, participation of Jews in Western culture had come to be regarded as the hallmark of spiritual equality, the indispensible condition for the attainment of full civic emancipation. Both had now been achieved, on the cultural side to such a degree that it had become a given premise, a point of departure, no longer remaining an aim. The critical position that may arise when, with a great effort, a goal is attained and then turns out to be a new starting point, one requiring a new orientation, was in this case aggravated by a double disappointment. First, although the vital energy invested by many Jews in mastering the task of cultural equality led to the rise of a number of individuals to leading positions in their respective fields, this did not necessarily secure recognition by the surrounding world. On the contrary, "racial" anti-Semitism asserted that nothing that any Jew could do, no point he could reach, brought him one whit nearer, and that innate characteristics separated Jews from gentiles and remained an insuperable barrier forever. Hence political equality, even when reached, had continued to be problematical.

There still remained participation in Western culture as an aim in itself. For a century it had been regarded as very precious because, so it was believed, such participation gave Jews the quality of an "individual." And this value had not altogether been shaken. However— and this was the second disappointment—the outlines of Western culture itself were by now so blurred that meaning dissolved into masses of facts, that each highly specialized branch of knowledge seemed to contradict rather than to complement, that, in short, a secure, common basis and aim of culture had been all but lost. With it had gone that confident trust in the future which the belief in progress imparted, and the link between timeless ideals and their realization in daily life, however approximate. Thus the Messianic hopes of Judaism that had given such strong emotional power to these beliefs in Jewish life had to be withdrawn from their Liberal setting. As a new goal, behind and above Western culture, Judaism reappeared in its timeless glory, giving meaning to life, conduct, and work, and unity and direction to culture. The quality of individuation that it could bestow helped to carry secular education in its train but no longer needed it as a carrier.

These two lines of development were by no means mutually exclusive. As the crisis of Western civilization enhanced the significance of Franz Rosenzweig's work for Jews at the Frankfurt *Lehrhaus,* he himself pointed out that a deepening of Jewish consciousness at the same time also increased the importance of Jews in their Western aspect. In the same sense, the influence of men such as Leo Baeck and Martin Buber extended far and wide to souls searching beyond the Jewish sphere. On the other hand, Albert Einstein's reputation helped to promote the building-up of Palestine, in particular of the Hebrew University of Jerusalem. By and large, however, it is probably true to say that as a rule the trend of development went either one way or the other, either nearer to Judaism or farther away from religion altogether, all the more so since, with the secularizing impact of the nineteenth century, the hidden religious quest of socialism and psychoanalysis exerted a powerful attraction that manifested itself as rejection of all institutional religions.

While in this postwar period German-speaking Jews retained or regained the spiritual leadership of the Jewries of the world, of which they composed hardly more than 5%, their simultaneous contribution to the scientific and cultural life of Germany and thus to Western civilization as a whole, was of an order to justify the pride of a great nation rather than that of a small splinter group of the population.

At the Kaiser Wilhelm Institute of Physics in Berlin worked Albert Einstein, whose general theory of relativity, published in 1916, had been confirmed in important aspects by astronomical observation in 1922. A milestone in the development of physics, yet equally stirring popular imagination by presenting matter as a form of energy, by accounting for the varying levels of reality with the nonspatial order of a four-dimensional space-time continuum, and by its cosmological implications, Einstein's work owed its revolutionizing force, as well as the constructive simplification it brought about, to his incisive restatement of basic notions usually taken for granted. The superficially most striking fact of the theory, that the observer's position is involved in the outcome of his observations, could seem to blur the sense of objective reality, reinforcing the disturbing effect of historical relativism as well as of the psychoanalytical findings of unconscious impulses determining conduct; to nonspecialists, this strange coincidence almost overshadowed the huge advance toward a unified view of the laws of the physical universe that the theory represented.

For, holding that "the eternal mystery of the world is its comprehensibility," as the expression of "a superior reason that reveals itself in the world of experience," Albert Einstein strove for the intuitive finding of a basic, comprehensive, unified law of the universe, out of a personal "immediate need," with the passion of a "cosmic faith" in "what Leibniz so happily called pre-established harmony"—a passionate faith that Einstein likened to the emotional state of the deeply religious or of true lovers. His was perhaps the purest and highest form of that secularization of a religious yearning that, beginning with Spinoza, went with inexhaustible perseverance and patience to seek God's revelation in the laws of nature. In Albert Einstein, the fascination of his calling had its roots in his youngest days. When at the age of five his father showed him a compass, the needle following its own laws was a wonder to him: "something deeply hidden had to be behind things." At the age of twelve he experienced a "second wonder" in a simple school booklet on Euclidian geometry, the "lucidity and certainty" of which, "an indescribable impression," gave him a first glimpse of those laws hidden behind the appearance of the world, the key to their unified representation. In the years of his manhood, striving to include in a comprehensive field theory the forces not yet covered by the theory of relativity, electromagnetism, and atomic structure, he felt safe in his confidence that "superior reason" would reveal itself, and scorned as a man-made image the idea of a personal God who cared for humankind. As an old man, however, almost alone among physicists in rejecting the interpretation of atomic physics by the quantum theory because it resulted in rules of mere statistical probability, Einstein gave as his reason for holding on to the concept of complete subservience to law instead of admitting indeterminacy, that he could "not believe that God plays dice with the world."

Though outstanding in the scope of his work, Albert Einstein was by no means the only distinguished scientist of Jewish descent. The half-Jew Niels Bohr, and James Franck were among the leading physicists, while Max Born worked in the theory of electronics. Colleagues of Einstein at the Kaiser Wilhelm Institute were the biochemist Carl Neuberg, the colloid chemists M. Polanyi and L. Freundlich. Richard Willstätter had gone from there to Munich; his work on the chemical structure of chlorophyll, plant dyes, and enzymes continued that of F. J. Cohn in its aim of elucidating the fundamental unity of life. Willstätter, as well as Einstein, Born, Franck, Haber, the half-Jew Otto H. Warburg, A. A. Michelson, the American physicist of German Jewish descent who measured the velocity of light, and the physiologist Otto Meyerhof were all Nobel Prize winners, while a number of their pupils who were to win similar distinction in their time were still unknown students.

Medicine and law, the oldest professional fields open to Jews, still attracted the greatest number—to an extent, in fact, that produced serious problems of overcrowding as well as stimulating brilliant work. In 1925, 26% of lawyers and 15.5% of doctors were Jews. In retrospect, these figures highlight another aspect of the German postwar scene— the widespread confidence which, despite a flood of anti-Semitic propaganda both Jewish doctors and lawyers, inconspicuous and famous alike, needed to maintain their professional existence at all and which they indeed obtained, since only a fraction of their number could have been sustained by the Jewish community itself. A characteristic common to both jurists and doctors was a more-than-average interest in the theoretical foundations and implications of their work, which brought about a typical combination of research and practice. A sense of social responsibility, often no doubt with an element of personal ambition, led many of them to representative positions in professional associations. A considerable number of legal commentaries, medical textbooks, and periodicals in a variety of specialized disciplines owed their inception to the Jewish heritage of the age of enlightenment of spreading precise and well-founded knowledge and keeping their standards up-to-date.

Among the numerous and important Jewish contributions to medicine, Sigmund Freud's work on neuroses, then gaining increasing acceptance, stands out by the depth and width of its revolutionary impact on the whole of human self-understanding, far beyond the confines of medicine, as well as by Freud's attempt to replace the shattered autonomy of rational consciousness with the wider concept of a single, basic human libido. Yet even on his own ground of psychological theory, Freud had to contend with Alfred Adler's "psychology of the individual." Examples of research in other medical disciplines, taken almost at random, are those of F. Blumenthal on cancer, of H. Finkelstein on infant welfare and pediatrics, of I. Boas on the diseases of the digestive tract, and of O. Minkowski on diabetes, as distinguished as that of his brother, H. Minkowski, on the mathematical aspects of the theory of relativity. As an instance of Jewish scholars born in Germany who attained eminence abroad, mention may be made of Franz Boas's pioneering work in scientific anthropology in America.

In philosophy and the historical sciences, the spiritual crisis of the time was felt with acute poignancy. Ernst Cassirer, a pupil of Hermann Cohen, carried on the tradition of Liberal idealism with courageous poise and dignity. His *Philosophy of Symbolic Forms,* while no longer trying to encompass the whole of civilization in one system and to lay down its laws, yet retained the synthetic quality of presenting the human side of the world in a comprehensive view, from its nonrational beginnings in myth to modern objectified forms of knowledge. This approach, while ordering the variety of phenomena, steered a middle course between the two conceptions evolved to evade the leveling influence of historical relativism: one, as we saw, that of Wilhelm Dilthey of types, the other that of "Gestalt," introduced by Max Wertheimer. In the history of literature, for instance, Friedrich Gundolf's books on Caesar, Shakespeare, and the German poet Stefan George—he was one of George's chief disciples—attained a monumental quality under a "Gestalt" aspect, whereas Fritz Strich showed classicism and romanticism to be typical forms of expression, irrespective of period.

In dramatic art, music, and literature the contribution of Jews, by the quality of their work even more than by their numbers, was not merely outstanding but instrumental in giving German culture, in particular Berlin, an international lead. If we seek reasons for such excellence as made unforgettable the performance of plays, operas, and concerts, we find them in the development of the Jews themselves as well as in the situation of the time. Freed from the fetters of former ages, no longer merely tolerated, they could give of their best. A loving care for the values of a cultural and literary tradition they had fully made their own, artistic sensitivity, and the secularization of religion that made art the foothold of the eternal on earth, gave them the power of deep conviction. On the other hand, being themselves, they could not stop the values of their own old culture—a "culture of the heart" as Heine had called it—from shining through them. Their feeling of living in a world that is meaningful as God's world even permeated, as in Franz Kafka's novels, a rendering of gloomy despair, while the sense of man's never-ending task to make this world worthy of being God's kingdom saved them from an attitude of self-complacency and kept their minds open to new ventures, ready to experiment, as critical of social as of artistic inadequacy.

The situation of the time, its very sense of crisis, favored that combination of insistence on basic and permanent values and of an open and critical frame of mind. With political and economic developments proceeding at an uneasy speed, with accepted cultural façades and habits crumbling before uncharted situations, the task of art to maintain a sense of traditional values, while at the same time mirroring and reinterpreting the changes of contemporary life, attained a sense of urgency that it lacked in more settled times. Theater, music, and literature in postwar Germany became the means of cultural integration and thus, together with the economic recovery, of national prestige. Art, and in particular dramatic art, which exerted a popular appeal almost equivalent to that of sporting events in England and America, served the double purpose of providing a brief escape from the demands of reality and of participating in the clarified and purified world of poetry and music.

Max Reinhardt's stage productions set a new standard of performance. Combining an imaginative sense of atmosphere and color with great precision of detail, with a flair for selecting star performers and integrating them into spectacular mass scenes, his grasp extended over the full range of his field. The tragedies of ancient Greece and of Shakespeare, the medieval morality plays in an open-air theater at the Salzburg Festival, the intimate comedies of Lessing, Molière, Wilde, and

Hofmannsthal, Maeterlinck's romantic plays, and the more modern ones of Strindberg, Wedekind, and Shaw—whom Reinhardt helped to fame even before he was appreciated in England—all these came alive with equal power and grace. Reinhardt's performances were almost equaled by those of a number of other Jewish producers and were supported by actors of magnetic appeal and human depth. Again a number of Jewish performers were outstanding in their art, such as Elizabeth Bergner, Fritz Kortner, Ernst Deutsch, Alexander Moissi, the comedian Max Pallenberg, and, among operetta singers and actresses, his wife Fritzi Massary.

The standards of musical life were just as high. Bruno Walter, pupil and friend of Gustav Mahler, whose torn and longing works had now attained a wide appeal, welded singing, acting, and playing into a unheard-of unity and harmony as a conductor, especially of Mozart's operas. Otto Klemperer's compelling force and precision of beat, the brilliance and devotion of soloists such as the pianist Arthur Schnabel, the violinist Carl Flesch, and a galaxy of singers were but the most widely known among artists of hardly lesser merit, for even smaller German towns maintained municipal opera houses, theaters, and orchestras, and a lively competition ensued for outstanding talent. Widespread and democratic as was this musical tradition in Germany, it received new, experimental ventures with reserve rather than with enthusiasm, and Arnold Schönberg's severely contrapuntal music in the new idiom of a twelve-note principle, in which he represented "the unity of musical space," was hotly contested.

In the new artistic medium of the time, the film, Jews were prominent as directors, actors, and producers. Carl Laemmle, born in Germany, ranks among the creators of the American film industry. Directors such as Ernst Lubitsch, Alexander Korda, Eric Cherell, G. W. Pabst, and Ludwig Berger strove to work out the intrinsic possibilities of the modern fairy tale in black and white.

Jewish novelists, essayists, and playwrights, a number of whom in their time attained recognition and fame throughout the Western world, both reflected and helped to shape its outlook. Politically they might take their stand on the extreme left, as in Ernst Toller's expressionist dramas of revolutionary pacifism or Kurt Tucholsky's satires lampooning political reaction and bourgeois self-complacency or as, in an isolated case, Arnolt Bronnen, a Viennese half-Jew who, on the strength of his nationalist and anti-Semitic dramas, became literary adviser to the National Socialists. These writers, however, whose works provided a formative influence while still widely diverging in outlook and depth, had a common legacy from the Liberal age, a vision transcending the moment, a belief in cultural values and in the bearing of historical tradition on the problems of the present—an optimistic faith that truth if earnestly striven for could be found and that its significance was not limited by national frontiers. They were all the safer in upholding a cosmopolitan feeling since they were securely rooted in the cultural soil from which they had grown. A tinge of the brooding heaviness of his Franconian background remained in Jacob Wassermann even when he branched out from the local lore of Nuremberg into themes of symbolic significance, such as the story of the foundling Casper Hauser or the search for justice in *The Maurizius Case.* The throbbing city life of Berlin, with its strong emphasis on the social problems experienced by a physician in a proletarian district, was portrayed in Alfred Doeblin's "Berlin Alexander-Platz" with James Joyce's prismatic technique of associations. The light, witty, elegant touch of Viennese music with its melancholic background found its counterpart in the writings of Viennese authors, in Arthur Schnitzler's delicate, bittersweet love stories, in Stefan Zweig's masterly novels, translations, and biographical essays in "The Builders of the World" with his discreet use of psychoanalytical insights, in Richard Beer-Hofmann's plays *Jacob's Dream* and *The Young David,* in Joseph Roth's *Job* as well as in his *Radetzky March.* The regional flavor might be less marked in works of strong social feeling such as Arnold Zweig's war novel *The Case of Sergeant Grischa,* in Lion Feuchtwanger's historical novels, and in Emil Ludwig's best-seller type of historical biographies. Yet the splendor of Prague's baroque churches may be felt in the writers hailing from this town, along with its fierce cultural struggles for nationality, which heightened the national consciousness of Jews, primarily as Germans but increasingly also as Jews. Franz Werfel, one of the most gifted lyrical poets of his generation, expressed this heritage in the musical architecture of his *Verdi,* in his drama *Paul among the Jews,* in his essays on religion and, foreshadowing the catastrophe of the Jews under Hitler, in the fate of the Armenians earlier in the century, in his novel *The Forty Days of Musa Dagh.* Max Brod's many-sided activities also centered more and more on religious problems, whether in a local setting as in his novel *Tycho Brahe's Way to God* or, turning with Zionist fervor to the Jewish past in *Reubeni,* or in his reassessment of the positions of *Paganism, Christianity, Judaism.*

Posterity is indebted to Max Brod as much as for his own works as for preserving and publishing, as the literary trustee of his friend, Franz Kafka's novels and tales even despite Kafka's own modest desire to have them destroyed. Thus it was possible to secure them their place as documents of a spiritual urge and quest that transcended the limitations of authorship, place, and time, and bore witness to the indestructible longing of man for God and for redemption. For these stories, told with humorous detachment and with a mature mastery of accurate detail sometimes taken from the Bohemian countryside, have a dreamlike, often nightmarish quality of elusive truth. Unseen and equivocal powers, manifested in unobtrusive and familiar yet eerie surroundings, in shoddy, obscene, ridiculous guise, appear to hold the secret of a happy life on earth and of redemption beyond; but these stories also inspire an unsubstantiated fear, an unknown or forgotten guilt, not revealed and never entirely accepted yet relentlessly driven home, more real than apparent reality. We may remark upon the features that relate this view of life to its time, the influence of positivism, which undermined the existence of spiritual truth; in art, the solidity of objects was reduced to the mere visual impressions by Impressionism; then Expressionists opposed inner symbols, often semi-conscious, to factual reality. We may see this development equally reflected in the loss of political and economic coherence that characterized the post-war era.

Another aspect of this development, and this also a Jewish aspect, was the loss of continuity of religious tradition and meaning and thus of a sense of spiritual security and of religious community. The loosening link with the past also endangered confidence in the future. This dilemma, the core of Franz Kafka's stories, produces Fear—a fear quite distinct from specific anxiety but rather "the Fear of all faith since the beginning of time," the fear of God, which had been lost in an overly optimistic hope of unending "progress" and material security. Deprived of the mediating help of religious law and ritual, the individual is exposed to the unmitigated impact of the absolute in all its ambivalence—a condition that in Germany may have contributed to both Hölderlin's and Nietzsche's deep mental disturbance. In Kafka, however, though experienced with the utmost intensity, this Fear was coupled with a childlike innocence and trust, still unified and free from conflict, with the ultimate certainty that "nothing decisive has happened, nothing really decisive in Heaven or on Earth . . . thus he can still be saved." Franz Kafka himself did in fact finally achieve a breakthrough from the agony of torment of personal happiness by studying the sources of Judaism at the *Hochschule* in Berlin and by regaining a sense of Jewish community from the message of Zionism, from guest performances of the Yiddish theater.

Yet, before reaching this final stage, he was spared none of the preceding steps. His spiritual quest drew him to the dark side of life as a possible means of redemption, the very opposite of middle-class respectability and absolute standards of moral goodness as emphasized for so long by Liberal Judaism. Not that Kafka denied these standards. On the contrary, by trying to live up to them he found "the dirt" to be his "sole possession—the sole possession of all people," and indispensable for salvation. In fact, in a position strangely resembling that of the Sabbatians of the eighteenth century, who held that for the sake of redemption Jews had to live in sin, but yet approaching it from the opposite angle, namely that "good" and "bad" were no longer clearly distinguishable, Franz Kafka rediscovered the relative value of guilt for redemption, the old midrashic adage: "Thou shalt love the Lord with thy good and with thy evil impulses"—the humanity of failure. The integrity of his feelings and his immaculate art of rendering them in images and symbols of timeless appeal raised his quest above the personal level and even above that of the Jewish position of the time to a generally human problem.

The Revival of Judaism

The Jewish scene presented firm contrasts between groups of widely diverging outlook and interests, city dwellers and country folk, capitalists and employees, "assimilationists" and Zionists, the older and the younger generation, between growing absorption into the surrounding world and enthusiastic rediscovery of Jewish values, between a fragmentation of Jews as a group and integration by the revival of Judaism. Though the cohesion, solidarity, and power of Jews that was alleged by anti-Semitic propaganda differed greatly from the real state of affairs, the very existence of continuing and mounting group antagonism contributed to a reinforced sense of Jewish solidarity. Very few of those who gave every outward appearance of drifting away took advantage of their right to terminate their membership of the Jewish community by a simple declaration, so that the tax revenue of Jewish congregations in no way reflected a critical situation. Nor was private generosity to charitable or educational causes, Jewish and non-Jewish alike, and personal interest in their conduct any less marked than it had been in previous generations.

The Jewish congregations continued to be centers of communal life. The Weimar Republic no longer objected to their joining together in regional associations. In Southern Germany such *Landesverbände*, long since recognized by the laws of their respective States, combined to form a larger association, while the corresponding Prussian Associa-

tion of Jewish Congregations, the largest of them all, still awaited legal
status pending the conclusion of a fair-minded "Concordat." In these
regional associations, where representatives of all Jewish groups
worked quietly and efficiently together, was centered much of the internal organization of Jewish life. In addition to communal administration, they subsidized small congregations that were no longer self-
supporting, maintained training institutes for teachers and rabbis, promoted religious, educational, and cultural ventures such as lecture
courses, choirs, and even sister institutes of the Frankfurt *Lehrhaus*,
besides supporting projects of Jewish scholarship. Their tasks multi-
plied when inflation swallowed up the numerous endowment funds for
communal hospitals, societies, charities, and institutions, funds that
represented pious legacies of benefactors over the centuries.

Although the economic recovery of the years following currency
stabilization enabled the central agencies to maintain the essential part
of this vast network of cultural undertakings, the capital that had been
their financial backbone could not be replaced. Furthermore, quite
apart from the needs of these institutions, inflation had left a huge
backwater of distress among individuals, predominantly older people
who had hitherto been able to contribute to communal needs from their
own income from investments or property but had now been completely impoverished. Apart from the increased burden that this meant
for the congregations, unobtrusive assistance was required in these
cases for those too proud and ashamed by the sudden loss of economic
security and independence. The Order of B'nai Brith had to amend its
principle of "Nothing for ourselves, everything for others" and to
switch part of its charitable support to the victims of a financial land-
slide.

The dynamic forces of German Jewry, as if attracted to two magnetic
fields with differing charges, were represented and led by two large
organizations, the Central Union of German Citizens of Jewish Faith
(Centralverein) and the Zionist Federation of Germany. At this time
the dangerous mass appeal of anti-Semitic propaganda could not be
overlooked, even though after the Hitler-Ludendorff *Putsch* of 1923
the specter of armed rebellion seemed to be laid for good. Jewish
cemeteries were desecrated; rowdy methods of intimidation, and unin-
hibited slanderous attacks on Jews called for action, so that the need
for a nationwide organization to combat anti-Semitism was self-
evident. The Central Union, represented down to the smallest village
congregation, drew its strength from this purpose. By then new means
of defense superseded in importance the legal assistance provided previously in individual cases, and the democratic parties gladly availed

themselves of the accurate and detailed informative material put at their disposal. These activities were complemented by an attempt at the academic level to present Judaism in its bearing on current problems and to encourage discussion among Jewish and gentile writers and scholars. The periodical *Der Morgen (The Morning)*, founded to this end in 1924 by Moritz Goldstein, became the leading Jewish monthly, filling the gap when Martin Buber's *Der Jude (The Jew)* ceased publication. As a mass movement, however, called upon to represent as well as to defend the attainments of the age of emancipation, the Central Union spoke for the Jew as an upright citizen equally aware of his Jewish roots and his Western allegiance, and made this synthesis the center of its work of internal education. However much Ludwig Holländer, the director of the Union, had the cause of Judaism at heart, the dialectics of a position between anti-Semitism and Zionism and, even more, the continuing momentum of emancipation in its hidden religious significance of a liberation from without, gave greater effect to the patriotic than to the Jewish aspect of the synthesis.

The outward-flowing tendency of the age of emancipation, the hope of salvation from a "normalization of Jewish existence," was even stronger in the Zionist Federation of Germany. Still playing a respected role, though after the collapse of German power no longer a leading one in the world Zionist movement, the Federation gained its growing appeal from the spirit of enthusiastic hope it inspired as well as from the disillusionment of the postwar situation. Not a few Jews shared the mood of a "weariness of Europe." The existence of widespread anti-Semitism and a contracting economic scope for Jews were undeniable facts. Kurt Blumenfeld, the leader of the Federation and the spokesman of the younger generation of Zionists, used his penetrating analytic powers to highlight the obsolete ideological basis of emancipation and the increasing hollowness of Liberal ideals. The realization of an autonomous National Home that had seemed within immediate grasp at the time of the Balfour Declaration again appeared remote but became all the more an ideal of fulfillment, of new Messianic hope. After the closer contact with Eastern Jews that the war had brought about, a wave of romantic discovery found a feeling of Jewish fellowship in Yiddish folksongs, tales, and plays. The combined attraction of the simple life, a spirit of sacrifice, and socialist convictions made the *Chaluz* or pioneer, tilling the soil of the Promised Land and living in communities without private property, a new ideal of concrete attainment. With the rebirth of the Hebrew language, the hope arose that the ancient greatness of the people of the Bible could be rekindled from contact with its sacred soil, and that a model of social justice would set an example to the world. Devotion to this ideal did not, however, suffice for the rehabilitation of Palestine as far as the financial aspect was concerned, and in appealing for funds for this purpose Zionism found response far beyond the limits of its own ranks.

While the two organizations appeared to be antagonistic and incompatible in their ideological tendencies, this divergence no longer threatened a split in the postwar years. In the discussions preceding the Versailles Peace Treaty in 1919 the Central Union had, without prejudice to its own policy in Germany, joined hands with the Zionists in demanding the establishment of a Jewish Home in Palestine and the granting of national minority rights for Eastern Jews. On the other hand, Zionist criticism of "assimilationists" did not mean a return to any form of ghetto by abrogating the Western culture of Jews. This common ground apart, which was less often emphasized than the differences, there were cohesive forces both above and outside the organizational level, not to mention practical cooperation in communal tasks. Franz Rosenzweig's *Lehrhaus* and Martin Buber's teaching attracted Zionists and non-Zionists alike. Similarly, Leo Baeck, both by his work and by his personal example, stood out as a living representative of the spirit of a higher unity of Judaism, capable of containing diametrical opposites and of a "true universality" combining Western culture with adherence to the Jewish community.

The strongest force outside the large organizations was the Jewish youth movement. It formed part of a far wider movement. Since the beginning of the century a growing rebellion had taken place by young people throughout Europe against the ever-increasing mechanization of life in the big cities, against "soulless" capitalism, against the formalized standards of bourgeois society, against one-sided intellectualism and narrow utilitarianism. Return to Nature promised a liberation from the sophistication and regimentation of city life. Informal dress, rambles in all sorts of weather, sports and athletics, cooking and camping in small groups, folk songs sung round a camp fire—all exerted a romantic attraction for boys and girls. In the revival of folk dances and long-forgotten lore a pagan element reappeared. Holiday trips gave adolescents a chance to hitchhike through the length and breadth of the country and even beyond its frontiers. On such trips they discovered culture in their own way. Gothic cathedrals, the stately dignity of old houses, the leisurely charm of marketplaces, relics of a bygone age, all instilled respect for the past and a longing to emulate its communal achievements and unity of life. With the growing momentum of this movement, youth hostels were founded and loose associations of smaller groups grew into larger bodies. From its beginning young Jews had formed part of this movement, sharing its spirit of revolt, its strict code of honor and comradeship of the sexes, its sense of community and voluntary discipline, in adventurous exploits and delights. With the emergence of larger, more closely knit associations groping for new forms of communal life, increasingly orientated on racial, Christian, or socialist lines, Jews became more and more unwelcome within the groups themselves but, in associations of their own, they continued to be treated in a spirit of friendly comradeship by the gentile groups.

The first Zionist association was formed as early as 1912 and during the 1914–18 war German-Jewish groups spread throughout the Reich. The feeling of common outlook and purpose among both types of youth associations made their divergent aims more a matter of personal decision than of ideological principles. Many of their members shared a preference for manual or agricultural work, and all of them had the formative experience of subordinating individual self-assertion to team work in a communal spirit. Having started from revolt, they learned to accept responsibility. Above all, however, they were united by an earnest search for true guidance, for abiding values amidst the crisis of tumbling ideals. Thus the rediscovery of Judaism, more often than not previously discredited by mere lipservice or lukewarm religious tuition, had a new tone of honest need and urgency. The revival of Judaism became a matter of concern for the inner life of this younger generation, though not for them alone.

"Through our Jewishness, not away from our Jewishness leads the path to our Humanity." With these words Leo Baeck indicated the reversal of a trend that had made Jews look outward rather than inward for a fulfillment of their human development during most of this period of emancipation. Leo Baeck was the outstanding spiritual representative of German Jews, not by virtue of any official position that did not exist, nor, wide and deep as was his learning, by peerless scholarship, nor on the strength of a rare combination of vision and organizational gifts, nor even by uniting in himself the thinker and the teacher, the historian and the theologian, but by the strength of his heart and "heroism of the soul." He attained a position of uncommon influence not only in the Jewish sphere of Germany but far beyond both its national and international confines. In addition to the busy life of a rabbi in one of the largest Liberal congregations of the Jewish community of Berlin and to playing his part in the communal administration, he educated the rising generation of rabbis as one of the most beloved lecturers at the *Hochschule,* both representing and administering the academic work of the College and of the Academy for the Science of Judaism in all its wide ramifications. As a mark of the confidence of his rabbinical colleagues, orthodox and reform alike, there was conferred on him in 1922 the office of President of the Union of German Rabbis, notwithstanding the leading position that he held in the international organization of Jewish reform congregations, which came to be expressed by his election as President of the World Union for Progressive Judaism in 1939. Beyond his professional activities Leo Baeck was the first rabbi to occupy the office of Grand President for Germany of the Order of B'nai B'rith, from 1924 until its dissolution in 1937. And as a non-Zionist he became one of the founders of the Jewish Agency for Palestine in 1929. This list of offices, although far from complete, depicts the breadth of his mind and interests, as well as the wide range of his Jewish activities in official bodies. His participation in these bodies was anything but one of formal representation. As quick at grasping the essential point of administrative tasks as of historical or theological problems, he combined a phenomenal capacity for detailed work and a modest sense of social service with a vision of the inner unity and historical continuity of Jewish life, so raising the level of committee work to an awareness of its functions above the mere turmoil of the day. Cautious in expression, tolerant of differing ways of approach, and of gentle courtesy, Leo Baeck might have appeared as flexible as a diplomat, and easily yielding. Yet his striving for peace, harmony, and toleration within the Jewish body politic as well as among religions came from spiritual strength. His humble dignity concealed rather than revealed great power. It cloaked a very definite mind and judgment and a core of resilient steel. On essential matters his "No" was final.

The rabbi Dr. Baeck of those years was tall but with a somewhat frail appearance, slightly bent at the knees when speaking, with a faint trace of professional smoothness in his quiet, warm voice, often conveying more than he actually said by the way he said it. He came to be known as a brilliant speaker and forceful writer who reached a wide public outside the Jewish sphere in his sustained effort to acquaint gentiles with the true meaning of Jewishness: "To live in the world for the sake of the world, to contradict the world for the sake of the world, to be different for the sake of the world, to say No to so much in order to be able to pronounce the great word Yes, to be ready to stand erect for the sake of the One God, the one command, the one humaneness against so much else, nay against everything else if need be, to renounce many a success for the sake of the future, to give every day its place and its due and yet, so as to safeguard the idea, to be able to oppose the day, to be prepared for any beginning yet never to lose sight of 'the end of days'—this is, for all our differences, what we as Jews have in common, this is the constructive task, the lifeline, the historical way of

Judaism. . . . We are the Noncomformists of the world for which we live."

Distinctions of garb, dialect, or even of religious law and ceremonial no longer applied, nor did they suffice to enable Jews to retain and deepen their religious identity within a perplexing variety of trends and valuations while preserving a humanistic openness of outlook. A new "fence around the Torah" had to be built of distinctive historical and theological consciousness, of more intensive religious feeling. This was the basic effect of Leo Baeck's scholarly activities. He rescued the Pharisees of old from much misunderstanding and defamation by showing that their movement was a heroic and democratic attempt at hallowing the life of the individual and the institutions of the State. He did pioneering work on the history of the Jewish sermon in late Greek and early Christian times, discovering its function as the spiritual bond of the community, its content as a clarification of Jewish doctrine in times of fermenting religious unrest. With great respect for Christianity, Leo Baeck yet demonstrated by typological comparison the contrast between Judaism as the "classical" and Christianity as the "romantic" religion. With consummate understanding, he traced the path of "Judaism in the Church," that is, the internal discussion of Jewish ideas in Christianity, ideas that were forcefully rejected in one age only to be happily rediscovered in another. He avoided the pitfalls of historicism by pointing to the specific idea of Judaism that permeated and shaped Jewish history throughout the centuries: "The teaching of Judaism is its history, and its history is at the same time its teaching." Yet he strongly resisted any interpretation of the basic doctrines of Judaism as dogmas in the accepted sense of the word, trusting the teachers of each subsequent generation to find the right expression at the right time rather than to seek the security of faith in fixed formulae.

Scanning the contemporary horizon with the vision of centuries, with eyes trained to observe large-scale developments behind the shifting scene of the moment, Leo Baeck saw thunderclouds forming in the still sunny skies. In the hopeful atmosphere of 1925, when the Weimar Republic had gained strength by overcoming the political upheavals of the postwar years, when currency stabilization and settlement of war reparations initiated a spate of economic recovery, hardly another person could have written what he then wrote to a friend and colleague:

> We discover two roots of our being within ourselves. . . . Men belong to the realm of the State and to the realm of God. Which law shall they obey when a conflict occurs? . . . The hour may arrive

when one is forced to opt—for the temporal or for the eternal. "Get thee out of thy country," God said to Abraham. To opt means to be ready to become a martyr, to recognise the primacy of religion and its commands, its primacy over everything. . . . All such martyrdom is the more grave the more the soul is attached to what must be given up for the sake of the higher allegiance.

It is a spiritual and moral disaster for Germany that so many men in leading positions have for a long time known nothing of the two realms, that the fact of being German has been turned into a religion. Instead of believing in God they, with the Lutheran pastors in the lead, believe in Germanism. This is nationalism unqualified—to recognise only one's own nationhood and not the world of God. (The spiritual aridity of many Jews is due to the fact that they too are trying to turn their German nationality into a kind of substitute religion).

Where men are estranged from the world of God, they are estranged from martyrdom too—from that which they are meant to prove in their own lives as well as that to which others bear witness. Why was the German revolution a revolution without martyrs? Where is the Junker or university professor who became a martyr for the sake of the Hohenzollern? Why is Jewish martyrdom understood so little or not at all in the Germany of today?

We Jews are rooted more deeply than others in the spiritual world, in religion. We are the people of God: this is why we have been drawn into conflict more deeply and more frequently—not only frequently but continually. That is the tragic trait in our history—tragic not in the small, bourgeois sense but in the highest sense which, through history, becomes spiritual and great. These last few years have turned us more strongly towards what is most authentically ours in ourselves. Once again we have experienced more deeply that we are rooted in the Kingdom of God.

Leo Baeck's "we" bore witness to a common experience and the concerted effort of many men and women of whom his was the leading and guiding voice. And indeed, for all the diversity of approach, the revival of Judaism in postwar Germany was characterized by a greater degree of unanimity than ever before. This appeared most strikingly perhaps in Martin Buber's inner development. From a position that had assumed Zionism and Dispersion, rabbinical Judaism and Hasidism to be incompatible opposites, from an attitude of "either-or" he had slowly reached a synthesis of "and." His own philosophy of religious existentialism was expressed in the book *I and Thou* which, published in 1922, as a textbook of social science came to exert a lasting and a far-reaching influence. From the intrinsic monologue of mystical experience Buber had gone on to discover the responsive and responsible relationship of dialogue, the meeting with a "Thou" in its own right, and lastly, the meeting with God as a "Thou." This was very near what

Hermann Cohen put into the very center of his philosophy of religion as the "correlation" between man and God, man and world, man and fellow-man—a modern expression of the biblical commandment "Thou shalt love thy neighbour as thyself," love each and both for the sake of God. Apart from its stimulating effect on ever-widening circles, Buber's conception of the meaning of relationship or "meeting" became most fruitful to himself as a new key to his understanding of Jewish religious history. For, viewed from the aspect of the impact on man of meeting with God, the ideas and images of old became valid testimonials of this experience, however conditioned they might be by the individual man and his time.

Thus to Buber the history of Judaism enshrined the voice of God, the true Voice, though wrapped in the limitations of its human recipients, yet capable of reaching any heart that held itself ready to receive its message at any particular hour or in any situation in life. This interpretation of the history of Judaism brought Buber nearer Baeck's view that Jewish teaching is coextensive with Jewish history. His own chief contribution to the revival of religious feeling among German Jews lay, however, in his emphasis on responsiveness to the Voice whose guidance, far from being fixed or uniform, as in Cohen's view of an eternal ethical command, responded to the varying needs of the hour. His insistence on intense and devoted readiness to follow its call made him a preacher with an inner spark as well as a historian and theologian. For, to his understanding, Judaism could no longer be expressed in a few fundamental concepts, as had been attempted by the Liberal reform, but was a multitude of meaningful human experiences legitimate in whatever form they took, in the main currents of Jewish history as well as in its subterranean streams. Jewish life in the dispersion was no longer rejected as meaningless: Buber realized a "theophany of exile," the appearance of God in the distress of dispersion. On the other hand, while remaining fully convinced of the national aims and the social ideals of Zionism, he became increasingly anxious lest the movement might turn into a secularised "nationalism of empty self-assertion," devoid of its religious raison d'être. He maintained that the Jews' own country, language, and culture still required "Hebrew man allowing himself to be addressed by the voice that speaks to him in the Hebrew Bible, and answering it with his life."

Indeed, henceforth the Bible became the center of Martin Buber's work. Together with Franz Rosenzweig he started in 1925, and completed by himself after his friend's death, the monumental task of rendering the Bible in a new German translation so as to make its quality of dialogue transparent, to bring out man's experience of the Voice in

its subtlest tones and repercussions, and to confront modern man with
it anew. The exegetical evaluation of their work in a number of articles
by both him and Franz Rosenzweig, paralleled by Benno Jacob's commentary on Genesis, came as a major Jewish contribution to biblical
scholarship, which had long been left to Protestant theologians. In the
field of theology Martin Buber used the new insight won by the translation for elucidating the central biblical conception of *The Kingdom of
God* (1932).

Franz Rosenzweig, the dynamic driving force of the renaissance of
Judaism, joined forces with Martin Buber in this translation of the
Bible. Their friendship and cooperation in this venture, as well as at the
Lehrhaus, signified the unity of this revival of Judaism on a higher level
of thought and in a deeper meaning of life. For a ray of the legendary
quality that came to illuminate Franz Rosenzweig's figure also shone
on their relationship. "One should not become a saint from choice but
from destiny," Rosenzweig had once casually said during the war. To
become a saint, in the Jewish understanding of a "verification" of faith
under supremely trying conditions, was what destiny had in store for
him. At the beginning of 1922 he fell ill with progressive paralysis,
probably the after-effects of encephalitis, which he had contracted at
the end of the war. Still only in his thirties, the doctors accorded him
but one year to live at the most. Actually he lasted for another seven
years, "probably a unique case in medical history," as his doctor said,
for the paralysis stopped just short of the vital organs. Even so, an
unsteady head had to be held in an iron frame, a speechless mouth took
hours to feed, a motionless hand or an arm supported by a cross-bar
could but vaguely indicate letters on the dial of a specially constructed
one-lever typewriter. His wife's devotion was his only means of communication. By spelling the letters he indicated and intuitively completing them into words, she took down word by word, sentence by
sentence what he wanted to say or write. However sudden the impact
of his illness, Franz Rosenzweig almost instinctively seemed to have
trained himself early to withstand it. As a young student he had told a
friend who chaffed him about the length of time it took him to get up in
the morning, that the moment of daily awakening from nightly death
was for him the greatest and holiest moment of the day, adding: "he
alone is truly blessed who is able not only consciously to experience
his daily reawakening, but also to remain conscious in the moment of
death."

In this affliction Franz Rosenzweig remained himself, serene, free,
humorous, and unaffectedly human, not excluding impatience and
rage. As far as possible, he maintained his position as the head of his

household, keeping up his wide connections and many-sided interests. His visitors, afraid of meeting a scintillating man converted into an incapacitated cripple, soon forgot his physical condition in the "wondrous intensity of life" radiating from him: "the incredible became the norm". The "unforgettably deep and warm look" of his eyes, his smile and his "conversation" took his guests out of their own limitations: "near Franz Rosenzweig one came to oneself" (Karl Wolfskehl). The image of this man in a book-lined study at Frankfurt, overcoming near-physical death by the strength of his faith, conveyed almost more than his words the meaning of what, in his *Star of Redemption* he had called experiencing eternity within life.

Besides maintaining his social contacts, without bitterness, sentimentality, or solemnity, Franz Rosenzweig just proceeded with his work. The *Lehrhaus,* continuing under his guidance and inspiration, flourished as a result of the devoted endeavors of a group of his friends, above all Martin Buber, who also accepted the chair of Jewish Studies at the University of Frankfurt for which Rosenzweig had been earmarked, and Nahum Glatzer. Altogether ten Institutes of Jewish Learning, modeled on the lines of Rosenzweig's prototype, came in the course of time to be founded in Germany, Switzerland, England, and America. Apart from his influence on the *Lehrhaus,* however, his illness forced him back to the written word, instead of the oral teaching that he had had in mind. Yet his literary work was perhaps the most astounding feat of spirit triumphing over the severest of physical handicaps. His writing, in its sparkling brilliance, human warmth, breadth of learning, and penetration, did not show the slightest trace of having been shaped under constant pain during sleepless nights, of having had to be retained in memory, of the fantastically cumbersome procedure of letter-by-letter dictation. The most that Rosenzweig allowed himself was an occasional reference to "technical hindrances" when thanking friends for assistance in providing him with books or references. Indeed, his writing at this time attained a new ease and grace. Much of it responded to the stimuli of the moment on a variety of subjects. His book reviews grew into little treatises, while a review of gramophone records was interspersed with original observations on the history of music. Rosenzweig's introduction to Hermann Cohen's *Collected Jewish Writings,* running into some fifty quarto pages gave a masterly portrait of his teacher as a man, thinker, and Jew, consciously visualized from his own different position. And the strong, almost compelling sense of Rosenzweig's own vision of Judaism permeated even his seemingly incidental notes and gave them convincing strength, enhanced by the legendary appeal of his survival.

Franz Rosenzweig's post-Liberal conception fused the three main lines of Jewish development into a new synthesis—Liberal in its courage, width and freedom of thought and religious feeling, orthodox in its care for traditional values, Zionist in its strong sense for Jewish community and solidarity, yet uncommitted to any of these movements as an end in themselves. And this new attitude of his, even more than any of his sayings as such, created a new type of Jewish feeling and thinking in Germany, still closely linked to, but no longer identified with the Western background. Rosenzweig collected his essays under the title *Zweistromland (Land of Two Rivers),* comparing by this title the Mesopotamia of old, situated as it was between the Euphrates and Tigris, with modern Jewish life, nurtured by the two rivers of Western civilization and living Jewish tradition. He was convinced that his approach to Judaism as a free, modern man was more than that of a passing phase: "only posthumously," he felt, would he "wholly speak out: because I don't concern myself with the means, I will clarify the unity of their goal for the Jews of the coming era. . . . I am subjecting my whole life to this posthumous state."

Rosenzweig widened the appeal of his message by trying to meet half way, by means of translations, those who could not read the sources of Judaism in their original tongue. In removing the barrier of language he did not wish to give modern readers effortless access to works of the past by rendering such works in a glib, fluent idiom of contemporary expression, but rather to confront them with a translation conforming as closely as possible to the original text. He was convinced that, fundamentally, all languages are sufficiently similar to make such precise and faithful reproduction possible, even though it might mean using forms that had not before been historically developed in the structure and grammar of the modern medium. Rosenzweig thus preferred to take the reader back with him into the past rather than to blur the significance of creative work by removing it from its original context. In his rendering of Hebrew poems of Judah Halevi he demonstrated that not merely the meaning but the artful and intricate rhyme, sound, and rhythm of a twelfth-century poet could reemerge in another language. It was not only the greatest Jewish poet of the Middle Ages whose work he thus presented, but a man of burning and longing faith, a philosopher and a theologian. Franz Rosenzweig referred to himself, half-jokingly, as "a medium-sized reincarnation" of Judah Halevi. In his commentary on the poems themselves, which spanned the gap of seven centuries between the poet and the reader, the translator expressed some of his own deepest experience:

The question as to how the Jewish people has survived all their sufferings has often been put, and there have been many more or less clever, which means more or less stupid, answers. The true reason, for which the plural "reasons" does not exist, emerges in this poem. It begins with a cry from an abyss of suffering, an abyss so terribly deep that He whom the cry is destined to reach, is at first merely a target for outcry, doubt and blasphemy. And in the very act of crying out doubt and blasphemy, which exceed all Biblical models because they are fed on the poisonous juices of a philosophy of doubt and blasphemy, the eye still recognises that He to whom the cry mounts is circled with stars. The unburdened mouth professes the power of Him who commands the hosts of heaven, the heart drowns in the ecstasy of beholding the glory of God—and all suffering is forgotten.

The Translation of the Bible

Having learned that such a degree of fidelity could be achieved in rendering Hebrew texts into the German of the twentieth century, Franz Rosenzweig and Martin Buber felt confident enough to undertake a new translation of the Scriptures. Quite apart from the technical problems of translation as such, numerous and complex as they were, the obstacles to undertaking the project at all were serious. The fundamentalist conviction of verbal inspiration and the belief in the infallibility of the Bible that underlaid the translations of former ages were no longer held by the translators themselves nor by the great majority of readers. Moreover, the Old Testament itself could no longer be naively regarded as a text of undoubted consistency, after "Higher Criticism" had demonstrated the greatly varying age and origin of its component parts. Approaching their task from a position of faith, though not a fundamentalist one, the Jewish translators could neither visualize a rendering of the sacred text as a literary effort, nor could they accept the solution of leading Protestant theologians, who confined the critical and the theological treatment of the text to separate watertight compartments: "If science and religion attempt to ignore each other," Rosenzweig wrote, "while yet being aware of each other, then neither science nor religion are any good. There is only one truth. No honest man can pray to a God whom he denies as a scientist. And whoever prays cannot at the same time deny God. . . . It is not a matter of belief versus science but of believing science versus disbelieving science. Or rather—since it is the proof of believing science that it includes the disbelieving whereas, conversely, to disbelieving science the believing remains inaccessible—the position is that of believing-nonbelieving science versus a narrow disbelieving one. And the word 'believing' does not mean a dogmatic commitment, but being held in a manner totally enfolding the entire human being. In this sense the heretic can be believing and the ultra-orthodox disbelieving."

Franz Rosenzweig and Martin Buber wanted to assist modern man to reexperience the creative and redemptive quality of divine revelation contained in the Bible. They were deeply convinced that, provided only that the reader was open-mindedly ready to listen and to receive whatever message or meaning he felt to be addressed to him, the word of God could still reach him, because "Jewish words, however old, partake of the eternal youth of the word," and because of the very fact that the Bible itself is a record of man meeting with God, and thus the beginning of an unending dialogue. So indeed had the Bible been regarded by generation after generation, each of which found answers to its own problems in it. Parallel to the text itself was the oral tradition of Judaism, layer upon layer of commentary. Though not crediting this oral tradition with an authority equal to that of the text as had been customary in the past, the translators accepted it in all its variety as a "unity of reading" of the Bible that they wished to preserve and maintain, so that the gleanings of former generations might shine through their translation. This wholehearted loyalty not merely to the text itself but also to its traditional interpretation, and its combination with a critical acceptance of the results of modern research, gives an idea of the magnitude of their task. However, they could face and master it because they were aware of a deeper unity underlying the diversity of texts. The Bible itself carefully distinguished between the individual aspects of the God of Abraham, the God of Isaac, and the God of Jacob, while at the same time emphasizing the identity of the God of the Patriarchs. Rosenzweig pointed out that all biblical statements about God, including even seemingly harrowing anthropomorphic ones, were equally true attempts to express a human experience, but were not "descriptions" of God. He and Buber accepted the symbol *R,* which scientific analysis uses to designate the presumptive final "Redactor," the editor of the Torah, but they reinterpreted it as *Rabbenu* ("our Teacher"), the master mind that conveyed the inner unity of the Bible. In their conviction this inner unity became fully transparent only when the cross-references in the text itself were viewed together in a synoptic manner, not merely in corresponding or complementary scenes and events but even in those hinted at by recurring words. Thus there was needed an unheard-of precision of translation. It not only precluded the rendering of synonyms by the same word but made it imperative to retain in the translation, as the basis of such subtler links, an indication of the original, basic meaning of Hebrew roots. This degree of fidelity made the new translation read very differently from any other, and it was frequently misunderstood as an endeavor at beautiful or decorative expression, although the courage and skill of the translators were widely acclaimed.

Franz Rosenzweig, undaunted by such misunderstandings, measured his and Buber's efforts not by the immediate reaction but against the achievements of their most distinguished predecessor in sixteenth-century Germany, Martin Luther, just as Luther himself, "with the reverence of a free man," had measured his translation against the Latin of St. Jerome some eleven centuries before his time. Rosenzweig saw their translation as one of the links in the chain of a "dialogue of mankind," each initiating a new phase of world history: "the translation into the language of tragedy, the translation into the language of the Corpus Juris, the translation into the language of the 'Phenomenology of the Spirit.' " Yet apart from this wide aspect of biblical interpretation, he foresaw that the Bible would attain a more immediate influence, thus opening a new access to its undimmed powers in an age of ever-increasing secularization: "when dogma and Law cease to be the all-embracing framework of the community and serve only as supports from within, then the Scriptures must not merely fulfil the task of all scripture, to establish the connection between the generations, but must assume an additional one that is likewise incumbent on all scripture:—to safeguard the connection between the centre and the periphery of the community. Thus, even if Church and Synagogue no longer arched the portal to the road of mankind, the Bible would still be available for consultation about this very road and, 'turning its pages again and again,' man could find 'everything in it.' "

The course of world history did not allow this translation of the Bible to bear fruit in the soil in which it was planted and out of which it had grown. What had been intended as a new beginning became the symbol of a heroic end. But every end can contain the seed of a new beginning: "He who is related to the God of Eternity, is reborn" (Leo Baeck). In December 1929 Franz Rosenzweig finally succumbed to his illness and was deeply mourned. Only two months before, the two hundredth anniversary of the birth of Moses Mendelssohn had been celebrated joyfully and meditatively, with the Academy for the Science of Judaism embarking upon the publication of a complete edition of his works. This edition was destined to remain unfinished. With the revival of Judaism gaining in power and depth, Franz Rosenzweig's death was felt to be the end of a blessed and courageous life, not the end of an epoch that it signified in retrospect. Only a few years later the German Jewry to which he so proudly belonged virtually ceased to exist.

Nevertheless, both Leo Baeck and Martin Buber took leading parts in the spiritual resistance of German Jews to the unprecedented persecution of the Nazi period, which made these final years as memorable as any previous achievements, and happily they both survived to safeguard the link with a rising generation. Beyond this personal link, the synthesis of Western Judaism that Hermann Cohen, Leo Baeck, Franz Rosenzweig, and Martin Buber combined to evolve and to represent, transcends the circumstances of its origin. While bearing the imprint of their time and being of historical significance, this synthesis is not therefore necessarily invalidated by changing circumstances. The very sense of insecurity and change inherent in the crisis of Western civilization tended to demand as its counterpart a modern restatement of the lasting and permanent foundations of Judaism, and the depth of this appraisal raised the work of these men above the limitations of the period.

Viewed as a whole, the synthesis of Western Judaism continued and extended Jewish tradition, both in its development throughout the centuries and in the particular, modern form it had taken during the period of emancipation of Jews in Germany. The Western side of this synthesis at the same time achieved a maturity of expression not previously attained—it became contemporary with its time, even taking the lead, whereas in previous generations Jewish ideology had more often than not lagged behind the general course of ideas. The work of these men is thus characterized by a specific combination of flexibility and permanence, of "now and ever," by the "touch of greatness," the large perspective, the vision of centuries that Leo Baeck demanded and welcomed, as much as by social responsibility and careful attention to detail. Being "rooted in the kingdom of God," each in his own way, they could retain an essential independence from their time while yet belonging to it and speaking its language.

Even in distinguishing the facets of individual approach within a concerted endeavor, Hermann Cohen's view of an "eternal perspective" of ethics, of a Messianic vision that, while extending into infinity, demands personal responsibility here and now, contrasts but does not conflict with Martin Buber's insistence on unconditional readiness to follow the voice of God, the call of which might veer within the hour. Both are aspects of Franz Rosenzweig's experience of Judaism as of eternity within time—of the fully lived moment in its perennial significance within the context of a life "before the Countenance." And his conception in turn encompasses the truth and the paradox of religious life—the paradox that Leo Baeck expressed by linking together the unfathomable mystery of divine revelation and the clear and precise commandment that it brings to man.

The details and emphasis of this synthesis of Western Judaism are bound to change in time. Yet its significance does not merely rest on having once been achieved. Martin Buber's call for a "renewal of dialogical immediacy between men," unclouded by the ideological differences of East and West, has lost none of its urgency. Jewish movements, groups, and parties will continue to reflect particular conditions of their age—Franz Rosenzweig's comprehensive feeling of "nothing Jewish is alien to me" retains its appeal and its challenge. The understanding of past periods of Jewish history is bound to vary; Leo Baeck's statement that the history of Judaism contains and expresses its idea will remain true.

Epilogue

A detailed description of the Nazi catastrophe lies outside the intention and the scope of this study. Any evaluation of the preceding period of emancipation, however, needs to be reassessed in the light of this holocaust. In the course of but a few years the work of many centuries was destroyed. More than half of the German Jewish population who could not save themselves by emigration, fell victim to the onslaught of fanatical race hatred. The whole of Jewish life in Germany, its old congregations with all the diversity of social institutions, synagogues, schools, hospitals, libraries, charitable institutions—the whole of this fabric of culture perished as if overnight. And not only German Jewry but those all over the continent of Europe were equally uprooted.

Germany under National Socialist dictatorship dominated the European Continent for ten years, came dangerously near their goal of world domination, and required a worldwide coalition to defeat it. The majority of German Jews, in common with many Germans and most of the Western powers, at first underrated the strength of the National Socialist movement and its hold on the imagination even of the majority of Germans who did not join it. This movement was able to arouse a spirit of sacrifice for the national cause stronger than the seemingly predominant economic interests and political realities of the time. Yet the explosion that destroyed Jewish life in Germany did in the end not spare the country itself.

This man-made destruction, for all its methodical execution, let loose an upsurge of irrational forces as incredible and seemingly unreal as a nightmare, deemed well-nigh impossible even while in progress within the ordered, civilized life of the twentieth century. The ideology underlying the meteoric rise and the rapid downfall of Nazi Germany is therefore of far greater importance than the temporal details of the movement. The widespread response it found even beyond Germany itself raises serious thought about the thinness of the layer of Western culture, which covers long-buried pagan strata, since these were capable of being evoked with such devastating results. Moreover, the

244

wildfire that set this pagan substructure aflame forms part of the finest Western tradition, though put here to sinister use: the Christian doctrine of one exclusive truth, secularized to the view of one nation alone being destined to world domination; Luther's view of faith regardless of conduct as the prerequisite of divine grace; Nietzsche's misinterpreted idea of a "superman" possessed of a "will to power" as unrestrained as a beast of prey, applied to the collective level of nationalism; Darwin's theory of "favored races," of divine favor manifesting itself in survival in the struggle of life, limited to but one "race" and put into practice by genocide.

All these components of the Nazi ideology were combined in the claim to the racial superiority of the German nation which, so it was asserted, Providence as well as Nature had destined to world domination, without any obligation on its part except the old Germanic readiness for heroic death in battle. Viewed against the conviction of the German historian Ranke that "every nation is immediate to God," the Nazi ideology has indeed a tinge of the pagan mythology of the "twilight of the gods," the self-inflicted catastrophe of the world.

With the holocaust ended more than an epoch in the history of the Jews that in Germany had spanned nearly two thousand years. The deep incision, if not finality of this fact enables the historian to visualise this era as a continuous whole.

Within this history of German Jews two peak periods stand out, one in the Middle Ages, when they were famed for their piety, the other the period of emancipation covering the last two centuries, from Moses Mendelssohn to Franz Rosenzweig. In particular the nineteenth and twentieth centuries demonstrate a degree of attainment by so small a group of the population as has rarely been equalled in any civilization. In the field of science, for instance, up to 1933, thirteen of the thirty-three German Nobel prize winners were of Jewish (or half-Jewish) descent.

Within the Jewish sphere most of the important modern developments had their origin in this German Jewry: the Science of Judaism, the religious Reform movement, Neorthodoxy. The national revival of the Jewish people, the Zionist movement that led to the establishment of the State of Israel, gained the dynamic force of its inspiration from Theodor Herzl's leadership.

When this period of emancipation is visualized as an era of Messianic expectation, a new light is shed on it. For this religious undercurrent can explain the unprecedented creative energy that, subdued and only latent in the eighteenth century, manifested itself among Jews since the nineteenth century, branching out widely and spreading over

many fields of human endeavor. The ideas of the French Revolution—
liberty, equality, and fraternity—were adopted by Jews as fulfillment
of their Messianic hope. In the fight for emancipation, this hope was
given a new opportunity for positive, active, and constructive expression; the expectation of redemption from within changed into the twin
hopes of liberation and salvation from without. This basic motif under-
lies and explains the dominant pattern of the period of emancipation:
the spiritual energies of Jews turned outward into the external environment. At the same time, however, this environment hardly ever ceased
to demand unconditional surrender of their faith, the abandonment of
allegiance to their religion and community, a severance of their very
roots as the price of civic equality.

This contradictory and paradoxical position is already inherent in the
structure of this phase of emancipation, which accorded all rights to
Jews as individuals while denying any to the Jews as a community. In
order to maintain their identity as a community, the Jews thus had to
adapt their religious forms of life as well as themselves to the environmental pattern. This reaction to the dangers of confrontation with
Western civilization could, with apparent justification, be interpreted
as a process of gradual but relentless dissolution and disintegration in
which all dykes and dams barely held the flood. With even greater
truth, however, the process can be visualized as the slow, long, and
painful evolution of a wider, more conscious form of Judaism, a form
that is potentially more capable of holding its own when confronted
with the full impact of Western civilization than the medieval tradition
would have been, that of continuing to seek refuge behind ghetto walls.
In this respect the age of emancipation paralleled the crisis of Judaism
brought on by its meeting with Hellenistic civilization in the first centuries of the common era, from which it emerged after a long struggle
with greater consciousness and resilience than before.

This enabled Jews to survive the Middle Ages, and I trust that the
synthesis of Western Judaism that was evolved in Germany in the early
twentieth century may likewise enable Judaism to survive as a living
faith, capable of further evolution and flexible adaptation. For while
this synthesis could not prevent the Nazi catastrophe, it has sustained
those who were saved and enabled them to withstand the emotional
impact of this abysmal event.

The new strength and resilience of twentieth-century Judaism as
compared with both that of the preemancipation and early emancipation period may be expressed in a metaphor. After the destruction of
the Temple, the Rabbis of the Talmudic period enjoined future generations "to build a fence round the Torah." During the Middle Ages this

fence was built up into a high wall. The generations of the early nineteenth century, filled by the hope of a fraternal mankind, felt it safe to take down the protective wall. Judaism of the twentieth century has rebuilt it as a demarcation line. Whereas the old fence, without doors and windows, was mainly held up by religious customs, which made it durable but rigid, the new consists of an intangible material, that of religious ideas. As has been exemplified in the unfolding of this book, the realization of their importance, of their vital power—vital in the strict sense of determining survival—has undoubtedly been one of the chief contributions of German Jews.

In the process of becoming westernized, they came to rediscover their own heritage in an environment the traditions of which seemed to be so very different. That Judaism itself is one of the pillars of Western civilization, a necessary counterpart to the culture of Greek antiquity, was indeed one of the basic factors that made the evolution of Western Judaism possible. This historical fact is evidenced by the part played by the Bible in this civilization, even without considering that of the Jews themselves, even in its growing stages, let alone in the last two centuries. The ever-growing awareness of the common ground of Christianity and Judaism has drawn them nearer to each other than ever before in their history, not merely owing to the antagonism of totalitarian movements to both of them.

Significance of Judaism beyond the Jewish Sphere

The present and future significance of Judaism beyond the Jewish sphere itself is much less easy to ascertain, involving as it does a consideration of two aspects: the process of secularization of its contents, and the problem of a wider, nay, according to consistent Jewish tradition, a universal validity of the messages of Judaism.

One of the aims of this study has been to show the unexpectedly large degree of a secularization of traditional ideas and values of Judaism, both collectively as a group and inherent in major contributions of individual Jews to the surrounding culture. On the collective side, it has been shown that Jews could find their Messianic hope expressed in the aims of the French Revolution or, later, of Liberalism, thereby preserving their own ground while growing into Western life. Such secularization, though not to the same extent, has taken place throughout the ages. It is a necessary process of exchange. Yet the fruits of secularization still bear witness to their origin.

Individual achievements of Jews are appreciated in the fields to which they belong but, apart from malevolent attacks or half-hearted apologetics, they have rarely been visualized as sparks from a common center of independent power. Taken together, though, they represent an indirect participation of Judaism in Western civilization that may be easier to overlook than to acknowledge.

There is another side to this process of secularization. While the revival of Judaism in the twentieth century markedly reinforced the conscious awareness of Jews of the fundamental tenets of their faith, this highlighting of the central aspect made the outlying branches of secularized ideas, though parts of the same tree, appear all the darker. Indeed, the identification inherent in secularization carries with it the danger that the Jewish origin of such ideas may no longer be recognized, that they may be regarded as entirely external to it. Ferdinand Cohn's discovery of scientific bacteriology in his search for the smallest units of nature, identified by him with God, should have its place in the history of the endeavor of Jews to probe the mystery of God's unity as well as in that of natural science. That such examples of secularization, in many cases unconscious, are no longer re-referred to Judaism means that they are lost as parts of its development. This has happened in fact on a large scale since the nineteenth century. The effect was an apparent weakening of Judaism at the time, whereas an awareness of the spiritual implications of, say, the scientific work of individual Jews would have served to maintain its evolution in step with the general development. To regain this bearing on religious conceptions of work in fields apparently far removed seems to me a permanent task.

On the human plane, a most serious consequence of this movement of secularization was the inner catastrophe of disorientation and despair that Nazi persecution inflicted upon those Jews who had lost contact with their own religious communal roots.

The sense of a wider, potentially universal, significance of Judaism, alive in particular among Liberal German Jews, referred above all to the social responsibilities of Prophetic ethics, which indeed continue to hold inspiring power. This problem, however, needs to be seen against an extended historical background. The Romans of old, for instance, could not understand why the Jews should keep their Sabbath free from work, as a day of worship, rest, and meditation. Modern man, taught by Christianity, understands it. Beyond such views common to both faiths, Judaism may still hold a message for the world at large. In the crisis of Western civilization this may be seen in the healthy balance that Jewish tradition maintains between spirit and nature, God and the world, the community and the individual, the loyalty to one's nation and to God's rule over all the nations on earth. Viewing life and world as God's creation, linking the material and the spiritual realms, neither idolizing nor damning nature but hallowing it, Judaism contains a most basic vision of our life on this earth, the outcome of long experience. Thus it is bound to expose any one-sidedness and to come under fire from any extreme. In the Middle Ages, which were bent on overcoming nature by spirit, Jews appeared as materialists, as usurers. In the age of positivism, Judaism was an obstacle to falling headlong into unmitigated materialism. Thus it was not merely accidental that the wrath and fury of the Nazis, claiming world domination on the strength of "racial," that is, natural, superiority verifiable only by survival, devoid of any collective responsibility, should be directed against the Jews. For these survived by the spiritual strength, the deep living sense of feeling that they were a Chosen People, by the grace of God that confers no claim to domination over other peoples but depends on responsible conduct both collectively and individually. This central belief of Judaism, an exemplary model of experience but no monopoly, might in the last analysis be found to be one of those which are of truly universal significance. Moreover, while Christianity is the religion of the individual, Judaism, as this example shows, may well prove to be a model of the spiritual forms of nationhood, which evolve once a nation has found its distinctive collective personality—forms that can even be reborn after having been lost through catastrophe or neglect.

The synthesis of Western Judaism as attained by German Jews meant a new beginning and a secure foundation for Jews both as individuals and as a community. Apart from the permanent task of maintaining the position of Judaism in the strategy of religious ideas, however, this synthesis itself, viewed in retrospect from the experience of the intervening period, still awaits completion in some important respects. The very fact of the Nazi catastrophe requires appraisal in terms of religious meaning, which in the comparable events of the destruction of the second Temple and the expulsion of Jews from Spain took several generations to achieve. Such reconnection with the darker sides of life, foreshadowed in Jewish tradition by those earlier reactions, may help to avoid a recurrence of similar explosive upheavals.

Moreover, the recasting of religious ideas in modern form while yet retaining and strengthening their sustaining and protective powers, in which German Jews took a leading part, has largely to be extended to a similar reinterpretation of religious law and ritual, the essence of the wisdom handed down by past generations. The attempt to live by faith, by obedience to the word of God alone, without the traditional support of its ordered expression in daily life, has enhanced the human attainment of many a German Jew, both great and small, yet it has also meant deep suffering. Happier times may yet carry on this readaptation of traditional forms in new environments, be it the State of Israel or the communities of the Dispersion. To Leo Baeck, the representative of German Jews in their last and, perhaps, finest hour, it was granted to emerge from the holocaust of Nazi persecution as the living symbol of Jewish survival. In the last year of his life he returned to the problem of the survival of Judaism in terms of a unifying principle in the long and varied course of Jewish history. He came to characterize Prophetic Judaism as a "spiritual revolution" and to understand its survival as the "rebirths" of one basic idea in ever new forms, as its renaissance by a creative response to the needs of each new age, thereby marking epochs of Jewish history. This basic idea, one of the very few "great thoughts" of mankind, is of equally decisive importance to all ages of Jewish history and provides the connecting link between them: the idea of a higher world, that of divine revelation and commandment, as permeating, forming, and unifying this world.

Index